Moving Over the Edge

Artists with Disabilities Take the Leap

Pamela Kay Walker

Introduction by Olivia Raynor, Ph.D.
Director, National Arts and Disability Center

ISBN 0-9771505-2-6

LCCN 2005906754

Printed in the U.S.A.
First printing, October 2005

Introduction by Olivia Raynor, Ph.D.
Book design by Molly Wanning, Wanning Design

This book is dedicated to everyone who enjoys the works of Andrew Wyeth,
and to the dear friend who has been in my life the longest, Al Byers.

TABLE OF CONTENTS

INTRODUCTION

PAMELA WALKER'S *MOVING OVER THE EDGE* is part autobiography and part chronicle of the disability rights movement and the activists, artists and issues that define it.

There are few personal accounts of the disability rights movement and even fewer about the role of artists and performers with disabilities. Many artists and performers with disabilities were discouraged in their pursuit of creative interests by stereotypic negative assumptions about creativity and disability, inaccessible environments or because of the manner in which they created their art, such as painting with a head stick or dancing using a wheelchair. Eventually, many people with disabilities began to challenge the system, the laws, ill-treatment, discrimination and segregation; artists with disabilities illuminated the complex social and political attitudes they faced in stories, writings, theatre, paintings, dance and song.

I have known Pamela for 10 years. We first met in 1996 when we were both speakers at the University of California Berkeley Art Museum/Pacific Film Archive. At that time, she was an arts administrator yearning to return to her work as an artist. I remember Pamela's presence on the stage that morning provoking the audience with her strong and eloquent voice for social justice and the arts, and speaking of the influential role of the artist in any political movement.

Moving Over the Edge includes Pamela's personal reminiscences along with commentaries from artists, performers, and activists of the time…Cheryl

Marie Wade, Judith Smith, Paul Longmore, David Roche and others. These commentaries offer additional first person accounts and perspectives to Pamela's reflections and opinions of her life's journey of 56 years. Forever the teacher and mentor, Pamela infuses the book with lessons learned and advice to others who may want to travel the path of an artist. Ultimately, *Moving Over the Edge* succeeds in its goal to recognize and celebrate the imagination and talent within the disability community and pay homage to those who paved the way for others to pursue their dream.

Olivia Raynor, Ph.D.
Director, National Arts and Disability Center
University of California Los Angeles

BEFOREWORD

I DON'T KNOW THE EXACT MOMENT I realized I was living in the middle of a creative whirlwind, but it was sometime between artistic projects as I was catching my breath. I thought, "Wow, something significant is happening here!" Not just for me, but for lots of people.

I have many fond memories of events and people, like the time I was in a touring holiday show. At one rest home where we performed, the only option we had for a dressing room was a small patio surrounded by bushes, with a door to the meeting room (stage). During a costume change, we realized that semi-truck drivers were high enough to see over the bushes and we had an audience both inside and outside.

Besides the fun adventures, I've had many intellectual ones on this long journey. Serving on grant panels and film juries with great minded people puts one right in the thick of it all. It has been delightful to meet and work with others who also feel passionate about this wonderful thing we call Art.

My experiences have been eclectic, from being a video producer to a talent agent. I've worked as a consultant for many acronyms, including the NEA, NADC, PBS, CAC and the BBC. Though I hit exhaustion many times, I know the feeling of being recharged instantly by witnessing or participating in Creativity. I find it nearly impossible to define why Art is important in our lives, but I know that it is with every cell of my body. Art IS. (period) And we are all enriched by it.

Enough about my work in the art world – that's not what this book is to be about. It's about how I and other individuals with disabilities managed to participate in that world, despite the figurative rain and sleet and snow that we encountered along the way.

I am writing these words before I write the book, though I imagine most authors write the foreword after the book. It doesn't seem right to me to do it that way. After all, "fore" means *before*, right? I write the beforeword first, to invite readers to join me on a journey of remembering. This method for starting a book isn't conventional, but then, neither am I.

The impetus for this book came out of a discussion with Olivia Raynor, Director of the National Arts and Disability Center. I told her stories related to the development of some of the Berkeley artists' careers. She found my ruminations fascinating and thought that someone needed to document the information. I said I'd been waiting for someone to do just that and I'd be glad to tell them all I knew. Alas, no one jumped to the task. It appears to be mine.

Believe me, I tried to talk myself out of it. I already have many half-completed projects waiting for attention. My voice dictation program isn't working well. And then there is the problem that I'm likely to upset SOMEONE by how I talk about them or, worse, by not talking about them. But, when all the eggs are counted, the task is mine.

Someone needs to write about the creative movement of artists with disabilities, to name unnamed heroes who were foster parents of a movement. I want to see the cultural movement documented as thoroughly as the political movement has been documented. And, so, I take off on another journey...

I embark upon it now and invite you to come along. I use a chatty style, one of looking back. I also jump about in time. I'm confident most readers can grog with this if they just sit back and let me tell a story, a story that might be told over several cups of morning coffee.

This journey will begin as autobiographical, but it will extend to include historical and sociological realms as I begin to talk about meeting other people with disabilities. Most of the events I'll describe were viewed first-hand, though some of the stories are second-hand, told to me by people who were there. I begin the book ignorant about art and its place in my life. By the end, I will have traveled many artistic roads and am considered one of the leading authorities on "art and disability" in our country.

In writing, I tend sometimes to make up words, to capitalize words that usually aren't capitalized and to break other literary laws. When I talk about something that is important to me, my speech reverts to Nebraskanese; when I get passionate in writing, I write as I would speak, natural and truthful, but sometimes I ain't gonna use proper english. It's not that I don't know any better, it's that I want to feel free to tell my story, person to person, me to you. I'll try hard to follow the rules of good grammar, but sometimes they just get in the way of telling a story.

Art is often capitalized because I believe it should be. Dream is often capitalized because this book is about reclaiming Dreams, making them capitals. Deaf is often capitalized in respect to Deaf Culture as a specific culture. If you see a capital where there "shouldn't" be one, I am making a statement by that choice, emphasizing the importance of a word. Likewise, if you wonder why a usually capitalized word is lower case, it probably reveals my sentiments about that word (e.g. special education).

If this book was a graph, it would portray a span of 50 years, showing the highest level of covered content to be from 1988 – 1993. If this book was a map of the United States, there would be a magnifying glass at Berkeley and San Francisco. It starts as my personal story, but becomes the story of many, and tells about other individuals who were part of this place in time. (See the Resource section at the end of the book for contact info on many of the artists and organizations I will discuss along the way.)

Remnants of this period exist in photographs, newspaper articles, videos, and other pieces scattered in the collections of the artists and people who were witness to this cultural period. Though some items are safely archived in a collection at the Bancroft Library of the University of California at Berkeley, many other pieces will be lost through the years, passed down to the families and friends of those who collected them, often going out in the recycling bin when the collector dies.

I find it interesting to notice which works of Art survive through time and which do not. Many of the historic artists that we are aware of today were not necessarily the best artists of their time, but they were the ones whose art survived. Some artists come to the attention of the right people at the right time to have their works immortalized, but there are many great works that never make it into the public eye, much less into collections.

This book is not going to be objective, but rather than pepper "in my opinion" throughout, I give the reader credit for having the smarts to figure out that I wrote the book, therefore, opinions are mine. I may poke at the cracks (and crackpots?) in the Disability Rights Movement, especially as related to the arts and individual expression. I am going to discuss some controversial issues, sometimes sticking my neck on the chopping block. Though I am strongly against censorship, I want this book to be read by young people and have tried to limit colorful word choices to a PG13 rating.

This book is about a subject that I feel is very important – the emergence of artists with disabilities, especially in the San Francisco Bay Area. I will be presenting several artists; many of them appeared in at least one Moving Over the Edge (MOE) show, a series of stage performances where many of us tried out our wings in the early stages of our creative careers. Even if good journalism dictates that writers remove themselves from their material, I chose to violate that dictate. This is the story of a movement I was part of. Objectivity is impossible.

Although I loathe long debates over terminology, some clarification is necessary. When I speak of Art or Artists in a general way, I mean all forms of art. However, there is a strong focus on performing artists in these stories, because they are at the core of this adventure. When I speak of people with disabilities, I mean all types. There will be significant amounts of information that apply across the board of disability. However, there will be a preponderance of tales about physical disabilities because that is my most obvious disability and, therefore, prevalent in my experiences.

The term "mainstream" can be confusing when used in a disability arts arena. It means one thing in the art world and another thing in the disability community. Mainstream art refers to art that is prevalent in the general public. However, among people with disabilities, the word mainstream refers to inclusion rather than separateness. My approach to this language hurdle is to use the disability definition when I use the word, meaning that mainstream refers to having access to what the general public has access to.

Regarding what to call us (e.g. Physically Challenged, Differently Abled), I like to think of us as Severely Labeled. A co-worker of mine put it this way: "Call me whatever you want, just don't call me late to dinner." I say, "What you call me is not as important as whether you look me in the eyes when you talk to me." If you haven't gleaned it from my words yet, let me be more direct:

I'm not going to be 100% Politically Correct (PC) in my word usage, and I'm not going to worry about it. (much)

OK, I think I'm ready for lift-off! I need to do one last check to be sure that I have all the bases covered:

Present self? Check!
Origin of book? Check!
Focus, subject and time period of book? Check!
Disclaimer regarding writing style? Check!
Announce lack of objectivity? Check!
MOE blurb? Check!
Terminology blurbs? Check!

Well, I think that about covers the Beforeword. Grab your coffee, tea or milk and come travel the story with me as it unfolds.

Enjoy!

Pamela Kay Walker

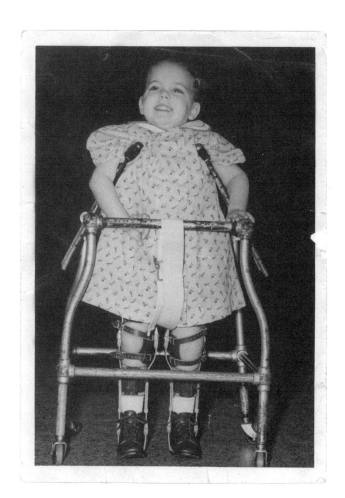

The author at five.

CHAPTER ONE

My Dream Shadow

I FIRST ENGAGED IN THE VENIAL SIN OF ENVY at age five. The temptress who led me down this path of jealousy was a girl my age, though she seemed much older. Barbara Sanderson was an only child, which may explain why she sought attention through her one-girl shows.

I had four siblings to share the performance antics of my childhood with, three sisters and a brother. I remember my oldest sister prancing in front of the mirror like a model, but the rest of us usually vied for attention as pranksters and teasers, rather than as mirror muggers. None of us would have the audacity to present ourselves for public exhibition like Barbara.

She was very organized about her performances. She would practice a show for a week or two and then hand out invitations to all the mothers on the block. Her shows would take place in her family's rec room. This was during the early '50s, when the latest craze for homeowners was to redo the basement into an entertainment center with a TV set and a bar. Mothers escaped the dusty heat of Nebraska summers by paying their nickel to descend into the cool world of Barbara's Dreams.

Children were not invited to Barbara's displays, but I often got dragged along because of my disability. I had had polio when I was a year and a half old, and I was still unable to walk. Mother would balance me on her left hip, where I jiggled down the stairs to Barbara's basement.

Barbara's performances were usually composed of show tunes. I have a vivid memory of her spinning around on a barstool as she sang a fancy rendition of "Volare." She took tap dancing lessons and managed to work in a sparkly-outfitted, heel-clicking act into most of her shows.

I was not impressed.

I thought she was a show-off and a boring one at that. I had internalized a message that said I could not dream of becoming an actress or a dancer. String bean Barbara could have these dreams, but I could not. Somehow, I knew this, and I was jealous.

I knew that I had inherited artistic genes. Although she poured most of her creative energy into cooking and sewing, my mother danced and sang as she cleaned house. I watched her from the couch while the other children played outside. I yearned for the life I imagined I would have had if I hadn't become disabled: a life of fame, fortune and signing autographs.

I wasn't allowed to talk to anyone about my disability. My parents felt that dwelling on it would cause me to feel sorry for myself. I had questions, but I had to sort them out in my own young mind.

Was I entitled to the same dreams as the other kids, even if I couldn't play outside like them? Why were my creative opportunities limited to segregated situations, like at the Crippled Children's Camp I went to one week out of every summer? Why could I only touch the world of art when it was heavily coated with a layer of therapy?

Despite my inner turmoil, I had a secret fantasy that stayed with me for many years: the Dream that I would become a famous singer. My belief in the right to this Dream was so tenuous that I didn't tell anyone. I sang when I was completely alone, except for the few times that I'd share an original song with my siblings. However, that didn't last long, especially after they failed to show the proper respect for my hit single "Don't Spill My 7-Up." What did they know!

I knew I had a good voice, because I'd heard it on the tape recorder that my parents had given me on my sixth birthday. How did I expect to get discovered if I kept my singing a secret? I had that all worked out. Every afternoon I had to go for physical therapy and, afterwards, I'd wait outside until my ride came. I would sing folk ballads quietly, but loud enough that anyone who came out the door when I wasn't looking might hear and "discover" me. He'd want me to make a record for him, and that would work because people would only hear me. They wouldn't know I was disabled.

I felt I had to keep my Dream a secret, because I didn't think a disabled girl could become a famous singer. I'd never seen a singer on TV or in movies use crutches, except for the occasional character who broke her leg. Yet, something inside of me clutched at the Dream and would not let the last note go. And, it almost happened! That is, from a child's point of reference, where having a solo on stage in a Shriners Crippled Children's Hospital show qualifies as famous.

I was seven when the Shriners had paid for my first airplane trip, flying my father and me from our small town to the city of Minneapolis. I felt like such a BIG girl – I'd even been allowed to get a new coat and my first hair permanent.

I spent the hours in flight playing one of those little plastic square games, arranging numbers from 1 to 24. My father would mess them up and see how quickly I could put them back in perfect order. He left me at the hospital to be fixed, hoping that a normal child would be returned to him, put back in perfect order. I was in the hospital for seven

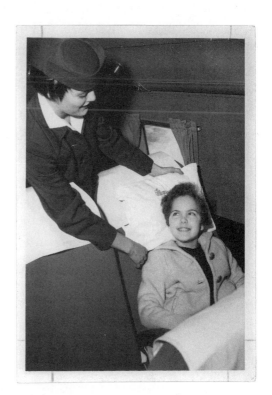

First flight

months, following surgery to straighten my crooked left knee.

The surgery and subsequent treatments were painful, and the hospital stay was lonely, but it was worth it if it led to my stage debut. All of the children in the hospital got to be in the show, so it wasn't a sign of talent to be on the stage. However, my voice stood out as one of the better ones and I was discovered! I was given a solo part in our butchered rendition of "One Little

Candle." I tried to be humble and not get too excited, but deep down I was thrilled.

I practiced my part several times every day, whenever I could find a quiet corner on the crowded girls' ward. Each night, after lights out, I said a prayer of thanks that I was going to be a Star at last! I was stuffed with confidence and joy.

Three days before performance day, I was discharged from the hospital and replaced in the show. I mentally beat myself up for not listening to that cautious voice inside me that said I should not get too attached to my Dream, that it was only a Dream, not something I could have for real.

I consoled myself with the fact that the Shriners had moved me one step closer to walking. With both knees straight and my legs encased in metal and leather braces, I was able to laboriously shuffle across the room.

Inspired by rehearsals on the Shriners' stage, I decided to try my hand at directing. My siblings became the victims of my attempt to make a taped version of Edgar Allen Poe's "The Raven." I read the poem and they added sound effects as I directed. We didn't get through the whole poem, just as we never completed rehearsals for the family rendition of "The Lion Sleeps Tonight." My foray into the world of child directing was rather brief.

At the age of nine, I slipped again and gave in to my singing Dream. On St. Patrick's Day my class was going to go to other classrooms to put on a musical play. My part was holding a baby while singing "Tura lura lural (That's An Irish Lullaby)."

Again, that cautious voice warned, but the Dream became excited... until a chair folded up beneath me just as I was about to sit on it. Since there was no curtain, all the other students saw me crash to the floor in embarrassment. I was unable to get up off the floor by myself, so the teacher had to pick me up. Pity stared at me from the room full of eyes. I was shaken so hard that I could not continue and was sent to the nurse's office. I wasn't physically hurt, but my Dream had been severely bruised and my ego was permanently scarred by the humiliation of the event. Ten year olds may act tough, but their emotional self-defense systems are easily penetrated, especially by their peers.

It was around this age when I saw a photo of Andrew Wyeth's painting, "Christina's World" in a magazine. I didn't know much about art, but I felt

compelled to clip that photo and treasure it. I couldn't consciously explain
it even to myself, but something in that photo gave me strength. In it, a
disheveled woman crawls across a field towards some run-down farm build-
ings. It might be viewed as a scene of despair and the painting has been called
"haunting," but it gave me encouragement. The woman's arms were skinny,
like mine, and she crawled the same way that I crawled. Somehow this filled
me with hope. I didn't know what was in the barn of my future, but I would
continue to crawl towards it, just as I saw every part of Christina's body reflect
a determination to move on. (I had that clipping for ten years before I learned
that Christina Olson was not a starving woman crawling towards a well for
water, but that she was actually disabled and got around by crawling through
the fields, refusing to use a wheelchair.)

Moments of grace, like finding the photo of "Christina World," helped me
to survive adolescence. I went to mainstream school. This was before laws
were passed requiring that children with disabilities be put in classes with non-
disabled children, but my parents had fought to get me integrated. Most of my
grade school years were spent at a Catholic school, where the nuns treated me,
for the most part, equal to the other students. There were some ways it wasn't
exactly equal, but at the time they seemed like small differences. In later years
I decided they were rather large differences, because they were usually situations that enabled children to develop social skills.

Cautiously, the nuns had let me go to the playground once, but I had fallen
from the merry-go-round and gave them a good scare. I had never been on
a merry-go-round before and I didn't know that centrifugal force would pull
me off if I didn't hang on. I enjoyed my battle wounds (a scrape on the arm
and a bump on the forehead) as proof that I'd had an adventure, but the nuns
considered them signs of their incompetence. After that I had to take a nap in
the nurse's office during recess periods.

I couldn't get into the school cafeteria because it was in the church basement and there was no elevator. I usually ate my lunch alone in the classroom.
Occasionally, a classmate would ask to stay with me. Tony Johnson was a shy,
quiet boy, but during lunch periods with me, it was as if someone plugged him
into a wall socket and turned him on. He'd sing and dance and perform as I
ate my peanut butter sandwiches. Like me, Tony had a Dream, but he kept it
a secret from most people. He didn't believe that a tall, gangly, freckle-faced

boy could seek fame as a performer. Ron Howard came on the scene just a few years too late to be a role model for Tony.

Annette Funicello was my role model, even though she was not disabled… then. Years later she would discover the wheelchair due to Multiple Sclerosis, a degenerative muscular condition, but that hadn't happened yet. She was my role model because she was a spunky, adventurous gal with an optimistic attitude towards life. I always had dibs on playing the part of Annette during the opening number to the "Mickey Mouse Club" on our TV at home.

In the fifth grade I was able to take my first real singing class. I learned that I was an alto, which explained why I'd been especially fond of singing folk songs. Towards the end of the year we were scheduled to go into the community to sing. We were going on tour! It was only for one school day, but it was still on the road!

After weeks of classroom rehearsals, the performance day finally came. Excitedly, I entered the school with my slow "4-star" gait (crutch, foot, crutch, foot). The principal came dashing up to meet me and pulled me off to the side. I could not go. I'm not sure if the problem was carrying me up and down the stairs or helping me in and out of the car, but the easiest solution was to leave me at school.

My consolation prize was that I got to be teacher-for-a-day and was left in charge of the first grade class while Sister Maureen, the usual first grade teacher, took my classmates on tour. Everyone made a big deal about the honor and trust I was being given and I even bought into it for while, but something nagged somewhere. I was learning that there was plenty of room for my brain, but no room for my Dreams.

I left Catholic school to go to public junior high and high school. I was totally immersed in academic studies, though I privately started writing poetry when I was 14. My older cousin, Ginny Amen, saw me sitting bored on the porch at a family gathering and suggested that I write a poem. I'd never tried to write poetry before, but I'd enjoyed Poe and other rhyming poets since early childhood. Within minutes I'd written the following in a free flow, without editing:

The circle of our life
Is to each of us our own.
We live among the ones we choose;
We learn by how we've grown.
We cry;
We laugh;
We work;
We play.
But none of us can truly say:
"I've lived my life the best."

It wasn't a great poem by any means, but what surprised me was how easily it flowed from me, through the pen, to the page. I momentarily entertained the idea that perhaps I was the reincarnation of Edgar Allen Poe.

Even though I exhibited creative talents, I was discouraged from taking fine arts classes because the teachers could not figure out how I could paint when I had no shoulder muscles for using a standing easel. I find it ironic that artistic minded people could not be creative in their thinking. Today this type of modification is becoming second nature to teachers because of the laws that require integration of children with disabilities into the regular classroom, but at that time no one thought of even the most basic modifications, like taking the paper or canvas off the easel and laying it flat on a table. My Dreams of the fine arts lived in solitude at home, with paint-by-numbers as my teachers.

My sister Mona took drama classes, but I was not allowed to. There were steps to the stage and no one thought of ramps in those days. Besides, I had to get good grades to go on to college. I had no time for that kind of nonsense and my parents, counselors and physical therapist made sure I knew that.

In 1967, I graduated from high school with honors. I used a two-year scholarship from Shriners to attend a local community college where the English teacher was also the drama coach. When I found out that the Drama Club was going to do "Arsenic and Old Lace," my repressed Dream for fame had a brief resurrection. I stayed after class one day and tentatively approached the teacher with the suggestion that one of the old ladies in a lead role could be disabled, that crutches would not interfere with the character. He enthusiastically encouraged me to audition and said he was willing to make it work if I got a part.

I left school that day feeling the thrill, enjoying the Dream... for about one hour. Then thoughts of me having to leave school just prior to the performance flooded my mind. But those were not as bad as my manifested images of falling down on the stage, in front of the students and teachers.

How could I ever expect to fake my way through the audition when I had never even had an acting class? What happened at auditions, anyway? I was too paralyzed with fear to find out. I didn't go to the audition.

The paralysis of fear was now destroying the remnants of the Dream that had been left after the paralysis of polio. Polio itself did not destroy my Dream, but there were stereotypes that defined what a girl who had been paralyzed by polio had a right to dream, and they didn't include acting or singing.

Finally, my Dream died. Ironically, Christina Olson, the subject of Wyeth's painting, died at this same time. Many years later I discovered that my Dream hadn't died, but that it had only been in a coma. However, I have much more to tell about before I get to the part in my story where my Dream takes flight.

Still unable to quiet my interest in creativity, I began to enjoy my Dream vicariously. I chose friends and lovers who were involved in theater or music. I went to their shows and cast parties. I enjoyed hearing stories about what happened behind stage. I especially enjoyed hearing about the mistakes that were covered up so well that the audience never knew about them.

After two years at the community college, I transferred to Denver University. My paint-by-numbers were left behind, low on the list of priorities when I could only take two suitcases. However, one of those suitcases was filled with my poetry. One Dream still had a pulse.

Even though I've been writing about my personal history, it is a history similar to that of many people with disabilities growing up during the '50s and '60s. However, in my case there was one important difference. I was mainstreamed in school, whereas most people who were disabled as children during that time were either schooled in "special" classes, "special" schools, or not at all. Something curls my stomach every time I hear the word "special." Isn't special supposed to mean things like birthdays or gifts? Does calling a class or a school "special" erase the word "segregated?"

My mainstream education led to college, but on a track chosen for me by parents, school counselors, therapists, rehabilitation counselors, and social conditioning. Regardless of whether one was mainstreamed or not, the message was internalized: We could not be artists. Yet many of us were driven by a need to be creative and held secret Dreams to sing, or write poetry, or paint… even if our only teacher was paint-by-number.

Postscript by my sister, Ramona J. Walker:

I was born into a family with three girls ahead of me. Pamela and I, two years apart, were drawn to each other. We built a life abounding with creativity disguised as child's play. Our activities included acting scenes from movies, making up scenes, and creating new song lyrics to make them more personal or into jokes.

Pamela urged me to take drama and supported my artwork. She'd visit my art classroom at lunch to see what I was working on. I never thought at the time that the things I was doing were denied her because of people who felt she could neither do, nor benefit from them.

I'm thrilled she responded to her creative side in spite of all the people who tried to limit her. She has taught me to look for the creative outlet in all individuals, because it is there in each of us. She has taught me to recognize art and creativity in everything, from the sliver of the moon in its final waning phase to the angle of a woman's head at the bus stop.

I would still be creative without having known Pamela, but I may not have ever realized it.

Dale Dahl

**C**HAPTER TWO Five-Oh-Four

1975 HAS BEEN NOMINATED as "The Worst Year of My Life." Since my life isn't over yet, we don't know if 1975 will actually win the trophy, but I'd say it has a pretty good chance.

Many difficult things happened to me that year, but the one most relevant to this story is that I got a divorce. I had gotten married during my last semester at Denver University. After I graduated, having seen enough snow to last a lifetime, we moved to Oregon and landed in a small college town. When we split up, I found myself living alone for the first time in my life, enduring rain instead of snow.

I had always lived with others. Coming from a large family and later having roommates, there were usually plenty of people around. Now it was just me. I shed about five layers of codependency that year, realizing that there was no one else to take into consideration when decorating the apartment or choosing what to have for dinner.

Despite the liberation, it was a lonely time. No one was automatically built into my environment to spend my spare time with. Leisure activities took on a whole new meaning and I found myself writing, not poems, but stories. Of course I didn't show them to anyone. I kept them secret as if they were contraband that would be confiscated and destroyed if I was caught with them.

The biggest problem for me in living alone was transportation, something I had taken for granted when I had people around to drive me places. My social life became almost non-existent. The few friends my husband and I had made in Corvallis felt uncomfortable around me after our divorce. Visitors to my small, dingy apartment included an occasional friend or relative, but mostly my employers. I had graduated with a Bachelor's degree in Psychology and Sociology and worked as a bookkeeper/typist, like many people with Bachelor's degrees in the humanities. I worked freelance and my clients either brought the work to me or provided my transportation.

I rarely left my apartment. To walk anywhere was out of the question. Since I hadn't anticipated the transportation problem, I failed to consider the importance of renting an apartment that was centrally located. It would have taken several hours for me to walk to any restaurant, movie house, or other public meeting place, and I didn't drive.

Although hand controls would make it possible for me to physically drive, I didn't feel confident that I would be a safe driver. Safe drivers are people who have good eye/hand coordination, and are able to judge distances and proximity when they are moving. These skills are learned in childhood as one runs towards a tree and smacks into it if he or she doesn't stop quickly enough. People learn these skills from catching balls or playing at recess with other children moving around at various speeds. Having had none of these experiences, learning to drive would have meant more training than just a Driver's Education class. I didn't feel like spending a year playing ping-pong to build up my reflexes, so I chose not to drive.

How was I going to get from A to B without a resident driver? Walking was out of the question, because it would take me ten minutes to walk one block. Corvallis was a small town, but not that small.

Remembering that my sister and I had ridden buses in Denver, I tried to ride a bus. However, I had forgotten that she had carried me up the steps into the bus. My attempts were met with failure – there were no lifts on any of the buses.

Up until this time, I had mostly lived in a non-disabled world. Other than going to physical therapy every weekday afternoon and an occasional hospital stay, I was rarely around other people with disabilities. In fact, I avoided them. They made me uncomfortable. I didn't want anyone to assume that I was like "them." And I didn't want anyone to get the idea that, since I was disabled, all my friends would be disabled. "Birds of a feather flock together" was a phrase that I did not want used on me.

I was subjected to the same attitudes in our society that non-disabled people are raised with. There are many inaccurate stereotypes perpetuated about people with disabilities and I was just as susceptible to being influenced by them as the next person. Today, many of my friends with disabilities have confessed to this same irony.

One day I fell in conversation with my neighbor across the street, John Wilson, and he mentioned that he was working with people with disabilities. I ignored the reference, acting like it had nothing to do with me. A few months later, after realizing that I could not use the buses, I decided to talk to John.

He brought over the cup of sugar that I'd called to supposedly borrow and as he turned to leave I said nonchalantly, "Did you say awhile back that you work with handicapped people?" ("Handicapped" was the term used in Oregon then.)

"Yes," he answered proudly, "at the recreation center."

"Oh, I see." I said tenuously.

John again turned to go out the door and I quickly added, "How do they get there?"

"Huh?" He wasn't going to make this easy on me, I could tell. Not only did I not want to affiliate with other people with disabilities, I hated to ask for help.

"If they are handicapped, they can't use the bus, so how do they get to the recreation center?" I was near tears, frustrated by two months of sitting at home because my pride would not let me address the problem directly.

"Usually their families or volunteers bring them to the recreation center," John replied.

"But what if they don't have any family or can't get a volunteer?"

John finally let me off the hook, "Are you talking about yourself?"

I said the words out loud for the first time, "I can't find a way to get around town. My father taught me that there was no such word as 'can't' but in the real world there is such a word. Is there a bus or transportation system here that helps people who can't get on the city bus?"

John didn't feel sorry for me, to my relief. I didn't want pity, just a solution to my problem. John could see that I was a fighter and a doer. He didn't give me pity, but he gave me a challenge that changed my life.

"No, there is no such service here," he said matter-of-factly, "so why don't you start an organization to work on this problem?"

That was Step One towards my becoming an activist. I had learned a lot about people during all my years of physical therapy, watching folks interact while they exercised. I had a Bachelor's degree in Sociology and Psychology. I could do this… I could start an organization to solve my transportation problem!

As I reminisce about my past, I cannot help but compare it to my present. I still live alone and I still don't drive, but when I had to go to the dentist today, I rolled three blocks (I use a power wheelchair now) and caught a bus to and from the dentist's office. The driver said cheerfully, "Thanks for riding; come back again real soon now!" What a difference a quarter of a century makes!

"Good bus" days are more frequent now, though things aren't perfect. Riders get told "the lift doesn't work" when it does, chairs aren't always secured properly, and some drivers have negative attitudes, resenting having to board a passenger using a wheelchair.

Back in 1975 bus days weren't good or bad, they were plain non-existent for most of us and that's what kicked me into activist mode. I was not the only person with a disability who was becoming activated. All over our country, people were beginning to see that they did not have to settle for inaccessible situations, that they could change them. An attitude of coping became an attitude of changing, and for many of us it seemed to happen almost over-night. Many things fed into this change, this shift in consciousness.

We had seen many other groups fight for their rights in the '60's: people of color, women, gays/lesbians/bisexuals. Although all of these groups still have distance to go, they have raised people's consciousness and have made headway towards a fairer shake from society. We saw their struggles and recognized similarities to many of our issues. We saw their successes and heard the word "rights." We looked in the mirror and saw our own humanity and decided that maybe, just maybe, we had a right to some pie too.

Another thing that gave impetus toward our shift was the Vietnam War. I hate war and I have demonstrated against it, experiencing tear gas at the hands of the National Guard. Even though my stand against the war perma-nently separated me from my conservative father, I could not morally agree with the things that our country did at that time. Yet, I have to acknowledge that the Vietnam War played a role in the evolution of the Disability Rights Movement.

Many of the Viet Nam Vets came home with disabilities. They quickly learned that some rights they had had before they went to Vietnam no longer existed. They had lost legs and arms in a controversial war and came back to find a lack of support and a lack of access. These men and women deserved support, regardless of how one feels about the war. They risked their lives for a country that would not allow them to go to the movie theater in a wheelchair because they were considered a fire hazard. The anger of Vets who became disabled in service added fuel to our movement.

There was another group joining our ranks around this time – young people who were injured in car, diving, or gunshot accidents. These are people who would have become death statistics ten years earlier, but medical science had advanced far enough that their lives were saved, though their bodies were left paralyzed with spinal cord injuries. Thirty years ago, Christopher Reeve would not likely have lived more than twenty-four hours following his accident.

The impact of the newly disabled on the Disability Rights Movement is important to consider. Unlike most people who had been disabled from early childhood, these people had had the benefit of a regular education. They had joined clubs, worked on school newspapers, and served as officers in high school. They had had rights that they took for granted until they became disabled. Because they had received a better education than most of us who had grown up disabled, they added skills and experiences to our movement that would be useful in fighting for our rights.

My college degree did not go to waste. I've watched this Movement and explored it from many angles over the years. It fascinates the sociologist in me.

Though it was a tough time for me, 1975 was the year that I began to shift from the personal to the political. I started a Corvallis chapter of an already existing organization, Oregon Architectural Barriers Council (OABC). For the first time in my life, I met other people with disabilities and we began to work together to eliminate the architectural and attitudinal barriers in our town. Now, fast forward to 1977…

Oh, wait – rewind. We're not quite ready. In order to understand 1977, we first have to understand what happened in 1973. A piece of legislation was passed called the Rehabilitation Act of 1973. The section of that Act that is of particular concern here was Section 504. Put in simple terms, Section 504 stated that it was illegal for any entity that received federal funds to discriminate against someone because of their disability.

Wow! What a wonderful piece of legislation! Let's take another look at that: *It was illegal for any entity that received federal funds to discriminate against someone because of their disability!*

This meant all kinds of doors would open for us… city council meetings, county services, universities, companies with federal contracts, buses… WHAT?! Did I say buses? Yep, *buses!*

If that was the case, why did I have to start an organization in 1975 so that maybe someday I could ride a bus? There is a simple answer to that question: I didn't know about the Rehabilitation Act of 1973, Section 504. In fact, most people did not know about the law.

After anti-slavery laws were passed in our country, many people continued to live in servitude because no one told them they were free. Likewise, people with disabilities led lives of isolation and dependency because no one told us we had been granted some rights.

Fortunately, in larger cities, there were people with disabilities who knew about "504." They also knew that the regulations that would enforce 504 were still unsigned. A three-year-old piece of legislation had no teeth in it. Although access was now required in many circumstances, it was being ignored because there was no penalty if it was not provided.

In 1977, the year after our country's bicentennial, demonstrators with disabilities began to fight for their rights. On the heels of our country celebrating 200 years of independence, people with disabilities bring attention to the fact that they are still being left out of the formula. Cities had spent money to paint fire hydrants red, white, and blue, while ignoring the law that said they should be building ramps to their City Halls.

People with disabilities and their supporters began to gather and take over federal offices across the country. I found out about it when Anet Mconel called and invited me to a sit-in with a group in Eugene, a short drive from Corvallis. Although regulations were written and sitting on the desk of Joseph Califano, the Secretary of Health, Education and Welfare (H.E.W.), he didn't want to sign them because they included alcoholism and drug addiction as disabilities.

I wasn't enough of an activist yet to trek down to Eugene on some issue that I knew nothing about, but I stayed posted on developments through the grapevine. Word-of-mouth was the only way to learn about what was happening, because the media was not covering the story. People with disabilities were becoming radicalized, but as far as anyone knew, we were comfortably being taken care of in institutions and back bedrooms.

The San Francisco occupation was the only one to have the strong support of a newscaster, Evan White, a reporter for a local television station. He and his camera crew stayed with the demonstrators through many of their activities. He documented the reasons people were demonstrating and the amazing behind-the-scene energy. He got in close and really listened, something that is still rare among reporters when it comes to disability issues.

Word got out about the takeover and many groups in the San Francisco Bay Area came to the assistance of the demonstrators. That is one of the reasons that it was able to last longer than any of the other 504 sit-ins across the country – they weren't starved out like the other groups. Black Panthers prepared food that was donated by women's groups, Glide Memorial Church, Safeway and McDonald's. Goodwill, unions, civil rights groups and many others helped, some bringing blankets and other supplies to the protesters. The Butterfly Brigade, a group of gay men, smuggled in walkie-talkies. Some of the federal employees who continued to work in the building during the occupancy smuggled in food and let demonstrators use their phones to secretly call home. Messages also got out by banners unfurled from windows or by Deaf protesters using sign language to pass information to people on the outside of the building.

I was not there, but I've seen photos and video footage of the sit-in. I've been able to listen to news coverage of the event, recorded and preserved by Ken Stein, a wonderful historian and ally for the Disability Rights Movement. I've heard many first-hand stories about those three weeks that are full of the spirit of finding something new, of coming alive. It was an incredible time in our history and I still get goose bumps when I think about it.

People with many types of disabilities gathered together for the first time and learned about each other's disabilities. Some of the people used respirators, some had to be fed. Volunteers joined the cause as attendants. Sign language interpreters volunteered to facilitate communications between Deaf and hearing protestors.

After three weeks, the demonstrators felt they were not getting anywhere. A plane was chartered to fly several members of the group to Washington D.C. to try to meet with Joseph Califano. Teamsters picked up the demonstrators at the airport, using delivery trucks with lifts to transport the wheelchair users. Reporter Evan White traveled with the group, documenting their night vigil in front of Califano's house and their march on the H.E.W. headquarters the next day.

This is where I come back into the story. I saw some of that footage, sitting in my easy chair in Corvallis, Oregon. Many people across the country saw that footage also. It was powerful enough to change my life permanently, and it was powerful enough to get thousands of people to call the White House and insist that the regulations be signed.

What did we see on our TVs that had such impact? We saw a woman in a power wheelchair driving up the hill towards the office of H.E.W. We saw a policeman running up the hill beside her, getting to the door a few seconds before she did. We saw him stand in front of the door, cross his arms in front of his chest, and push on her wheelchair with his foot. His kick only caused her chair to roll a few inches backwards down the hill, but it was enough to make people, including myself, sit up and take notice.

The most common reaction was, "All this time, I thought they were being well cared for." People all over the nation now heard stories of discrimination and of poverty resulting from a lack of access. They learned that there was a remedy, but that the remedy was being stalled. They let the White House know that something was wrong with this picture.

After demonstrators spent twenty-five days sleeping on floors of hallways, stairwells, and offices, they finally reached victory. The 504 regulations were signed! The longest takeover of a federal building came to a close as demonstrators emerged from the building, cheering, hugging each other, and singing "We Have Overcome."

At that time in his career Evan White was only a cub reporter and was not usually able to feed footage into the national airwaves. Lucky for us, there was a reporter's strike and news programs were hard up for footage. Otherwise, Evan's story would have been seen only in the San Francisco Bay Area instead of across the country.

Earlier, I hated admitting that something useful came out of Vietnam; likewise, it's hard to give credit to an anti-union event. Sometimes one has to make difficult decisions. Crossing a strike line, in most situations, is a no-no in my book, but the key phrase here is "in most situations." If Evan White had not fed footage into the national airwaves, the passage of regulations for 504 might not have happened for a long time, and they may have been severely watered down by the time they were passed.

Some of the footage taken in San Francisco exists today, but all of the footage taken in Washington D.C. was lost. The same reporter's strike that enabled our story to get told nationally resulted in the destruction of the video footage of that story. A shortage of tapes meant they had to be reused and visual remnants of previous stories were wiped away.

In 1977 I hadn't yet recognized the power of what was taking place. I became an activist for totally selfish reasons. All I wanted was to ride the bus. I felt instead like I was being pulled into a movement that I didn't want to be in, forced to associate with "those" people.

For awhile there it even looked like I'd be able to sit back in my easy chair while other people with disabilities put their lives on the line and got laws passed that would benefit me. Then I learned that the section that related to buses was gutted from the final signed version of the regulations. There would be many more years of demonstrations before buses would be required to have lifts.

Even watered down, 504 was an incredible piece of legislation. It quickly caused major changes across the country, benefiting thousands of people with disabilities. However, it would not impact the problem most relevant to me at that time. Like it or not, disability politics were going to become a big part of my life.

Postscript By Bill Blanchard:

As one of the occupiers of the Federal Building in San Francisco, I have many memories. I recall pangs of hunger, physical discomfort, long periods of boredom, anxiety over the outcome, and embarrassment from having my disability related personal care needs tended to in clear view of passing strangers. But what I remember most clearly is who the people were who led us to our ultimate victory. The leaders of our sit-in were, for the most part, women with disabilities. Women have often played major roles in social change, often without recognition. At the Federal Building in 1977, everywhere I turned there was a woman in a wheelchair in charge, a woman with a disability out front. These were strong, courageous, intelligent, and articulate women who in many cases were having to come up with ideas and implement them at a moment's notice. Not that there weren't capable and equally courageous men with disabilities in position of leadership, because there were, but the number of disabled women willing to put themselves on the line did not escape my notice, women to whom I and others owe a debt of gratitude. May there be many more women of such conviction and courage.

**Ch**APTER THREE   From Chaos to Creation

EARLY IN 1977 I WROTE IN MY JOURNAL, "Out of chaos comes creation!"
At the time, I had no idea how prophetic those words were. By the same time
the following year, I had fully entered the chaotic world of activism, which
eventually set me on the path of reclaiming my right to be creative.

Social change usually happens gradually. Years go by as society slowly morphs.
Sometimes, though, there are specific moments that can be pinpointed as
having a major impact in a short period. The time immediately after the passage
of the regulations for 504 was one of those moments.

There were many individuals involved in the 504 demonstrations who
were affected in various ways. There were also many bystanders, like me, who
were motivated to become part of this evolution. Individuals grouped to form
organizations and administrations. Eventually, all of society noticed, as people
with disabilities finally began to enter the mainstream.

Issues of self identity, group identity, and social identity subconsciously
swirled around in my head. Occasionally these thoughts rose to the conscious
level, but for the most part I only knew that I was in a process of change. I
understand it better, retrospectively, after talking to many other people who
went through this same metamorphosis.

As an individual, I was both drawn to and repelled by the idea that I had
found a group that I belonged to. The closest I had ever come to feeling any
sense of belonging was in my own family. I knew that I was one of five children

who were raised Catholic and poor in the Midwest. However, even with my siblings I didn't quite belong. Though my family tried very hard to never treat me "different," I was different. Others in the household didn't take half an hour every morning strapping cold metal braces to their legs, and none of them had to spend two hours after school at physical therapy.

Group identity was a new concept for me. Did I want to embrace it?

I had tried hard to prove that I wasn't disabled. I had self-identified as a non-disabled person, even though now and then there were reminders that I didn't completely belong. When I began to associate with other people with disabilities, it felt great to not have to explain myself to people who intuitively understood a part of who I was – a part of me that no one else had ever validated.

Two things helped me to embrace my new identity: (1) I attended a Governor's Conference on Employment of the Handicapped with 200 other people with disabilities; I saw such a variety of people (rich/poor, old/young, liberal/conservative, straight/stoned, straight/gay, citified/countrified, nice/mean…) that I realized it was true – we were all individuals. (2) I met a blind person I couldn't stand and found it freeing to feel that way and admit it.

I have heard stories about the Little People cast in "The Wizard of Oz" coming together and discovering others "like themselves" for the first time in their lives. The result was one of ecstasy. They became wild at their hotel, drinking and carousing with each other. I imagine they were riding on the high of finally feeling they belonged.

A current advertisement for new technology says, "We are all connected by our need to be connected." Many people with disabilities felt connection for the first time in their lives when they came together in the 70's to demand that their rights be recognized and met.

I wrestled with wanting to belong, and yet not wanting to be stigmatized as being one of those "cripples" we were taught to pity. Other people with disabilities were also working their way around this dichotomy. At the same time that our internal conflict churned, we were trying to make concrete changes in our communities, to enforce laws that existed but were being ignored. In many cases, our motivations started as self-serving ventures, but the more we became part of a group dynamic, the more we began to work for the "cause," to improve things for all people with disabilities.

I found that there were few resources in Corvallis for people with any type of disability except developmental disabilities. So I started a hotline out of my home to network and counsel people with disabilities. I ran an ad in the local newspaper, listing my home phone number.

As president of the only local disability-run organization, and by having this hotline, I became an information and referral expert on several types of disabilities. I learned a lot by just listening to the people who called me with their problems and concerns. I became a one person Independent Living Center.

After 504 was implemented, colleges and universities were required to provide support and access for students with disabilities. Even private colleges were mandated to comply with 504 if they processed National Direct Student Loans. Literally overnight, college administrators realized they needed to hire someone to coordinate services for disabled students. Since I had experience providing services that helped people with disabilities, I got the job as the first coordinator of Handicapped Student Services at Oregon State University (OSU).

In 1977, my degree in Psychology finally paid off. I was hired under "instructor" status; they would have preferred that I had a Masters degree, but I was the only one of ten applicants who had experience with various types of disabilities. I believe only two out of the ten were disabled.

My supervisor, Sally Wong, had been the main person assisting students with disabilities prior to the passage of 504. It was only one part of her job, but she had managed to provide an amazing amount of support for students with disabilities even though it wasn't legally required at the time. With the influx of disabled students that the college was expecting after 504 was implemented, Sally knew she'd need help coordinating all the services that would be required.

On my first day of work Sally took me around to meet various campus personnel, including the head of our department. Imagine my surprise when I saw a print of "Christina's World" on the wall behind his desk. As a young girl, the painting had conveyed to me that I'd make it OK through adolescence; now it imparted a new positive message to me: that even though I felt like a fish-out-of-water in an academic setting, I'd be welcomed and respected. After all, if a man with a Ph.D. and I both appreciated the same art, we couldn't be that different. (I didn't know then that this painting, released the year before I was born, was one of the most popular ones ever done by an American; but even if I had, I'd still have taken it as a good omen to find it in the office of my new Department Head.)

Sally took me under her wing and taught me how to be an administrator. She also taught me how to diplomatically fight like a bulldog when I knew I was in the right about getting something that was needed. I learned that a calm, yet persistent voice could move a mountain, as long as one was willing to patiently listen to all the arguments about why something couldn't be done. Once the storm blew over, a smile, a bat of the eyes… "OK, I can see it's going to be tough to do, so how will we do it?" More rationalization. Smile, calmly restate the question. Eventually, persistence can wear down some mighty big boulders.

OSU was strong in the sciences and most of the students I worked with majored in computer science or mathematics. However, my fourth year working there, Justin came along, majoring in Art. He was newly disabled, still afflicted with a strong case of the anti-Birds-of-a-Feather Syndrome. I'd conquered mine by this time, but I could recognize it in others and approached with caution.

Justin didn't keep his Dream a secret. He actually majored in art even though he used a wheelchair! The art building, Langton Hall, was not wheelchair accessible; part of my job was arranging for classes to be moved to alternative spaces in inaccessible situations. I ran into major problems with moving most of Justin's classes because many involved equipment and extensive supplies.

The "solution" arrived at by the administration was to set Justin up with a space of his own. Instead of taking some of the classes that they decided were immovable, he would do independent studies.

I did not like this arrangement, but Justin accepted it as passively as I had accepted that I could not take fine arts classes in high school if I couldn't draw on an easel. There was a slight difference now and that was that they couldn't completely exclude Justin from the class. Still, he was not getting inclusive treatment. Part of the learning in art classes comes from seeing the work of other students and hearing teacher's critiques. They lowered the easel for Justin, but he still was not being taken seriously as an art student. [I'm happy to report that Justin is a working artist today, selling mostly through the internet.]

At the same time that I fought for access for Justin, an exhibit of Art students' work was going to take place in Langton Hall and the event was advertised prominently all over campus. The poster used for advertising the exhibit showed Christina of Andrew Wyeth's "Christina's World" crawling towards Langton Hall to attend the event. The image of Langton Hall was superimposed on the poster, replacing the farmhouse with a building that she would find inaccessible once she got there.

This incredible painting had found its way into my way life again! What was it telling me this time? Perhaps that I needed to be that bulldog that Sally had taught me to be. Just because there was a law and regulations, it did not mean everything was hunky dory. It would take time to make changes, but meanwhile it was important to find alternatives that were inclusive. As long as people were showing good faith towards eventually making the necessary changes, I could be patient. However, there were many people who made only token efforts to change, some who made excuses for why they couldn't change, some who ignored the new law completely, or some who were just making foolish mistakes.

People with disabilities had to become watchdogs and even vigilantes. There was no government entity checking up to see if people were obeying the law. The only way the law got enforced was if an individual filed a federal complaint with H.E.W., and then it could take three years for the complaint to be investigated.

Today it is still pretty much the same – unless there are complaints, there are no government inspections to be sure folks are following the law in regards to 504 or our new Civil Rights law, the Americans with Disabilities Act (ADA). The difference in enforcement, however, is that ADA compliance issues can be tried in the courts. We don't need to wait for a bogged-down federal branch to get around to investigating a complaint.

In case you are wondering what the difference is between 504 and the ADA, I'll give you my simple explanation: 504 applies only in cases where federal funds are involved, the ADA applies everywhere in the U.S. Both include programmatic access as well as physical access.

In the last chapter, I mentioned my friend Anet Mconel who was involved in the Eugene takeover of a federal building. She was my first role model of a disability activist. I met Anet at the Governor's Conference on Employment of the Handicapped. She caught my eye as she whizzed around in her wheelchair, frizzy red hair blowing about. Like me, Anet was post-polio and her body had been affected in similar ways to mine. Yet she used a power wheelchair while I struggled on braces and crutches.

Anet was an extremely interesting person and an example to me that people with disabilities could have things in common besides disability. Both Anet and I were involved in women's issues and had similar opinions on national politics. I enjoyed reading fantasy and science fiction, and she was married to a well known Sci-Fi writer. She had two children and a house full of the hubbub that family life provides, and I loved children.

I had often said that people with disabilities had full lives involving many things besides their disabilities; now it was coming home to roost for me as more than just a catch phrase in speeches. I was beginning to believe my own words.

Anet and I had been raised differently – my father was adamant about my not using a wheelchair. Studies show that there are fewer negative stereotypes piled on someone standing than on someone sitting in a wheelchair, even when the person standing has an extreme disability and is struggling to stay upright.

I saw Anet zoom all over with her wheelchair, able to accomplish much more than I was able to do at my slow, unsteady pace. Anet had a major impact on my life by suggesting that I get a wheelchair.

"I don't need a wheelchair, I can walk!" I was staying true to my father's party line. Besides, all those years of painful and exhausting therapy will have been for nothing if I give up walking, I thought to myself.

"You wouldn't need to use it all the time, but wouldn't it come in handy sometimes, like at shopping malls, for example?"

I wasn't about to tell her that I'd only been to a mall once in my life and that it had been a frightening experience. It was not a friendly place for an unsteady walker with people dashing about, bumping into each other.

"You could do things that you don't do now because of the crowds," added Anet, making me suspect her of mind-reading.

"I go lots of places and do plenty as it is," I said matter-of-factly.

"Yeah, and are you going to try to tell me that you don't collapse with exhaustion after a few hours out and about?"

"I'm not saying it's easy," I countered, "but the exercise is good for me and helps strengthen my muscles."

"Any muscles that aren't strong by now have atrophied," Anet said bluntly. "Do you feel like it's giving-up to use a wheelchair?"

"Well, that's what my father would say." I didn't add that I was concerned with other negative stereotypes, too. After all, I was talking to a woman who used a wheelchair.

"It's not about giving up, it's about mobility." Anet looked me directly in the eyes. "It's not about dependency, it's about quality of life."

It took a few months for me to process and absorb what Anet was trying to tell me. I had buried my father in 1975, and gradually I was able to bury his power over my life. I looked at the matter of getting a wheelchair realistically and saw that it made sense. At first I regarded it as a minor decision, one of convenience, but I quickly realized that it was much more.

At age 30, I bought my first wheelchair and my life blossomed. I got a power chair because I have no shoulder muscles, which makes pushing a manual wheelchair impossible. I went places unassisted for the first time in my life. I had never been to a grocery store alone, because I could not walk with crutches and carry groceries at the same time. Now, I was charging off at 5 mph, asking my neighbors if I could pick up anything for them.

I was able to enjoy activities without fear of falling or running out of stamina. I was able to have a life! Getting

My life turned upside down

a wheelchair turned out to be a major positive change for me, not a luxury or mere convenience, as I'd perceived beforehand.

Transportation was not a big problem anymore, because the town was small enough that I could drive my wheelchair from one end to the other in a half-hour. However, now the problem of architectural barriers reared its ugly head. I could get to the theater, but could I get in? I could get to the art gallery, but could I use the bathroom? I could get to the museum, but could I see the information for each painting if it was placed above my head?

I came across an announcement for informational materials called "Accessibility to the Arts," available from the National Endowment of the Arts (NEA). I sent for them and was not only surprised about how quickly they arrived, but also how thorough they were. A huge packet with red, black and white designed brochures covered a wide range of topics about making venues accessible to people with a variety of disabilities. These publications were full of technical information for accommodating audience members with disabilities.

As director of the Special Constituencies Department at the NEA, Paula Terry was the woman behind the making of these materials. Thanks to Paula, many changes have been made in artistic and cultural facilities across the country. In recent years, she has been instrumental in addressing issues not only related to people with disabilities as spectators, but also as artists. Little did I know back in the '70s that I would meet Paula Terry one day and work with her. She has been a strong ally to artists with disabilities for many years.

I later learned how the creation of Paula's position had come about. Andrew Wyeth's son Jamie, an artist himself, is married to a woman who is disabled. In 1972, Jamie Wyeth was appointed a Council member of the NEA and was instrumental in having the Council commission a study on access to art organizations. The study revealed that there were many things that needed to be done. As a result, the position of Special Constituencies Coordinator was created to educate and assist grantees in making their facilities and programs accessible. Paula Terry has been in the position since 1979 and it has been elevated to a "director" position and an office (rather than a position only). In 1997 the name of the office was changed to the AccessAbility Office. (Cheers to another "special" going the way of the dodo bird!)

Encouraged by the materials I'd received from Paula, I began to look at my interest in art again, though admittedly I looked out of the corner of my eye, merely glimpsing. My gut was telling me that something was shifting, but I wasn't quite able to identify it.

I became interested in everything I could find about theater groups that involved performers with disabilities. I made contact with a man in the state of Washington, Martin Kimeldorf. He was writing plays for theater productions using actors with developmental disabilities. He gave me one of his videos and I was impressed by some of the trend-setting work he was doing.

Martin told me about a friend of his, Rod Latham, who started a theater group called Access Theater in Santa Barbara, California. Rod's company served as a model for others who wanted to give opportunities to performers with disabilities. His productions integrated performers with and without disabilities.

When I heard about the work of these two men, I created a fantasy theater company in my mind, called THE (Theatre Housing Everyone). It was a pipe Dream, but at least I was dreaming again. I was beginning to see that ALL of society was not saying that I had no right to dream of being an artist... I had found three allies (Paula, Martin, Rod) who were actively encouraging people with disabilities to realize their creative Dreams.

Looking back on life is fascinating to me. We come to crossroads and choose which path to take based on something someone says or does, or the example they show us. That's one reason I feel compelled to mention the names of people who helped me choose which direction to go as I approached one of life's intersections. Often people never realize the impact they have on others.

Working at OSU I learned a lot about deafness and Deaf Culture. OSU's first Deaf student who used sign language as her primary language was a feisty and brilliant woman named Suzanne Rebillet. Overnight I had to become an expert on hiring qualified interpreters. Fortunately, Suzanne was a patient and good teacher.

Suzanne majored in Anthropology. She focused much of her work on issues related to Deaf Culture as a true culture, having all the aspects of a distinct cultural group, including language. As a graduate student she taught a class in Deaf Culture and one of the teaching tools that she used was a video of a television program that had aired in San Francisco called "Rainbow's End." It was an educational program for children, produced in an integrated way, for both hearing and Deaf children. Years later I met the producer of that program, Dr. Susan Rutherford, and the starring actress, Jane Norman.

You may be getting tired of me mentioning how "years later" I met so-and-so. I'm not trying to name-drop; I am showing how synchronistic my involvement in the arts has been. In the '70s I heard about people who were involved in new, exciting projects, and in the 80s and '90s I found myself working with those people. Life is so surprising sometimes! I feel honored to have met some of these early scouts in the area of art and disability.

The evidence was beginning to pile up… Perhaps doors were starting to open for artists with disabilities.

When I became an activist in 1975, speaking engagements became a part of the job. I would need the fingers and toes of all the Rockettes to count the number of times I gave the Disability 101 talk. I was often asked to speak about people with disabilities and the barriers they encountered. Gradually the topic of images of disability was becoming more and more a part of my speeches.

I have been aware, since early childhood, of ways that people with disabilities are portrayed in movies. We are either on one end of the spectrum or the other, but rarely just ordinary people. One extreme has us as villains and recluses, with Captain Hook being an excellent example. The other extreme has us as super crips who do incredible things and overcome all odds, such as the 1967 movie "Wait Until Dark" in which the recently-blinded heroine defeats two bad guys who have trapped her in her apartment. These two extremes don't leave much for a child with a disability to look forward to – either a pathetic life or one of obsessive over-achievement.

As a child looking for role models, I failed to find any acceptable ones among these images. Instead, I looked to Shirley Temple and to Annette Funicello (despite those stupid mouse ears) and to Heidi. Shirley Temple starred in the 1937 movie "Heidi," which includes a subplot where she helps an "invalid" girl, Klara, to walk. It's interesting that I did not see Klara as my peer, but turned rather to Shirley Temple's feisty character.

When a role did call for a disability, usually a non-disabled actor was cast to mimic the disability. This was done despite the fact that there were many qualified actors with disabilities, such as Jane Norman, Henry Holden and Victoria Ann-Lewis (other names I would someday put faces to).

I became an expert on the subject of images of disability. In addition to the things I had noticed on my own, I did research. I could talk for hours about how people with disabilities were portrayed in books, in movies and in songs. Did you ever listen to the words of "Ruby Don't Take Your Love to Town" by Kenny Rogers? The husband forgives his wife for cheating on him because "it's hard to love a man whose legs are bent and paralyzed."

I was beginning to formulate an opinion that is still my driving philosophy today: It doesn't matter how many laws we change if society still looks at disability in negative and stereotypical ways. The key to changing attitudes about people with disabilities is changing the images of disability.

The powers-that-be at OSU encouraged me to go back to school. I was a sore spot on their employee list, the only person in the department with just a Bachelor's degree. They offered me reduced rates to take classes towards a master's degree in anything, so that I would someday have a more prestigious paper to hang on my office wall. I took classes in Adult Education, Educational Media, Journalism, and Broadcasting. I wasn't sure what I would do with these classes, but they got the department head off my back. Little did I know at the time that I had given birth to a career change.

The broadcasting classes were the ones that hooked me. I had two instructors, Dr. Richard Weinman and Don Sands, who made accommodations for me to take radio and television production classes. I fell in love! The first time I saw a Grass Valley Switcher, I thought I would be high for a week! If you don't know what a Grass Valley Switcher is, imagine levers and knobs and switches that change the shapes and colors on the television monitor. If you are old enough to remember the television show "Laugh In," you can picture all the fun things that can be done with a Grass Valley Switcher.

Besides having a blast, I was good at it! I learned that I had an excellent radio voice and a good television presence. Dr. Weinman was another one of those people who said the right thing when I hit a crossroad, something like...

"You talk a lot about how poor the images of disabled people are in the media," he said. "Maybe they would be better if people with disabilities were the ones making those images."

"There aren't very many people who have had access to education to get to a place where they could do that," I answered.

"What about you," he challenged.

"I've only had a couple of television production classes and one radio broadcasting class," I reminded him.

"It's a myth that you have to have a four-year education in broadcasting to make media," he said.

"Who's going to take me seriously if I don't?" I asked.

"Don Sands doesn't have a degree in broadcasting or production, but he made a video on a subject he was passionate about." He continued, "That video won awards because it's a good video, not because of his education."

Once again I found myself challenged. After giving it some thought, I decided it was time to quit talking about what was wrong with the media and to start changing it. It finally dawned on me that I could talk all day about problems related to the current images of disability, and though this made people more aware of how to interpret them, it did nothing to change the stereotypical images being fed to the general public.

Even though the Disability Rights Movement was busting out all over, images of disability were still primarily made by non-disabled folk and were still reinforcing inaccurate stereotypes. Not only is media one of the most effective ways to define images, it is also an industry that can easily be made accessible for workers with disabilities.

I decided to change careers, to shift into working in the media, but it didn't have to happen overnight. One class at a time, I moved towards my goal. I kept my job at OSU for a few more years, but change was happening. I was not going to give up my Dream this time, even if it took years to realize.

Dr. Weinman planted the seed that started my career change. Corbett O'Toole provided the final motivation for me to leap, not knowing where I'd land.

In the early '80's Corbett coordinated workshops for disabled women and girls in the northwest. OSU was one of the conference sites. It was during the summer, so the dorms were available for non-campus activities. Due to my position at OSU, I assisted with conference logistics before and during the three-day event.

The purpose of the "No More Stares" conference was to provide information and esteem-building experiences to women and girls with disabilities. I didn't go to any of the workshops, but I spent a lot of time hanging around with the staff. Corbett and several other women with disabilities had come from Berkeley to facilitate the conference.

I had often felt like the Lone Ranger in Corvallis. Most of the other people with disabilities I knew were followers, not leaders. Many were of the do-not-make-waves variety. That summer I found myself surrounded by strong, independent disabled women who supported each other and worked together to make things happen. I realized how tired I was from doing things alone.

Their last night there we went out to dinner and I cried through the whole meal. After seeing the strength that was possible for women with disabilities to have, I did not want to go back to my less-than-fulfilled existence. I didn't want to fight battles single-handed anymore. I decided to move to Berkeley.

To work in the media, I needed to go where I would have opportunities and access. Many people with disabilities live in the Bay Area and, as a result, Berkeley is one of the most accessible cities in the country. I liked the idea of living in a community where I wouldn't have to first build the ramp every time I wanted go somewhere.

Meeting Corbett and the other women that were involved in the "No More Stares" conference pushed me to the point of action. I applied for jobs in Northern California and was able to secure one within a year, at the Center for Independent Living (CIL) in Berkeley. I was hired to coordinate a five state conference on serving youth with disabilities. Although the job was not in art or media, I would be living in an area where there were many opportunities to get experience as a beginner.

I had worked as an instructor at OSU for six years and had made many wonderful friends. They threw me a going away party that was both emotionally difficult and rewarding. The biggest surprise of all, however, was when the Department Head handed me a large wrapped package. I didn't dare hope that it was what I suspected, but uncovering it proved that my hope was fulfilled. He was giving me "Christina's World" to take with me to Berkeley. Now that's what you call a good omen!

I moved to Berkeley in the fall of 1983 and within one year was co-hosting and co-producing a radio show with Judy Heumann. Anyone who has read about the Disability Rights Movement is aware of Judy's political work. She was one of the movers 'n shakers at the demonstrations that led to the signing of the 504 regulations. I was fortunate to also see the artistic side of Judy. She has a beautiful singing voice and is a talented radio host. Though most of her life she has worked in politics, she has always been a strong supporter of the arts.

Our show was called "Disability Rap" and aired weekly on KPFA, a Pacifica Radio station. We didn't get paid to do it, but we had a lot of fun. It was a public radio half-hour talk show on a variety of topics related to disability. We'd interview two or three guests each week on a particular subject. Judy liked to do political shows, but I liked to do artistic shows, resulting in a good balance. My favorite was a one-hour special we did where we played songs either by singers who were disabled or songs about disability. We covered a wide range, both good and bad examples, and discussed how those songs might affect the public's image of disability. Did you ever think of the song "Short People" by Randy Newman as a disability song? "Short people got no reason to live."

At that time, the KPFA studios were not wheelchair accessible. Philip Maldari, Public Affairs Director at KPFA, made it possible for us to do our show. He drove us in Judy's van with a wheelchair lift to Oakland, where we used the studio of Youth News to record our programs. Philip also did tech for the taping and taught us a few this 'n that's to improve the program. The first time I saw Youth News, I was taken by surprise at how small it was. Lot's of lights blinked off one wall and another was filled with bulletin board notes. We were smushed in tightly between. It was very different than how the movies depict old time radio shows, where speakers stand at microphones that are at least three feet apart.

There was another KPFA host who used a wheelchair, but he chose to crawl up the steps to do his show. The advantage was that he benefited from interacting with the other KPFA folks and was able to be part of the whole KPFA scene. Judy and I chose the route of less wear and tear on our bodies. [Note: KPFA has since moved into a brand new building with good access.]

We did the show for a year-and-a-half and won awards for it, but eventually I felt I had to move on to my real interest: video. I wanted to play with images, to alter reality through manipulating visual material. I wanted to find a Grass Valley Switcher!

I didn't find a Grass Valley Switcher, but I did find the East Bay Media Center (EBMC), a nonprofit organization in Berkeley that encourages individuals to make video. Their motto is "Be your own producer!" They hold workshops and rent equipment at affordable rates, believing strongly that media production should be available to everyone, not just the economically advantaged.

Mel Vapour as the manager and Paul Kealoha Blake as the president make a dynamic team, putting media into the hands of people who usually do not have access to it. As the quality of video formats improved, they spoke about the "Video Revolution." By this they meant that video was allowing common folk to tell their stories. Before the availability of high-quality low-cost video, media making excluded a lot of people. Now, underrepresented and disadvantaged people can tell their stories and the tired excuse about "broadcast quality" holds less water.

As champions of the underdog, Mel and Paul give encouragement to youth, women, people of color, and others who often find themselves excluded from media production. They opened a huge door for me and greatly enabled the documentation of the 1980's Bay Area disability arts community, often granting the use of camera equipment and editing decks. Many of the Bay Area artists that I mention in this book were documented on video thanks to Mel and Paul.

When I first started hanging out at EBMC, I volunteered to answer phones and to do other clerical things. I had taken some of their workshops, but I didn't have the confidence to consider myself a media maker yet. One day I showed up to work in the office and Mel stuck a video camera in my lap and said "Go out and make video!"

In less than a half-hour I was on the street making a tongue-in-cheek documentary of obstacles I encounter out in the world, such as cars blocking curb ramps and skateboarders cutting me off at the pass. I got a friend to pull into and park in a "disabled-only" parking spot on his motorcycle. It was great fun and extremely satisfying.

For eight years after that, I produced and edited videos as fast as I could. I was still working at CIL, but most of my spare time was spent at EBMC. Even though it's cheaper than film, video can be an expensive hobby: camera rental, videotape stock, editing time. But before finding EBMC, I'd had a drug habit that cost me a lot each month, financially and physically; I decided that an addiction to video was much healthier and traded in my self-destructive habit for one that was truly fulfilling.

I was also a host for a cable access program that Mel and Paul produced, "Barrier Free TV." Blaine Waterman was the first host and I took over when he left. The program was similar to the radio program that Judy and I had done, although it was for television and sometimes involved location shoots and supplemental video clips. Steve Potter, another media maker with a disability, frequently operated one of the cameras, especially for the out of studio shoots.

I produced many videos of my own, including the blood-sweat-and-tears inducing "Into the Echo Chamber" (glorious and gory details in Chapter Fourteen). I also worked on other people's videos as an editor or consultant. Perhaps most importantly, I documented many artists who were beginning to explore issues of disability through their art.

In the '70s I had struggled with identifying as a person with a disability. In the '80s I embraced that identity as I joined the community of artists with disabilities.

In the '70s people with disabilities came together to form political organizations and independent living centers, and to learn about themselves and each other. In the '80s many of those same people began to create Art.

Out of Chaos came Creation!

This book is not a definitive work about artists with disabilities, but more of a dialogue about a group of artists that mushroomed during the '80s and '90s in the San Francisco Bay Area, especially in the performing arts. I count myself among them, finally recognizing and reclaiming my artistic Dream.

Postscript by Corbett O'Toole:

The cavernous, cold, concrete-floored former mechanics garage and now "back room" at the Center for Independent Living in Berkeley was packed with people. Native American Lynette explained her nose ring to Tani, a black blind Baptist. Kari and Darcy, a white lesbian couple, were dancing cheek to cheek. Dale, a white deaf man who'd just appeared one day at the front door with a big smile and a 6-pack of beer, was wearing a doctor's coat and holding a plastic speculum aloft in his right hand, weaving his new electric wheelchair through the dancing crowd. "Want an exam?" he signed. For the non-signers he looked at the speculum and then pointing towards the front office to demonstrate his suggestion. Guy, a very straight white man with cerebral palsy, was holding Maria's hips trying to learn to move to her Latin rhythm. Bob held Jan on his lap so his shortened arms could caress her front. An electric wheelchair with a stuffed mannequin "driver" weaved in and out of the dancers. Don and Joe used their bar flirting techniques to ignore the noise and cruise cute guys. It was a typical 1975 party at the Berkeley Center for Independent Living.

*Chap*TER FOUR   The "Disability Awareness" Fad

WHILE ARTISTS WERE SLOWLY EMERGING from the disability community, some folks in the general public were starting to "get it." Get what? The buzz-word became "Disability Awareness."

After the implementation of 504, Disability Awareness became a fad that lasted at least two decades. Many people began to "teach" about disability. Sometimes "teachers" were individuals or groups of people with disabilities; other times they were special education teachers, therapists, or other professionals who worked in disability related fields. Disability Awareness took many forms.

Speakers In the early stages of this fad, professionals in disability related fields were paid for speaking to classes and groups. Gradually, people realized that lectures about disability would be more authentic if the speakers themselves were disabled. However, people with disabilities were expected to speak for free. We weren't paid as "professionals" even if we had lived with a disability most of our lives and been involved with other people with disabilities through various organizations. There was an unspoken expectation, on the part of both disabled and non-disabled organizers, that we should do it as our contribution to "the cause."

Simulation Exercises   People sometimes get into a wheelchair, or blindfold themselves for a short time, and think they have learned what it is like to live with a disability. These exercises can be helpful, but they need to be accompanied by materials and verbal information, and involve more than a five-minute test drive. They open peoples' eyes, but they are only a launching pad towards understanding disability issues. If a person is given a wheelchair to use and a list of ten things to go out and accomplish, the exercise has more impact because it has practical application. The simulator might then discover things they had not known, such as that bathroom doors are often too narrow for a wheelchair to enter, that a sidewalk is often sloped slightly, and that not every corner has a curb cut. Since the disability experience is not only a physical condition, but strongly impacted by societal attitudes, the best simulation exercises put the person into public situations where they encounter strangers who assume that they are disabled.

Advisory Committees   Some groups, including University administrations, became enlightened enough to create advisory committees on disability issues and to appoint people with disabilities to seats on those committees. However, many fail to recognize the difference between a person who knows only about their own disability and one who has worked with, and is informed about, many other types of disabilities besides their own. Especially in situations where there is only one "disabled seat" on a committee, having the former type of advisors shows tokenism rather than true commitment to the concept of "nothing about us without us."

Friendships   Having a friend who is disabled can teach a person a lot about disabilities, though sometimes the motivation is patronizing. It's one thing if someone meets a person who happens to be disabled and extends a friendship past any fears. However, it's a completely different thing when someone seeks out a person with a disability to befriend because of their disability, perhaps with well-intentions of learning about disability or doing a good deed. The second intent reminds me of the "take a Black to lunch" fad that hit our during the Civil Rights Movement.

Altruism   Doing deeds to "help the handicapped" is an activity that many altruistic organizations have embraced. I still chuckle about the time a fraternity at OSU approached me saying that they had decided to throw a party for the disabled students. When I relayed the news to a student who was blind, her response was, "I'm tired of people throwing parties for me to give me a social experience. If those frat boys really want to help me, one of them can ask me for a date!" Tokenism? Perhaps, but on our terms.

Disability Art Events Artistic disability awareness events also emerged post-504, though not as fast as the academic or hands-on events. Film screenings on disability subjects and art exhibits of works by people with disabilities were presented, frequently sponsored by disabled student organizations. Disability Awareness Fairs or performances cropped up. Art is one of the most constructive ways to do consciousness raising. Many people can be reached through art who would not go to a lecture or educational event about disability.

* * *

More damaging than the Disability Awareness Fad, though, was the Exploitation Fad. It hit like a whirlpool after the passage of 504, but like a tidal wave in 1990, after the Americans with Disabilities Act (ADA) was passed. Capitalistic Vultures descended on Americans with expensive equipment and services, falsely claiming that the ADA required them. It reminded me of what I'd read in history books about the carpetbaggers who found nefarious ways to make profits from the emancipation of the slaves..

Whether an individual or group is trying to learn more about disability, do something for people with disabilities, or include people with disabilities, the key to doing it right is to involve people with disabilities in the process. Everyone benefits if people with disabilities are called on as experts. For example, at OSU I reviewed blueprints for planned renovations, and because of this, money was used more efficiently. One time, there was a plan to lower five drinking fountains in a building that had no wheelchair access. Since that was the total accessibility budget for the year, I advised them to put paper cup dispensers beside the drinking fountains and use the money to build a ramp into the building. Common sense has a greater chance of prevailing when those who will be impacted are part of the planning.

An excellent example of including people with disabilities at the planning stage was the City of Berkeley's Disability Arts Fair, held annually during the

1980's. When I came on the scene, Elaine Belkind was creating and producing the Fairs, advised by a committee of folks with a variety of disabilities. She did an excellent job of finding a diverse group of performers to play on the stage at Martin Luther King Jr. Park, pulling together talented folks from a variety of classes, ethnic groups, ages, disability types, sexual preferences, etc. She beat the bushes to be sure she didn't leave anyone out. Some acts were groups, but at least one of the performers was a person with a disability. And she was actually able to pay the performers!

Some years a poetry anthology of writings by people with disabilities was published in conjunction with the Fair (e.g. "Closer to the Truth" and "Range of Motion"). Elaine also obtained window showcase space on a side street of downtown Berkeley for exhibiting works by visual artists with disabilities. The showcase ran in conjunction with the Fair and for a period before and after.

Elaine is a true ally to artists and audience members with disabilities. Her events were always sign language interpreted and materials were available in alternative formats for people with visual disabilities. Diversity was high on her priority list as she looked for artists and advisory committee members.

The events were free and included more than the arts. Vendors and organizations had booths, sharing information or selling merchandise. Some years the Fair expanded into the nearby Veterans Memorial Building where videos by or about people with disabilities were shown. Using the indoor space also accommodated poetry readings, dances and other performances that did not work well in an outdoor space.

The talent was excellent and you couldn't beat the price, but attendance at the Fair dropped year after year, despite Elaine's efforts to make it bigger and better. Many artists with disabilities were starting to bud, but audiences were decreasing for an annual event that gave these artists exposure. There are several probable factors that played a part in this decrease in attendance.

Possibly the name of the event became a problem. When the Disability Arts Fair originated, the name told people instantly what it was about. As people with disabilities began to develop a sense of self-pride and recognition of their rights for inclusion, they began to feel differently about events that separated or stigmatized them. Although I don't feel that the events themselves did this, the name of the Fair may have kept people away. People without disabilities would not go to a Disability Arts Fair because they thought that it had nothing to do with them; people with disabilities did not go because it made them think they were being pigeon-holed.

By the late '80s, people with disabilities were getting tired of being called "special," tired of non-disabled people doing simulation exercises to learn about disability, tired of giving Disability 101 speeches, and tired of being treated differently. There wasn't anything wrong with the Disability Arts Fairs, but people with disabilities were starting to be more suspicious and less innocent. Cynicism was growing among a group of people that had previously learned to "be nice" and always smile.

Another reason the Disability Arts Fair may have had difficulty was because it was primarily an outdoor venue. Weather is never dependable and rain can always spoil months of planning. The area where the audience sat had no shade and sunny days were extremely hot. Outdoor venues can provide more technical problems than indoor venues, and because of the openness of the seating, people tended to wander off if there was a delay in the programming.

The Disability Arts Fairs opened opportunities for artists with disabilities at a time that none existed. These artists didn't come out of nowhere. Like me, many of them had been secretly singing or writing for years, but we had accepted that "being an artist" belonged only to the non-disabled world. A lifetime of experience had taught and reinforced our misinformed perceptions. Artistic genes can lay dormant for many years, sometimes for a lifetime. (Frank Moore, who I'll talk about in the next chapter, was an exception, literally putting his body out there for art long before most of us knew we were artists.)

Even those of us who went to regular classes and schools had not had much exposure to art. Minor adaptations were made to see that we got the academic basics, but art, music and drama were not considered vital to one's education. We were dealing with unenlightened attitudes towards Art as well as towards Disability. People were expected to cope with the realities of their disability, meaning that we were to just accept that we couldn't do certain things. This was the message society gave us and this was the message that we, as members of society, also held.

However, the 1970's had brought a new approach to being disabled: empowerment! We did not have to just cope with inaccessible situations.

Things could be changed! Theaters and museums that received federal funds were making accommodations for people with disabilities. However, most changes were for audience members, not for participants in the arts. We'd slowly gained recognition as receivers of services, but not as providers of services. Breaking THAT mentality is one of the biggest challenges facing people with disabilities in our country even today, so it's no surprise to find it in the art world.

As we'd moved from re-actionary mode to pro-actionary mode, people with disabilities came together (many for the first time) at demonstrations and began to share their stories with each other. The political gatherings led to social gatherings where there were discussions of shared experiences, sameness and differences. The social gatherings led to cultural gatherings where people began to express those discussions in artistic ways. One by one, spectators emerged from audiences and became openly involved in making art.

Somehow creative people with disabilities started finding each other. It doesn't matter whether it was Kismet, fate, karma, synchronicity, part of THE Big Plan, or just old-fashioned coincidence. Birds of a feather were starting to flock together.

Work, mutual friends, or political activities put artists with disabilities in contact with each other and we were compelled to keep that contact going. Gradually we started sharing our lives with each other and we realized that there was a common denominator in our friendship: we had secret Dreams of being creative, despite programming that said this wasn't allowed for us.

We began to feed each others' starving Dreams.

The first stage was recognizing ourselves as artists in a society that wanted to keep us only in art therapy.

The second stage was trying out our art "in house," experimenting in our own safe communities, at events like Disability Art Fairs.

Today, we're at the third stage, the explosion – we're moving our art out into the world. We're taking it to the streets and we're doing it in all forms... fine arts, video, performance, dance, written word, computer art. Artists with disabilities are showing up everywhere creativity is explored. This sometimes manifests itself as showcases of artists with disabilities produced in mainstream venues and widely marketed to the community at large, not just to the disability community. It also includes cross-pollination events, where artists with disabilities are showcased alongside artists without disabilities, based on subject or genre, but not disability specific.

Am I saying that there were no artists with disabilities prior to the Disability Rights Movement? Of course not, one flip through an art history book would disprove that notion. (Beethoven, Sarah Bernhardt, Goya, Frida Kahlo, Mozart, Toulouse-Lautrec, Van Gogh… to name a few.) However most of them did not identify as disabled, much less see themselves as part of a disability community. An exception might be some of the performers in circus side shows.

I was 30 years old before I shared my creative Dreams with anyone and before I started to entertain the idea that I might be part of something bigger. This happened around the same time I attended my first Disability Arts Fair in Berkeley, and coincided with my agreeing to do the "Disability Rap" radio show with Judy. Very cautiously, I brought my poems out of the suitcase they had lived in since my college days, and I began to read them to other people.

It was as if winds of change had whispered to me, "It's okay to bring out your Dreams now."

Postscript by Hannah Joyce Karpilow:

I joined the disability community shortly after this "fad" began, when I started doing attendant work in 1981. I was fortunate to have excellent teachers, which in turn provided unique opportunities to further my education within the Movement.

Disability Awareness is not something you achieve by reading a book, taking classes, or even necessarily by becoming disabled. It comes from being part of a community, from having an assortment of characters as tutors. Certain qualities benefit the absorption of this education; being nonjudgmental, respectful, intuitive, attentive, and not presumptuous. Being curious about people, not their disabilities, but their humanity.

I attended many events discussed in this chapter. The Disability Arts Fairs at Provo Park were great occasions for becoming exposed to the Culture. I liked the casual style, and they were free. The performers and the audiences were my teachers. Combining my interest in the arts and my involvement in the disability community was a win-win situation. While I don't always appreciate the art for art's sake, I sometimes learn something about Disability Culture from it. Being a witness to this Culture in its infancy and watching it develop is a privilege. Being involved in this book is an honor.

Chapter FIVE

I CAME ALIVE IN BERKELEY! Some called it a disability Mecca, others call it a disability ghetto. There are so many people with disabilities living in the Bay Area that Berkeley has become one of the most accessible cities in the world.

Some of the access is subtle, like a lack of stares as one travels down the sidewalk in a wheelchair. Other types of access are related to disability being so natural that a waiter taking an order from a person with a physical disability automatically asks if the customer would like their meat cut up. In so many ways I hadn't realized how many architectural and attitudinal barriers were oppressing me until I moved to a town where they were missing.

In an environment that is not only accessible, but provides a supportive community, it's only natural that artists with disabilities would emerge and flourish. Although all the pioneers of the Disability Arts Movement deserve recognition, I have chosen four artists to focus on. I present these artists to you because their lives demonstrate variety in respect to art types, their disabilities, their influence on me, and choices they made along their creative paths.

Dave DeWeerd, Kathy Martinez, Frank Moore, and Cheryl Marie Wade have all explored a variety of forms in their art, though each specializes in a different area. All of them performed on stage, probably Frank the most and Dave the least. Kathy and Frank were born with their disabilities; Cheryl and Dave became disabled over time, beginning in mid-childhood. I have interacted with each of them to various degrees, Frank the least and Dave almost

24/7 for five years. All of them lived in Berkeley at the time when I began to let the artist in me out of the closet.

These four artists have greatly impacted me and many people through their artistic expressions and their lives. They are some of the artists who taught me, directly and indirectly, that I was an artist. I present them here in the order that they entered my life.

Kathy Martinez was a young girl when she starred in "More Than Meets the Eye," a Lassie episode about a blind girl who gets lost. She was a natural and appealing child actor, but the industry was too short-sighted (pun intended) to see her potential. Although she was a union actress, offers of roles were rare.

Kathy enjoyed taking gymnastics, but because of her blindness, people at her school became concerned about safety and pulled her out of the class. Her family fought the issue for a long time and eventually they won, but by that time Kathy was disheartened and gave up her interest in gymnastics.

This and other stories are told in "Tell Them I'm a Mermaid," a film based on an original idea conceived and developed by Victoria Ann-Lewis. The work is a musical theater presentation in which seven women with various physical disabilities describe their attitudes towards being disabled.

Besides being an actress, Kathy is also a percussionist and a singer. She got her first drum set when she was twelve. Her early influences were Motown and the Top 40 on KJLH in Los Angeles, a radio station in Watts. Her parents enjoyed and encouraged her drumming, though they viewed it as a hobby, not a potential career choice.

I met Kathy in 1983, when we both had jobs at CIL in Berkeley. She is all business at work, but a bundle of fun on breaks. Her quick wit and infectious laugh match her impish smirk and raised eyebrows. When jokes are told, she sits still, listening intently, but once the punch line hits, her whole body conveys delight and joy.

From 1988 – 1993 Kathy performed with Sistah Boom, an all-percussion women's band that marched in parades and played at parties and celebrations. They worked out ways to cue Kathy so that she knew when the band leader motioned for a change in formation or direction.

Kathy played traps with a rock 'n' roll band called "No Stinkin' Badges" for four years. She was the only woman in this otherwise band of sighted men. One person would give the verbal cues when Kathy needed them, so that she didn't get confused with more than one voice. She also played in various jazz combos.

One of Kathy's teachers was Carolyn Brandy, a pioneer for women percussionist. Kathy especially enjoys playing Afro-Cuban/ Brazilian music, Samba, Salsa, and traditional Yoruba music. She finds the rhythms that correspond to our heartbeat to be hypnotic and healing. She studied different percussions, not only their rhythms, but also their traditional and religious connections.

Kathy became so interested in the spirituality of African music that she traveled to Cuba to study the Yoruba rhythms. These were carried to Cuba from southwestern Nigeria where there were different rhythms for different gods. The drum is viewed as the voice of the ancestors who watch over the moral life of a community. Proper drumming reflects a sense of respect and gratitude to the ancestors. Music and dance is used to restructure and refocus the community's integrity and as a source of strength in the lives of its members.

I have always been strongly affected by drums in a visceral way, whether it's the wild pace of the long version of "In-A-Gadda-Da-Vida" or the slow background blues beat of an Aretha Franklin song. However, I never thought much about it until my conversations with Kathy. She helped me to recognize and understand the power of a beat to transform, stimulate, heal, and soothe the mind.

In the late '80's, I invited Kathy to work on a collaborative project. It was because of the magic of her drumming that I'd involved her, but I was delighted to discover that she also had a beautiful singing voice. Using a synthesized effect on the microphone, her voice came out in an other-world eerie chant, haunting but beautiful.

Working and hanging with Kathy is always a time of laughter. She sparkles and enjoys having fun and playing with music. Any time Kathy is involved in a creative project, she brings a sense of energy and jubilation. She taught me to relax and enjoy a creative ride.

In recent years, Kathy has given less time to her artistic side and more time to her work as an activist and "change agent." She's worked at the World Institute on Disability for many years, traveling frequently to help women with disabilities all over the world. She's also worked on AIDS awareness and assistance projects in several countries.

Kathy provides an excellent example of someone who has an incredible gift for being an artist, but who has made a choice to use her energies in advocacy. As an artist, you can only go so far without making a large commitment to either "go for it" or stop. Kathy came to that point and knew that the work she was doing around the world was very important. She has focused on Disability Rights work through most of her life, putting her artistic goals second.

Of course, finances also influence artists when they have to make these kinds of choices. It's very difficult for an artist to make a living at their art. Kathy has usually worked at a livelihood where she has felt good about the difference she's making in the world. Although her art makes a difference too, she has made enormous contributions to people in other ways. She hopes that soon she will be able to travel less and have more time to return to drumming.

Kathy does not draw boundaries between what is political and what is art. She sees the world as a circle. She talks about the sacred Bata drum, which was traditionally played only by men. Women were not allowed to dance and sing. In her way of saying a lot in a few words, Kathy will say "Things are changing, women are drumming."

Whatever she is doing, whether it has to do with drumming, with service work, or in politics, I always think of Kathy as "drumming."

Frank Moore is a thin, wiry man with a body full of energy. His arms and legs spasm and shake with the beat of cerebral palsy. His speech is difficult to understand, so he often communicates by using a pointer on his head to indicate words or letters on a board.

Frank typically dresses in tie-dyed clothes from head to toe, and his power wheelchair is brightly decorated. He wears humongous glasses and drools through his misshapen teeth. Wild hair flies around his head and his chin is covered by a straggly beard.

Have I just described an erotic genius?

Yes.

Frank usually has a crowd of people around him, adoring him, touching him, being close to him. He has helped many people learn about their erotic energies and to express themselves more fully. He focuses on touch in much of his art, encouraging people to be playful. His performances have a reputation for being wild and shocking, yet moving.

During the 1970's Frank performed with his cabaret, "The Outrageous Beauty Revue," at a San Francisco nightclub called the Mabuhay Gardens. Men in wheelchairs singing "Macho Man" with pride and gusto is one example of the types of things they did.

The first story I heard about Frank tells of his entering the stage in his power wheelchair, totally nude. Several women lifted him and laid him on the floor. They poured spaghetti on him and the performance consisted of their eating it off his body.

For Frank to expose his body the way that he does helps many people to feel less self-conscious about their bodies. Body acceptance is a beautiful thing; lack of body acceptance is an ugly thing. Frank shows that the line between "beautiful" and "ugly" has more to do with how one feels than with how one looks. He does this as work/play/art.

After seeing Frank proudly display his unusual body so easily, with no sense of shame, I began to flaunt my atrophied legs almost as much as I exposed my cleavage. I began to feel comfortable in shorts on hot summer days, and to attend gala functions in short skirts and nylons. Frank's influence enabled me to attend the "Exotic Erotic Ball" in a revealing outfit that led to four compliments on my legs, three sexual propositions, two requests for dates and one proposal of marriage. For several years I have also danced scantily clad in San Francisco's annual Carnival, resulting one year in a photo of me in "Utne Reader." Whether on stage, at a costume event, or in the public, my legs don't have to be hidden. I wouldn't go so far as to say that Frank turned me into an exhibitionist, but his head-stick euphemistically pointed me in that direction.

Frank also taught me to be freer in creating my art, to worry less about who it might offend. He is always pushing boundaries. In 1990, he was one of the handful of NEA funded artists that Senator Jesse Helms demanded be investigated for "obscenity."

I admire the work that Frank has done regarding free speech and anti-censorship. I heard him on public radio once, at a time when many artists were being censored. Knowing that it is almost impossible to understand what he says, Frank went on the air and said the seven dirty words that are not allowed on radio. It was hysterically funny, one of the cleverest broadcasts I've ever heard.

Speaking of censorship, I want to take a side road for just a moment to talk about the current threat to freedom of expression in our country. If society wants to protect itself from "difficult" images, disability is a prime candidate for censorship. Many people are uncomfortable with disability related material, sometimes even finding it disturbing or offensive. People can be afraid of us and they may fear becoming disabled themselves. These fears not only create obstacles to inclusion, but they give an impetus for people to avoid us.

It is important for artists with disabilities to be able to express themselves, even (or especially?) related to sexuality. We've been told that we are not sexual beings, but some of us are challenging that through our artistic expressions. It is important that artists with disabilities not be censored. Freedom of expression is our ally.

The trickiness of anti-censorship is that if we want the freedom to say what we think, we need to let others say what they think. I have a right to talk about how I think my body is beautiful; others have a right to call my body deformed. I have a right to say that it is my opinion that many people with disabilities who want to die need better support, not death; others have the right to say that it is their opinion that a severely disabled life is not one worth living.

Unfortunately, under a "freedom of speech" banner, sometimes people deviate from anti-censorship to action or incitement to action. An anti-abortionist group had a web site that listed the names and home addresses of doctors who performed abortions. It encouraged anti-abortionists to cause physical harm to the doctors and their families. Freedom of Speech means that the anti-abortionist group had a right to have a web site stating their opinions about abortion; it does not mean that the group had a right to encourage violence.

Jack Kevorkian has a right to his opinions about assisted suicide, but so do the Not Dead Yet folks. Kevorkian can easily get the press to cover his side, but where is the press when a spokesperson for an opposing organization has an opinion? One form of censorship is failing to tell both sides or suppression of a story.

Censorship/anti-censorship can be a fine line that will likely never be permanently drawn. Frank Moore states on his website:

"...there will always be thought-cops and other forces of repression with their cold mugs of hemlock. We artists who deal in cultural subversion (some call it corruption of morals) should always be prepared to take that bitter drink."

Frank's work is considered controversial – pushing boundaries of body acceptance, eroticism, pornography, and sexuality. I don't always like the messages he conveys, but I respect his work immensely. And, sometimes I have thoroughly enjoyed his work…

…like the time he performed on stage with Nina Hartley, a famous adult movie star. Frank sat in his wheelchair while Nina danced with him, wearing only thong panties. Three nude people moved in circles around them, wrapping them in white toilet paper, tin foil and Saran Wrap. It was beautiful, erotic, playful, and completely wacked. Typical Frank Moore.

Frank is respected as an artist across the country, from Greenwich Village to San Francisco. The last time I saw him perform was at a benefit for Annie Sprinkle, a famous erotic performance artist whose houseboat had burned down. Dressed as Sonny and Cher, Frank and his wife Linda sang "I've Got You, Babe."

Frank is so far over the edge that most of us cannot even see him. He's the kind of trailblazer that is a hard act to follow. I interviewed him in his home once for the Barrier Free TV show, but the experience was so surreal that my memory of it is a dream-like fog. People tend to either love him or hate him. One thing that most will agree on: The man's got guts!

Frank Moore's name belongs in art history books, in a chapter on erotic artists. That is saying a lot when you think about the fact that society considers people with disabilities as asexual. My greatest respect for Frank is due to his persistent and primordial twisting of minds around that stereotype.

Cheryl Marie Wade was slowly emerging from her artistic cocoon while Frank Moore was thrashing about on stages. Cheryl has had rheumatoid arthritis most of her life. Her hands and joints are gnarled and she uses a power wheelchair. But, as one of her poems states, she is a Woman with Juice (!).

Cheryl started writing when she was 17. She went through a period of isolation and wrote daily in a journal of life, but it wasn't her life she wrote about. She wrote from the life she wished was hers, as if it was real. That's a creative twist on the Imaginary Playmate concept!

In college during the '70's, Cheryl began to write poetry, but a critical teacher affected her so strongly that she stopped doing poems for a few years. She continued writing short fiction and had one of her works published in

"With the Power of Each Breath," an anthology of works by women with dis-abilities.

I met Cheryl not long after I moved to Berkeley. She was writing a book of biographies featuring people with disabilities. Someone suggested that I might be an interesting person to interview. She never finished the book, but it provided the on-ramp for the relationship we have traveled over the years. Although she was working on a book when we met, I didn't know she was a poet and that she had Dreams of performing. Our lives came together and we became friends, but it was through joint ventures on stage and with video that we developed our creative relationship.

Many of us were unaware of the fact that we were artists. Cheryl was writing a book, and had already had some of her writings published, but she considered herself a talented writing hobbyist. I was producing and hosting a radio show, yet I didn't see myself as an artist, nor did I know of Cheryl as one.

Years of internalized oppression, like blinders on a race horse, kept us from seeing the obvious. Once I began to recognize myself as an artist, I began to see the other artists around me.

Cheryl discovered that she had a unique power with language when she started performing her poems with Wry Crips Disabled Women's Theater. With this mind-blowing group of women with disabilities, she wrote material, individually and during improvs, and performed staged public readings. When Cheryl received enthusiastic audience feedback for her works, she realized that she had something special. She returned to poetry and three years of prolific writing followed.

Cheryl also became involved with AXIS Dance Company, not so much as a dancer, but as a creative consultant. She has a quick eye for seeing when something works and when it doesn't. AXIS was trying to find ways to integrate dancers with and without disabilities in a way of equality. Cheryl provided constructive feedback in the beginning stages of their development.

Cheryl is known most for her written and performed poetry. She reworks pieces until they are perfect. Her thoroughness and her amazing way with words led to many of her writings being published in national magazines, small press anthologies, and academic papers. On stage she lulls audience members into a false sense of security with her rich, lush voice; then, before they know it, they are turned upside-down and maneuvered through new territory, even-tually to be returned to their seats, safe, but altered. Her full-bodied hair and the intensity of her eyes electrify a room on her "good" days and remind us of our humanity on her "bad" days.

   Cheryl excels at both rhyming and non-rhyming poetry. Her words carry an impact either way. I usually depend upon rhyme to make my pieces work. Cheryl does not need a rhyming crutch, as you can see in this poem by her:

I am not one of the physically challenged--
I'm a sock in the eye with gnarled fist
I'm a French kiss with cleft tongue
I'm orthopedic shoes sewn on a last of your fears

I am not one of the differently abled--

I'm an epitaph for a million imperfect babies left untreated
I'm an ikon carved from bones in a mass grave at Tiergarten, Germany
I'm withered legs hidden with a blanket

I am not one of the able disabled--

I'm a black panther with green eyes and scars like a picket fence
I'm pink lace panties teasing a stub of milk white thigh
I'm the Evil Eye

I'm the first cell divided
I'm mud that talks
I'm Eve   I'm Kali
I'm The Mountain That Never Moves
I've been forever   I'll be here forever
I'm the Gimp
I'm the Cripple
I'm the Crazy Lady

I'm The Woman With Juice

Reading Cheryl's words is a powerful experience. Seeing Cheryl perform her words is an emotional rollercoaster ride that includes passion, sorrow, impishness, and an occasional burst of blues. In delivering her poetry, she alternates flirtation, anger, and tenderness, grinning with delight at the exuberant audience reaction that follows each reading. Having Cheryl on the bill insures a packed house, and I have never seen an audience less than WOW-ed by the unique expressiveness of her words, hands, face, tones and gestures.

Cheryl has been a major influence in my life, as an artist and a friend. We have shared many giggles and guffaws. When that girl gets on a roll, wit flies faster than a skateboard going down a San Francisco hill. Directly and indirectly, Cheryl taught me to be bold, to make strong artistic choices. She dragged me, kicking and screaming, to the view that editing and re-editing my words often greatly improves them. (…Pamela grudgingly admits as she reworks this chapter for the eighth time…)

By her encouragement and example, she gives us permission to express our own style, to know that though I could never be a Cheryl Marie Wade, she could never be a Pamela Kay Walker. Cheryl builds relationships based on celebration, not competition. She knows and helps others to know that all voices and styles are valuable, each of us contributing something only we can create.

Cheryl does not call herself an artist. She feels it would be pretentious to do so. She acknowledges doing things that have become art over time and she recognizes that she has a powerful way of communicating, but she feels that it's up to others to decide if her works are art.

Although she continues to write and now adds playwriting to her talent bank, Cheryl is not able to perform often these days. The body of a crone (over 50) with a disability tends to be temperamental. With unpredictable pain flare-ups, energy fluctuations, and the wear-and-tear of a lifetime of living with a disability, her body isn't cooperating with her creative side.

Cheryl and I have contemplated with each other about how much more we would have produced if we hadn't spent so many years not knowing we were artists. She and I have helped open doors so that young people with disabilities today will have more access and support for giving life to their artistic Dreams.

Don't get me wrong, Cheryl has left a rich legacy. Many of her writings have been published and some of her performances have been captured on video. However, at least 20 years of her creative expression were lost because of internalized oppression and physical and attitudinal barriers.

I don't like playing "if only" or "what if" games, but it was important to mention this issue. There are many artists who were thwarted in their development for other reasons (gender, incarceration, economics, class…), so this problem is not specific to disability. However, it is disability that I'm talking about. Disability – the bastard child of sociological dissection.

Who knows what Cheryl would have become if she'd had support for her art early on. But we do know what she is…

…Cheryl Marie Wade, Queen Mother of Gnarly, Spunk on Wheels, Poet Laureate of Disability Culture… A Woman with Juice!

Dave DeWeerd ("The Weird One") was a quirky, creative adventurer. He usually dressed in a fedora hat and safari clothes from Banana Republic. Sometimes he walked with a carved cane. His art was one of the few examples of experimental work from the Bay Area disability community of the '80s.

Dave developed juvenile diabetes at the age of five, resulting in his being a scrawny kid who didn't tend to play outdoors. He had to go home for lunch because of dietary restrictions and his need to take insulin, so he did not develop lunchroom friendships. He was pretty much a loner, except for two creative friendships and his deep relationship with his brother Tom.

His artistic interests were obvious at an early age and his family was very supportive. Because of the diabetes, Dave was hospitalized many times during childhood and adolescence. He used this time to draw, to scribble down new ideas, and to write.

He obtained an animation camera, and with his two buddies, spent hours in the basement creating short cartoons. They did all the art work, wrote the script, and shot the animation sequences. We're talking before the boys were ten years old!

Dave took a correspondence course to become an artist, one of those schools that advertise on matchbook covers. I laughed, but when I saw the artwork that he produced as part of the course, I was thoroughly impressed, especially considering he had done this before the age of 15.

After high school, Dave moved to Los Angeles, to find fame and fortune as an animator. The closest he got to fame was a job with Filmation as an inbetweener on animation series of "Star Trek," "Lassie's Rescue Rangers," and "The Brady Kids." An inbetweener is a person who draws one piece of the picture over and over, making slight changes, so that when the frames flash by quickly, we see movement.

Dave found inbetweening to be boring and moved north to Gilroy, where he worked on a restoration project for the Mission at San Luis Obispo. A mural had weathered over the years, and in some areas of the building it was impossible to recognize the original artwork. Dave researched the design, the colors and the methods used when the work was first done. With pride, he showed me Alfred Hitchcock's "Vertigo," because a scene in it is filmed at that Mission, a synchronistic blend of his creative passions for fine art and film.

Dave's interest in film had grown, fed by the Hollywood influence during his Los Angeles years. He began to write screenplays. Hospital stays became the place where he worked out new movie ideas, pushing animation into the background. However, there was one animation project that he never left behind: a work that he called "Struggle," about his life. It involved several bodies climbing over each other to get to the top. He obtained the music rights to Gustav Holst "The Planets, OP. 32" to use for the soundtrack.

Eventually, Dave moved to Berkeley, and attended the California College of Arts and Crafts, studying animation and film. His film short, "Made From Scratch," was screened at several festivals. It consists of flashing words and images scratched directly onto the celluloid and accompanied by a chaotic soundtrack. Some of the sounds are similar, like the whistled tune from the Andy Griffith Show. Sometimes the soundtrack and the images seem linked, but only for a split second – "A Bicycle Built For Two" plays as a bicycle flashes across the screen, almost missed if you blink. Other times there are no linear connections between what is heard and what is seen, such as randomly scratched shapes to the theme song from "The Good, the Bad, and the Ugly." The common thread throughout the 3-minute collection of seemingly unrelated icons is a male voice pronouncing words that often scratch into sight, hinting at a message – words like Mediocrity, Perpetual, and Nebulas.

Though "Made From Scratch" has had more screenings, Dave is remembered most at the school because of his video "Phoenix Rising," subtitled "A Celebration of Touch." Originally the work was to be called "Liquid Satin" and to feature Nina Hartley. The intent of the piece was not pornographic, but artistic and erotic. Nina was to lie on a satin sheet and close-ups of the texture of her body and the sheet would blend and move to a Brian Eno soundtrack.

A couple of days before the shoot, Nina got sick and Dave had to completely revamp what he was doing. He had already bought the expensive sheet, so he was invested in using it. The studio and camera equipment were scheduled and he had to produce something for his class assignment. He found replacements and the final piece is a 15-minute colorized collage of images of three nude people playfully engaged on the satin sheet. Digitized close-ups and fluid camera movements create a flowing tapestry of indistinguishable body parts. (Was that a knee, a shoulder, or a breast?) Images of physical intimacy resolve into liquid patterns of light, shade, color and sound.

Dave DeWeerd with art installation "Passages" (computer animation inside cut cardboard)

Dave called the work "Phoenix Rising" because it is what rose from the ashes of the original plan. Even though it did not turn out the way he had originally planned, the work won Best of Festival at a video refusé and shooting it made him a celebrity on campus. The rumor mill still has him as the student who used school facilities to shoot a porno video with Nina Hartley.

I got to know Dave while he was editing "Phoenix Rising" and I was editing my first video, "Strong, United and Proud." We were both putting in long days at the editing decks and ran into each other often. It didn't take long before we were artistic co-conspirators, lovers, and best friends.

By this time in his life, Dave's diabetes was affecting him in major ways. He'd had a kidney transplant and needed to take immuno-suppressants to keep his body from rejecting it. This made him more susceptible to infections and, as a result, he lost a leg. He walked with an artificial limb and most of the time would not have been recognized as disabled, though he was still very thin.

He was also starting to have problems with his eyesight. This, more than anything, frightened him. Visual art had been an important part of his life as far back as he could remember. He was terrified of losing his vision.

Our meeting was one of those gifts that the Universe gives people now and then. Dave taught me to appreciate art, even that which I didn't necessarily like. He taught me to respect Picasso and turned me on to Fellini. (I still don't like Picasso, but I do see his value now.) Dave was also very instrumental in helping me to comprehend the concept of experimental art and to extend my own artistic expression beyond traditional boundaries.

Dave also benefited from our relationship. Prior to meeting me, he was like I had been in 1975, coping in a non-disabled world, passing as much as possible for a non-disabled person. His eyesight was declining gradually enough that he could hide or deny it. He could turn down an invitation to go to the movies at night by telling himself and his friends that he had something he wanted to watch on television, not admitting that his night vision made it hard for him to navigate in the dark. I was someone he could begin exploring these issues with.

In the world he portrayed himself as a confident man, full of energy and a love of life. These things were true, but there were times that his energy started to run out and he kept going, not admitting that he needed to take a break. The eventual result might be a week of recovery at home, causing him to fail a class or to not be able to take part in the final steps of a project that he'd worked hard on. Dave had to look his disability in the face when his diabetes progressed to the point that it was causing serious problems, some of them avoidable if he'd admit that he was disabled.

For example, his artificial leg often rubbed sores on his thigh. If he continued to wear the leg, the sore would become infected and he would wind up in the hospital. He had two choices to not wearing the artificial leg: (1) stay at home until it healed; or (2) get a wheelchair to use for the times that he could not wear the leg. However, getting a wheelchair meant admitting that he had a disability. I pointed out to him that he could not edit video from home (or the hospital, for that matter), but he could edit video from a wheelchair. So, which situation was disabling?

After Dave began to talk openly about his disabilities, he made a huge transition in how he dealt with problems. He got a wheelchair and did many other things that improved his quality of life. Consequently, he found he had more time and energy to devote to his Art.

There are many Dave DeWeerd's out there. I want to acknowledge those nameless artists who may not be visible, but who are enjoying a life of creativity and enriching the lives of those around them with it. And, I want to encourage closeted artists with disabilities to see that getting support does not make one less of an artist, but that it can actually enable one to be more of an artist.

Dave lived for five years after we became involved. Over that time, he and I worked on several projects together, learning how to adapt as his disability progressed. One of my favorite works we created together is a collage of body parts clipped from magazines and laid out to be hills and mountains in a landscape scene. We called the work "Belly Button Moon" and we even made an animated short of it, using moving clippings of straight hair to create the impression of a waterfall and curly hair to create the foam that bubbles when falling water meets the bottom.

Dave taught animation and video to children and adults. He worked professionally and on his own independent projects right up to his death in 1992, though the last year was very hard. He died actively, meaning that we talked openly about his dying and said all the things we wanted to say to each other.

When he died, Dave left a trail of drawings and sketches for his life work, "Struggle." It never became a completed work, though he had worked on it for several years. Before his death, he realized that "Struggle" was not an animation, but more of a journey and process. Working on "Struggle" had been his outlet for the times that life threw him too many curve balls, too fast.

In 1992, just after Halloween, his favorite holiday, Dave completed his performance art piece "Struggle." (How's that for a metaphor for "died?") East Bay Media Center honored him with a retrospective of his animation, film, and video work as a part of their annual video festival.

Dave did not become a nationally recognized artist with a massive body of work, but the work he did produce was rich. The people who had the fortune of working with him benefited greatly from the way he opened us to expand creativity into unknown territories. Unique territories. Fun territories. Territories with no boundaries around the Muse.

* * *

Each of the artists in this chapter taught me important things that enrich my own creativity. They helped me to learn that I am an artist. Dave was the one who actually made me say it out loud for the first time.

Kathy taught me that everything has a beat, and that the important thing is to find the beat of my own Dreams and to keep drumming.

Frank taught me to be nonjudgmental about my art and to laugh playfully while dancing with the Muse.

Cheryl has been a creative sister, demonstrating that editing doesn't take away, but adds to the juice of a work. Her vibrancy on stage has pushed my own performance persona to greater heights.

Dave helped me to understand that, for some of us, art is a lifestyle. From hand-drawn menus when he served me breakfast in bed to dressing like an adventurer in the exploratory world of creativity, Dave frequently demonstrated that "Art" is a verb.

These artists emerged at a time when there was little support and rare access for artists with disabilities in the mainstream art world, yet each of them made important creative contributions to that world. Equally important, they left a roughed-out trail for future generations of artists with disabilities to follow.

Postscript by Cheryl Marie Wade

Who Is Art?

It begins with the body different...electric.

"I can probe and pry your secrets with these almost boneless fingers"

Some people are born artists. Divine imprint on the DNA. Most of us enter with a fuzzy wash, defining as we sample dribs and drabs of possibility in the world around us.

It's my poem, the story of my life, it's their poems, the story of our lives.

"I'm an epitaph for a million imperfect babies left untreated"

"I'm an ikon carved from bones in a mass grave at Tiergarten, Germany"

For Cripples, possibilities are offered in dull colors and muted tones: be careful, be realistic, be safe....

It's a love song, it's a cry for help, it's get the f*** off my back, it's rock n roll. Theater. Performance Art. On one in the spotlight. Transformation....

Art fueled by activism took me from a girl who hid her deformed hands under a shawl to a center stage diva waving her Queen Mother of Gnarly paws in the Booga Booga spotlight. Activism gave me a stage, juice, an audience; a way to find my voice. Art fueled by activism gave me the chance to set free and empower the isolated teenager I was, a girl desperate to find some image of herself that didn't carry with it the burden of shame.

Who is art? It's you, it's me, it's anyone willing to walk, roll or crawl into that white hot sweaty spotlight and push it, push it push it push it, and then push it...further....

Chapter SIX

SINCE YOU ARE READING THIS AFTER THE FACT, you won't have noticed that I neglected you for some time. I apologize, but I have a good reason, an exciting reason!

I had a regular pace going, working on this book every morning before I did anything else. Then, I got a phone call that threw my work schedule off. I made it to the second round of an extremely competitive grant process. This is not bad news, mind you, but it meant prioritizing my time differently for a bit.

A new source of grants for artists, Creative Capital Fund, had 1800 applicants their first year and I made it to the second round! I entered a proposal in the performing arts category, and only 56 were asked to submit second proposals. Fifteen of those will be funded. Better than 25 percent chance! How could I refuse to turn in the second proposal?

This inspired me to apply for another grant that was open to residents in the San Francisco Bay Area. I had held off writing the proposal, leaving it to Fate: If I made it to round two with Creative Capital, I would go for a grant through Theatre Bay Area's CA$H (Creative Assistance for the Small company and Hungry artist) program.

I found myself with two weeks to write two proposals. Is that a good enough excuse for neglecting you?

If I get funded I will start a small theatre company and produce a show that I am currently writing, "The Rise and Fall of the us/them Empire." It explores "us" and "them" issues, especially related to body differences. This includes differences for which an individual has no choice (e.g. gender, ethnicity, congenital disability) and chosen differences (e.g. tattoos, dress). The production will be a multi-media performance and include interactions with the audience. It draws from modern, historic, and fictional references, from armpit shaving to German purification, from Hephaestus to Mary Magdalene. Disability is used in a pivotal way to explore these issues, but it integrates with other themes.

Does this sound like something you'd like to see? Well, hopefully I will have good news to share with you about the work by the time I get to the end of this book.

Another thing that diverted me from working on this book for the past two weeks is much less exciting – a lawsuit against the Social Security Administration. This has more to do with advocacy than art, but it is definitely related to the survival of artists with disabilities.

For those of you who do not know about SSI and SSDI, let me give you a simplified crash course. Even those who know about it might want to stick with me here, because I am going to mention some things that may be helpful to artists and other self-employed folks receiving SSI. (There won't be a test and the SSI subject will be covered more thoroughly in Chapter Seventeen.)

SSI is Supplementary Security Income that comes from the feds. Some states add to it minimally. [Update: In 2005, the federal portion of the benefit was raised to $579 a month for an individual to live on.] People with disabilities who have never worked and are poor, with little or no assets, are eligible to collect SSI. They also get Medicaid (in California this is called Medi-Cal) which pays 100% of covered medical expenses. The word "covered" is key here, because not all things are considered eligible expenses, such as many medications.

SSDI is Social Security Disability Insurance. This is what you get if you have worked at a job where you have paid into the Social Security pot. (There are a few other ways you could qualify such as if you were disabled before age 22 and are eligible for a parent's benefits because they are disabled, retired, or dead.) There is a mysterious formula used to determine how much you are able to draw each month if you become disabled. If you get the maximum, you get more than you would on SSI, but you are still probably at poverty level. With SSDI you also get medical coverage, but what you get is Medicare. Medicare covers many things that Medicaid will not cover, but it will only pay 80% of approved charges.

Some people, like me, receive both SSI and SSDI. This is because I have worked enough to earn SSDI, but not enough to put me above the allowable monthly income limit for SSI. At the time of this writing, I receive $665 a month on SSDI and $30 a month on SSI in California. I get both Medi-Cal and Medicare. This may seem like a great situation to be in for medical coverage, but there is sometimes a question about whether or not certain things are "covered" and, if so, by which one? There was a time when it was almost impossible to get a power wheelchair "covered" because vendors did not want to have to deal with paperwork bouncing back and forth between Medi-Cal and Medicare, each one claiming that the other one was responsible for the purchase.

Now that you have had your crash course, let me try to explain the reason for my lawsuit. I will try to keep this simple, though nothing having to do with the Social Security bureaucracy is ever simple.

If you are on SSI and you earn any money, you must report it. If you earn less than $65 a month, they do nothing. This is also true if you are on SSDI, but it's a different set of rules. If you are on both, you must follow both sets of rules simultaneously. On SSI, there is something about the next $20 above that which they ignore. I have never understood this, and I'm a bright woman. Suffice it to say that you can earn $85 a month without having to pay anything back. You still have a paper work nightmare to deal with and you may get called in for a review, so they can be sure you are still disabled, but you won't have to pay anything back. If you earn over $85 a month, you have to pay back one dollar for every two dollars earned.

Although I doubt that this system ever made any sense, it probably came closer to sensible at the time that it was started, when minimum wage was much lower than now and when most people in our country worked 40 hours a week or not at all.

The nature of work is not as cut and dry as it used to be. More and more, people with and without disabilities work out of their homes, part time, and/ or are self-employed. People provide labor in other "atypical" ways, such as through barter exchange and co-op ventures. Most important to the subject at hand, there are people who don't work often but make real good money when they do work.

Like me.

If I get a paid gig, I usually get paid very well. I can make a lot of money in only a few hours. The amount I get paid does not reflect how many hours I can work in a day, or how long I can keep that up.

One of the things that I do is acting. As an actress I filed self-employment for many years. At the end of each year, I claim all of my income and expenses on the proper IRS forms. After expenses, I usually don't make a whole lot in a year. "Self-employment" is a whole different animal than what SSI calls "part-time employment," but I'll get to that in a minute.

A great thing about self-employment is that instead of looking at how much you make every month, SSI waits until you file your taxes and then divides your income by 12 (months). They use the figure you get AFTER you deduct your expenses in determining whether or not you have earned over the allowable amount per month.

An ungreat thing about self-employment with SSI is that most of the people who work at the department of Social Security don't understand this method, though it is totally legit. Anyone who uses it frequently has to educate case workers and other Social Security personnel about the method.

In contrast, "part-time employment" uses a monthly figure and no expenses are allowed to be deducted from it. [An exception is "Impairment Related Work Expenses (IRWE's). In my examples below, though, assume I am not using an IRWE.]

For example, If I do a consultant job for two hours and earn $250, I will have to repay my SSI for that month if I do it as part-time employment. However, if I do it as self-employment, it will be calculated with my taxes at the end of the year and my expenses will be deducted from it. Suppose I paid an administrative assistant $100 to assist me in preparing for the job, $50 to attend a meeting with me to take notes, and $40 to type a report. That leaves me $60 that I actually earned for the job.

In the above example, I'd lose my SSI for the month if I were viewed as part-time employed. However, if I were viewed as self-employed, expenses would be deducted first, leaving the $60 to be divided by 12. SSI would determine that I had made five dollars a month.

What if the above was the only paid gig I had for the whole year? According to the part-time worker method, I'd have to repay my benefits for one month. According to the self-employed worker method, no problem comes up unless my income significantly exceeds my expenses. As you can see, for people who work sporadically, it can be a great advantage to be considered self-employed rather than part-time employed and, therefore, owed them nothing.

REQUIRED READING FOR ANY ONE FROM THE SOCIAL SECURITY ADMINISTRATION WHO READS THIS BOOK, ESPECIALLY MY CASEWORKER: Because of pain, low energy and stamina, I barely have 15 good hours in me per week. That doesn't mean I can work at a paid job for 15 hours a week, because I also have to take care of the things of life during those 15 hours – like writing bill payments, balancing my checkbook, and filling out forms from Social Security. This book is being written one hour a day, five days a week, using Dragon NaturallySpeaking (a voice dictation program). I pay an administrative assistant to manually cleanup the mistakes that the program makes, like when I say "run" and it thinks I've said "Ron." IN OTHER WORDS: Writing a book does not eliminate my disability nor my eligibility for SSI or SSDI.

While I was a non-union actress, all my jobs were on contract. I had no problems with Social Security considering me self-employed. However, all of that changed when I joined the union, American Federation of Television and Radio Artists (AFTRA).

AFTRA requires that all actors' paychecks be processed through a payroll company, and that is where the trouble started. The payroll company takes out deductions and, on paper, looks like an employee. However, it is nothing but a contracted third-party for processing checks.

SSI decided that I am an employee (Of who?—the payroll company?), and they will no longer allow me to claim self-employment when I work as a union actress.

I appealed. I appealed again. I was heard by a judge who ruled against me. I appealed again. I petitioned in District Court against the Social Security Administration.

This process has been going on for six years and I've been doing it on my own. I have not been able to find a lawyer to help me because those who work on SSI cases usually work on ones that have a large back-payment coming, so that they can take their cut. In my case, the money involved is less than $50, but I'm fighting the principal because, for some people, SSI is their only regular income. Also, SSI eligibility can tie into other benefits such as subsidized housing, attendant care, wheelchair repairs and other medical costs. Losing SSI can be like knocking over the first standing domino of a precarious row.

Many people complain about how we don't see actors with disabilities on the screen and how non-disabled actors borrow a wheelchair to play a disabled role. The issue I'm talking about here is one of the reasons for this. Actors are not taken seriously in the industry unless they are in the union. But an actor on benefits who joins the union jeopardizes his or her benefits, including medical coverage.

One of the reasons I had to ignore this book for three weeks is that I had to file more paperwork to the District Court. It is now in the hands of the judge. I hope to report a favorable outcome to you before I finish this book, but don't hold your breath. It's taken years to get this far.

Before I leave this chapter, I must tell you two fun things that I did during the three-week hiatus in our relationship. I went to two concerts: Jethro Tull and Inti-Illimani. Both were great and reminded me why art is so important.

Jethro Tull was dynamic and playful! I had never seen them in concert before and had no idea what a delight they bring to the stage. Their performance reminded me that I always want to keep playfulness in my art, whether as part of the process or as part of the product.

Inti-Ilimani was fabulous also. They have some incredible guitar players, including one who makes the guitar sound like two different instruments at the same time.

As I watched the guitarists pluck the strings, I remembered a time when I was obsessed with learning to play the guitar. I learned a few little riffs, but my interest waned as I realized that going any further would take lots of practice. For me, playing the guitar was one of those adolescent phases that got tried and discarded.

Being the introspective and questioning person that I am, an internal dialogue churned as I watched the stage. What is the difference between a Dream and a phase?

Children with disabilities have the same right to explore creativity as children who are not disabled. I did not get a chance to explore singing in order to find out if it was a Dream or a phase.

But I did get a chance to explore guitar playing and I got that one settled early on.

I often feel like a fifty-year-old adolescent now, testing things out to see if they are Dreams or phases.

Or are they the same thing, but with different timelines?

When is art a hobby and when is it a career?

When does one get to say they are an artist?

These questions are not specific to people with disabilities, but it certainly makes it more difficult to answer these questions if one has not had the opportunity to explore scribbling, being in school plays, or singing to other groups in music class...

...Or spinning on a bar stool in a basement while all the neighborhood mothers watch.

Postscript Concept by My Pseudonym, Calico:

Pamela's World (Parody of Andrew Wyeth's "Christina's World")

PHOTO BY RAMONA WALKER

TALKING ABOUT COMEDIANS INTIMIDATES ME – I feel pressure to be funny and clever. I will swallow my inhibitions, and tackle this subject anyway, because I think our comedians are an important part of our emergence to power. If we can't laugh at ourselves, who can?

Humor is an important part of surviving and coping. Even extremely off-the-wall, tasteless, over-the-top jokes can have purpose. There have been times that I have sat in an audience, listening to a comedian who I think is a jerk with no sense of anything, but I realize that he or she is actually reaching a good number of the people (i.e. with jokes about bathrooms, The Great Equalizer).

We need it all. We need the high brow and the low brow comedy. Fortunately, the disability community has both, as well as some who are in a league of their own.

I tried stand-up comedy once and, frankly, I don't understand why anyone would thrive on being a comedian. It's hard work! You spend weeks coming up with a script, figuring out the motions to go with it, practicing in front of a mirror, and boring your friends with private rehearsals. Then you get on stage and try to make it look spontaneous, like you are saying things you just thought of at that moment. Bing, bing, bing, ten minutes or less go by and it's all over.

The bit I did was about sex. It didn't go over very well. I didn't understand this at first, since sex jokes usually crack an audience up, and my delivery was good. Later I realized I had been telling these jokes to an audience of mostly people who knew nothing about disability. It was probably strange enough for them to have a woman in a wheelchair on the stage in the first place (a stage that I had to be lifted on to). Then, she talks about sex? No doubt it confused them greatly, since it's a known "fact" that people with disabilities don't have sex.

Sex is a topic some comedians consider a cheap laugh. There are those who pride themselves on never having to use sex or body noises to get a laugh; then there are those who pretty much base their full show on these types of jokes. I think we need them both, because both reach a different type of person.

There are many nationally recognized comedians with disabilities who have appeared in television sitcoms, in movies, and on popular late-night talk shows. Geri Jewell is probably the most famous, starting from the time of her early '80's appearances in "The Facts of Life" TV series; she's now a regular on HBO's "Deadwood" and CBS's "The Young and the Restless." A PBS documentary, "Look Who's Laughing," was produced by Randy Johnson and features Geri and other comedians doing stand-up comedy. (You'll see my name in the credits as associate producer!)

This chapter is about some of the comedians with disabilities who came out of the San Francisco Bay Area scene. I learned about many of them from Mike Dougan. He had videotaped hours of performances and interviews with five local comedians who had disabilities. He had edited a rough draft together and asked me to take a look at it and give him feedback. It was great! I don't think he made too many changes from the rough edit to the final edit of his one-hour documentary "Able To Laugh."

The individuals featured in Mike's video came to comedy from different directions. Some participated in a group led by an excellent professional speaker, Lee Glickstein. Lee's method has people get up in front of each other and take the leap, to be vulnerable. They work with what they know best – their lives, their hopes, their passions, their fears, their stories. Then they find the comedy in these things.

At the time, he called these groups "Humor in Recovery" because his methods drew on the 12-step approach where people simply tell the truth about themselves. Now he calls these groups "Speaking Circles." He encourages people to find their own comic style and pace, not to try to imitate the rapid-fire or the one-liner-zinger approach. The results of his influence are powerful.

Lee's students with disabilities felt ready to put on shows for the public. At his full house "Access To Comedy" show, I first saw Joel Rutledge. Joel walked on the stage with no visible disability. Since the event was billed as one featuring comedians with disabilities, audience members played an inner game show of "What's His Handicap?"

Joel Rutledge comes across as the kind of guy who would help the neighbor lady carry her groceries into the house. Opie of Mayberry without the freckles, taller, blond instead of red-headed. The Boy Scout type. But, it's all done with trick mirrors. Joel Rutledge has a wicked wit and an invisible cruel streak that he exposes so subtly to his audiences that they have to acknowledge similar twists tucked away in their own psyches.

Joel can't read crib notes unless they are about two inches from his eye, but his humor barely touches on this disability. He ruthlessly tackles the subject of growing up as a stuttering child with an alcoholic father. His routine turns the meaning of the phrase "passive aggressive" inside out.

 The first time I saw Joel, I laughed through his whole routine. My favorite part he does is about a conversation between a "Type A" personality and a stutterer: The Type A listens intently, anxiously waiting for the moment they have enough information to complete the sentence of the stutterer. As the blood drains from the Type A's face, the stutterer eventually says "No, that's not it...."

Joel and I have become good friends and I try really hard not to complete his sentences. Actually, his stutter is barely noticeable now that he has learned to take his time speaking. His speech has a pace of its own. I wouldn't really say that he speaks slow, but rather... that... he... speaks... steadily.

Joel's pace is atypical for comedians, but it works! He knows that the speed with which he delivers his lines is slower than audiences are used to getting them, but he structures his material so as to take advantage of his unique timing. He is a comic genius and an excellent role model of someone who doesn't let a disability exclude them from a particular field. He makes people adjust their thinking by showing that "different" adds variety. Just because most comedians deliver rapid fire, who says you have to do it that way?

In addition to being a comedian, Joel is also a nationally recognized public speaker and a published writer. Oh, and he also plays the accordion. But, he's just a regular guy who I have enjoyed sparring with for endless hours of deep, often serious, conversations on life.

Mike Lee, on the other hand, is rarely serious. He's a never-ending comedy routine. Having a conversation with him, even a business phone call, is a series of one-liners and short vignettes. Many times I have been "caught" by Mike, listening attentive to a story about something that happened to him, discovering that I've been "had" when he gets to the end and drops the punch line.

Mike is blind and has a companion dog, not only to assist him in getting around, but also as part of his comedy routine. His material borders on disgustingly sick, but the kind that makes you laugh hard anyway, because of the visual image created. For example, Mike tells about cleaning up after his dog had an accident in the house. Think about how you would go about finding and cleaning up doggie patties if you could not see. Audience members politely chuckle at first, but Mike's gregarious nature eventually wins them over to roaring laughter.

One favorite is his story about the time that some of his friends took him to a nude beach. After everyone supposedly took their clothes off, his friends went off somewhere, leaving him alone. His punch line mentions something about wondering why he could hear so much traffic at the beach. They had taken him to a freeway island.

I've never been able to determine if the nude beach trick really happened, because it's almost impossible to get a straight answer out of Mike. It made for a good bit that had non-disabled people rolling in their seats, though. People were more cautious about laughing at some of his other jokes, though, because they weren't so sure his jokes were politically correct (PC).

Mike is also a motivational speaker and I'm sure he goes over extremely well with the Type A personalities that Joel frustrates.

David Roche was another comedian that I met at this time. He intimidated me at first, being a very wise man, but eventually I realized we were peers. David was born with a facial disfigurement. The medical pseudo-wizards used radiation therapy as an attempt to treat a growth on his face. The radiation burned him, adding to the discoloration of the area and who knows what else. One of David's jokes makes the observation that the words "radiation" and "therapy" are a contradiction in terms.

Sociological and psychological studies about how people view those of us who are "different" have derived some fancy statistics. The highest level of discomfort, according to these studies, is caused by conditions that involve the face. David's childhood would support this evidence. He is one of the most beautiful men I've ever known, both inside and out, but his facial difference made other children treat him like a monster. Adolescence (aka hell-on-earth for many youth) brutalized him further.

JUDY GIER

Reverend Dave of "The Church of 80% Sincerity"

I did not see David go through his struggle of self-acceptance, but he shares it with the world in his one-hour performance piece, "The Church of 80% Sincerity." His stories are powerful, humorous and encouraging. Through David's stories, audience members learn about themselves. He starts out talking about his face, but by the end of his performance, his face has become a metaphor for the human condition we all experience.

In the time I've known David, he has gone from doing stand-up comedy in a noisy coffee house to performing at the White House. As I dictate these words to my computer, David is heading for the airport. He has been invited to perform for President and Hilary Clinton and members of Congress. I spoke to David and, of course, he was a bit nervous. I told him to just keep in mind the fact that they all use The Great Equalizer.

David has a new performance piece that I've seen as a work in progress, but he's been so busy traveling with his "Church" show, and doing speaking gigs, that he hasn't had much time to work on it.

(Why is it that all these performers are also public speakers? Public speaking is the day job that supports what they really want to do. They make at least twice as much money for the same material if they present it as a motivational speech. Heavy sigh. Why is Art so disrespected in our country that artists have to compromise their lives this way?)

The show that David is working on is called "Catholic Erotica." I think it will be a masterpiece!

Ben Stuart aka Benjamin Rodriquez, was the bad boy of this group. The three comedians I have described so far are clean cut, well-dressed, well-mannered gentlemen. Even though Mike Lee's humor strays a bit off the path, these guys stay fairly well within the bounds of good taste. They'll talk about sex, but in a Dr. Ruth way. Ben Stuart talked about sex in a Howard Stern way.

You might notice that I speak of Ben in the past tense. Unfortunately, he died at a young age (early 30s?), which sort of cuts a comedian's career short.

Of course, his career was already about as short as one can get.

I just made a bad joke that I think Ben would appreciate. You see, he was a man of short stature. He used a power wheelchair, so I never saw him stand. I'd guess that he was about three feet tall.

The PC way to refer to this disability is that he is a person of short stature or a Little Person. Some people don't mind being called dwarfs, but some do. "Midget" is a term that is usually used incorrectly. Technically, dwarf means short limbs, not proportionate to the rest of a body; midget means short, with everything proportionate.

Whatever, Ben was short.

Ben performed regularly at the Holy City Zoo, a well-known comedy dive in San Francisco, the same place where I did my one and only stint as a stand up (sit down) comedian. His routine was full of cusswords, drug jokes, dirty jokes and crude jokes about ethnicity. His classic line was, "I'm one of Jerry's Kids... Jerry Garcia."

Though Ben was the hoodlum of the comedy gang, he was very important. He may have offended some people, but he reached others that the white shirt comedians couldn't reach. He gave our community balance and I miss the flavor of his presence. He took risks and made it work.

Kenneth Littleton Crow is another comedian we have lost to Lady Death. As a comedian, I found Ken's material to be fairly average. The bit that has stayed with me over the years is him singing a country western song, "Oh, I'm wheelchair bound…" (As in "California bound"… get it?)

Though I think he was par as a comedian, he was great as an actor. For several years, he was in the "Shakespeare in the Park" series in Golden Gate Park in San Francisco. Then he went to Ashland, Oregon, playing in the famous Shakespearean company there. This is an amazing accomplishment when you realize that he delivered his lines from a wheelchair. When an actor is good at their craft, complaints about a wheelchair interfering with authenticity disappear.

Alexis Maguire was the only female comedian to regularly come out and play with the "Able to Laugh" bunch was Alexis Maguire. She was dyslexic, which made for great word play with her first name. In addition to doing stand up comedy, "Alexis the Dyslexic" was working as a teacher at the traffic school. They use comedians to teach their courses so that students will pay more attention.

Each of these comedians mentioned their disability at least once during their routines, though the degree varied considerably. Some of them based their routine almost entirely on their disability; others mentioned it one time, in passing; others threw it in every now and then as a zinger, reminding audience members who, by this time, had forgotten.

Whether or not the comedians do material about their disability, they are important. I think it's a mistake when people put pressure on members of a group to address issues related to their group in everything they do. Just because a comedian is disabled, their material does not have to be about disability.

This same thing can be said about any performer with a disability, whether an actor, a musician or even a radio disc jockey. I think it helps if they don't hide their disability, but the degree they use it as part of their art is their choice.

Now I'm going to argue the opposite opinion...

During my high school years in Nebraska, Rock 'n Roll was played on the radio for only two hours every night. The disc jockey was named Mel Sauer, and he was great! I listened to him for several years before I found out that he was blind. He never mentioned it, but small town gossipers did.

Out of the blue one night, between songs, he mentioned his blindness. He was joking about having gone bowling the night before and somehow explained to the audience why that was so funny.

Learning that Mel was blind did a lot to change my stereotypical image of blind people. Until that time, I had no real-life reference. I had never known a blind person. My perception of blindness came from literature and movies that portrayed them as unfortunate victims who were helplessly dependent on other people. Certainly they were not contributing members of society, or bowlers.

Finding out that a successful, well-loved radio disc jockey was blind made me re-evaluate internalized images that I had held. Even more importantly, any blind children or teenagers who learned about Mel Sauer could know that life held possibilities for them.

Mel changed me and many others when he came out about his blindness that day. He probably also changed himself, because he gracefully demonstrated self-acceptance – he didn't apologize for his blindness, but spoke of it naturally and with humor.

Michael J. Fox has Parkinson's disease. It has progressed far enough that he can no longer hide his shaking hand in his pants pocket. Instead of retiring and hiding it away, he is openly talking about it. This type of revelation helps to chip away at the wall that says our disability should be a stigma, that we should be ashamed of it.

Whoopi Goldberg has a learning disability. I've never heard her mention it in her comedy skits, but she doesn't hide it either. Danny Glover has a learning disability and speaks publicly at events to raise funds to support programs for people with disabilities.

It is not black and white. Did Mel Sauer have to prove himself first, to his employers and to his audience, before he revealed his blindness to us? Would we have accepted it the way we did if we hadn't already been a fan of his? If Michael J. Fox was not an extremely popular actor, would directors and producers continue to hire him with Parkinson's disease? How many performers are out there, hiding disabilities, for fear that revealing them will thwart their career advancement?

For a performer to reveal a disability (if it is hidden) or to focus on a disability (if it's not hidden) is a personal choice. But, it is a choice that has "big picture" significance and should not be made lightly. The more open a performer is about a disability, the more damage can be done to the wall of ignorance between the general public and people with disabilities.

[....getting down off the soap box now....]

I think of the title "Able to Laugh" and I see many possible interpretations. One is "Look, folks, we can laugh, too! Betcha didn't know that." An interpretation I don't like is "Isn't it wonderful how they are able to laugh despite what they have to live with?" I prefer to interpret it as "We are able to laugh at ourselves, as humans, including the humorous side of our disabilities."

Speaking of laughing at ourselves, I have a story about how I used sick humor to break the ice in an uncomfortable situation that I found myself in.

I was hired as an actress to be in an industrial video. Many actors make their bread and butter doing jobs that pay well, but that have little exposure, often seen in-house only. These are called industrial videos. I did one for Bank of America that was about employee benefits.

I played the part of an employee at the bank who just happened to be disabled, though the disability had nothing to do with the part. It was a reflection of the level of awareness on the part of the director, Michael Coll, that he wanted to reflect diversity in the video. Unlike many directors, he includes disability in his definition of diversity.

Only employees of Bank of America saw the above mentioned video. I was in another video that only prison administrators and workers would likely see. I am a union actor, but people have usually never seen me in anything unless they work at Bank of America or at a penitentiary.

I digress... my story is about the time I was hired to be in an industrial video made by a company that produces training materials on topics related to management and communication skills. This video was about how to resolve conflicts in a group discussion.

Six actors were hired to work on this video. I was the only one who was disabled. I was totally intimidated by the other actors. All of them had much more training and experience than I had. The director had told me that other actresses who had auditioned for my part were better than me, but that he chose me because he thought I'd be easier to direct. I wasn't sure if that was a compliment or an insult, but it did let me know that I was the weakest actor in the group. Needless to say, I didn't feel very confident when I showed up on the set.

A couple of the actors had seen each other before, but none of them really knew each other. We started out equal in that way, but levels of interpersonal exchange quickly developed between the other actors. By the end of the first day, they were laughing and joking with each other. I wasn't ignored, but I wasn't really included either. After one day of shooting, a bond had formed between the other five actors; I was not within the circle of that bond.

This is not an easy concept to explain, and it could be relegated to the realm of "all in my head," but, I know what I felt, and it was not a sense of belonging. I returned to my hotel room that night in tears. I contemplated the issue while soaking in a hot tub. Had I created this division by my own insecurity? I looked at other angles, including the usual one: am I unlikable?

Suddenly, I knew the problem. It wasn't personal, *it was the disability*!

Every now and then this sneaks up on me – my disability is so natural to me, that I forget that others might have discomfort about it. When I feel myself being excluded or treated oddly, I usually fail to consider my disability as the cause until I have eliminated several other possibilities.

Duh… it was my disability.

The next day I would try a strategy to break the ice: humor.

When doing a professional shoot, actors usually have a lot of "downtime." The director gets busy or the technical crew has to do some things. Meanwhile, the actors have to stay in their places and keep their energy high because shooting could resume at any moment.

I enjoy downtime, because it can be a lot of fun with the right bunch of actors. On the second day of shooting, during our first lengthy downtime, I demonstrated one of my specific skills as an actor – doing animal imitations. Soon, we were all taking turns showing the bizarre things we could do.

This was the warm-up, showing them I was human and not afraid to be silly. Then I brought out the big guns – I started telling cripple jokes. I wanted them to know it was okay to admit that they had noticed my wheelchair.

How bad were the jokes? They were pretty bad (groaners), or do you mean were they PC? You be the judge. If you become too offended, stop reading and go on to the next chapter.

So.....

What do you call a man with no legs and no arms who is on your wall?
Answer: Art.

What do you call a man with no legs or arms who is on your doorstep?
Answer: Matt.

What do you call a man with no legs or arms in your swimming pool?
Answer: Bob.

What do you call a man with one leg on skis?
Answer: Skip.

What do you call a woman with one leg?
Answer: Ilene.

And my personal favorite: What do you call a dog with no legs?
Answer: It doesn't matter, he won't come anyway.

There are many more, but my intent was only to give you a taste of the horrible jokes I used to break the ice that day on the set many years ago. The jokes did the trick and I became one of the group. Humor can build bridges, break down doors, break ice, open eyes… it's a powerful tool to sharpen and use.

If we can laugh at ourselves, we are more approachable. One of the reasons non-disabled people are uncomfortable with us is because we remind them of the fact that they are mortal. Laughing at the quirks caused by our disabilities is one way of saying "Yeah, I'm mortal. So what? Aren't you?"

When the video "Able to Laugh" first came out, there was some worry about how it would be received. Mothers try to keep their children from staring at disabled people and here was a group of people with disabilities who were making fun of themselves. But the video was very well received and continues to sell for use in classrooms as an educational tool.

It even won Best of Festival in Superfest one year! And, that leads quite nicely into my next chapter which is all about Superfest.

Postscript by David Roche

I get nostalgic when I think of those years. We were real pioneers.

I get resentful sometimes because artists don't get credit as disability activists. It's important to change laws, but it's just as important to change imaginations.

I feel proud that I make a living performing, speaking, coaching.

When I first was performing, people used to tell me how good I was and how I changed their lives. I never believed them, I thought they were just being polite. It took me about five years to catch on. In 1997 I quit my day job and co-produced a show that I thought was going to make me a couple thousand dollars. I went on stage in front of about 30 people, facing a loss of a lot of money. Somehow, in the middle of the show I got this epiphany where all of a sudden I realized it was a great show and I was going to make it financially and I did indeed change peoples' lives. That sense has never left me. I still get anxious but I feel I can go anywhere in the English speaking world and be a hit. My art changes peoples' lives.

Chapter Eight Superfest, CDT, and Chat About Allies

SUPERFEST INTERNATIONAL MEDIA FESTIVAL ON DISABILITIES has been around, in one form or another, since 1970. It has had various face lifts over the years, and at least one period where it was comatose, but it thrives today. It is a fantastic venue for keeping a pulse on videos and films that are being produced about disability or by producers with disabilities.

As the publicity for Superfest says, "These are not how to tie your shoe if you are disabled" videos. Recent entries are thought-provoking and exciting, including a satire on telethons, a depiction of schizophrenia through dance, documentary portraits of people with disabilities working in the sex industry, a man's story of the drug Ecstasy alleviating symptoms of Parkinson's Disease, a historic journey into the history of Circus Freak Shows, and clever Public Service Announcements used to recruit people to work as personal assistants for people with disabilities.

Superfest is the child of the Corporation on Disabilities and Telecommunication (CDT), a nonprofit organization whose mission is to encourage positive and realistic images of people with disabilities in the media. Part of that mission includes providing support to media makers and artists with disabilities. After all, one of the best ways to affect the images being made is to be involved in the making of those images.

Superfest was started by Neil Goldstein at Children's Hospital in Los Angeles as a small screening of works about disability. Under his guidance, it grew to an international festival, with entries submitted from around the world. Awards were presented, often at gala events, Hollywood style. Over the years, many stars gave support to Superfest, especially at the Awards events… puttin' on the Ritz!

One year Neil was able to get a PBS special aired, showing the award winners. This ninety-minute program was hosted by brothers Tom and John Ritter, sons of Tex Ritter (singing cowboy star of "B" Westerns during the 40's and 50's).

Tom became involved with CDT in a big way, serving as Board President for many years. Having lived with a disability (cerebral palsy) all his life, he knew the value of the organization.

At the time that Northern California became involved with Superfest and CDT, Tom was Board President and Neil was Executive Director. Superfest was held every two years. The Bay Area was one of several sites where works were judged.

Mony Flores-Bauer is the one to blame for introducing Superfest to the Bay Area, along with her cohort in crime, Bob Fitch. I am affectionately teasing them, because I greatly appreciate the hard work they gave to Superfest over the years.

For a few years Northern California's primary involvement in Superfest was hosting one of the judging sites. Neither Bob nor Mony are disabled, and they did not feel that it was appropriate to have a room full of non-disabled people judge videos about disability. Mony started calling around to find people with disabilities who were involved in the arts or media. She did not look for token disabled people, but people actually involved in media or art.

That's how I got involved. I started judging Superfest in the '80s and I pulled in other creative folks who we could talk into giving up a Saturday to look at some great (and some awful) films and videos.

It has been interesting to watch the change in submitted works over the years. When I first judged, many entries were medical in nature or promotional videos for things like prosthesis or other equipment. In the '90s Superfest began to see not only more videos from a first person voice (i.e. produced by a person with a disability), but works that were experimental, multidimensional, and thought-provoking. Although a very large number of works are still traditional documentary, they have moved from "inspirational" to "informational."

One year Northern California was asked to host the Awards event in San Francisco. Superfest was a huge gala event at Fort Mason in San Francisco. Tom Ritter and I hosted, and Bay Area celebrities gave out the awards. Superfest and CDT made a big splash that night and people wanted more.

Mony had organized the event and had done such an incredible job of pulling people together that we didn't want to stop. Thus, the Northern California chapter of CDT was formed. We contacted Los Angeles and asked them what they thought of the idea. It was a go!

Lots of things happened over the years, and although I don't want to bore you with too much detail on the marriages and divorces of the organization, I do need to give a brief overview:

Nationally Neil resigned as Executive Director, moved east and started another chapter, CDT East. Dave Deweerd, Kathy Martinez and I became national board members from Northern California. The organization staggered and stumbled, as often happens with changes in leadership, priorities and direction. Jim Hammitt replaced Tom Ritter as Board President, but Tom stayed involved. Tom brought in Cindy Allen, who took over the role as treasurer and main organizer of Superfest.

[Cindy has done more work as an extra in television shows than any other wheelchair rider I know. She is a blond in some of her earlier roles ("In Living Color") but becomes black-haired in later ones ("Shasty McNasty"). She was even an alien in a wheelchair in one of the Made-for-TV "Alien Nation" movies! If you see a black-haired, wheelchair driving woman in the background, it's probably Cindy. I wish I had her agent!]

CDT East CDT has always been about more than just Superfest. When Neil started the chapter in the East, he used media to educate people about Lyme disease. He also worked on a statistical study about how often, and the manner in which, people with disabilities are portrayed on television.

CDT Northern California This chapter grew larger than any of the others, probably because of the number of people with disabilities who live in the San Francisco Bay area. Before long, the chapter was doing more than judging Superfest. Monthly meetings were held with programs related to art or media, such as a slide show of paintings by a fine artist with a disability, or video by a local media maker. Eventually, performers started to filter into the organization and it took on new objectives, frequently hosting events for performers to strut their stuff. Initially this was the cause of a lot of friction, because the media makers in the group felt that CDT was about media and should remain about media, that to include theatre would water-down the resources and goals. After several debates it was decided that there was enough overlapping of the two (i.e. multimedia performances, taping of performances for video), that it made sense. (I voted against it, but I've seen how the organization has developed since that decision and I'm glad the vote went as it did.)

Networking CDT also became involved in collaborative projects with several other national media organizations that had nothing to do with disability, primarily through the Northern California Chapter. One such project resulted in the establishment of funds for independent media makers through the national organization, Independent Television Service (ITVS). Networking with other media organizations greatly increased the visibility of media makers with disabilities and works about disability. CDT impacted the other organizations in many specific ways too: Several members of CDT served on judging panels for other film festivals (e.g. San Francisco Film Festival; National Educational Media Festival); CDT wrote an article for the National Association of Media Arts Center's newsletter on the use of the internet by people with disabilities; CDT assisted Bay Area Video Coalition in getting captioning equipment at their video editing facility. Go Networking!

Fast forward a few years and we have a big shift. CDT Northern California became the national organization and the other chapters dissolved. Superfest became an annual event with other things happening locally throughout the year. Shifting and growing, shifting and growing.

For several years, I was the president of the Northern California Chapter. Shortly before it became the national organization, I passed the baton to Liane Yasumoto. Liane is grace on wheels, a beautiful and powerful woman who incurred a spinal cord injury in a car accident when she was a teenager. Liane has grown to be a strong leader and took over the role of Executive Director of CDT when the base of operations moved north to the Bay Area.

Three exemplary projects that CDT has been involved with in Northern California are described below. These worked out well and might be fodder for other organizations trying to do similar things:

1. Disability Culture Gathering CDT held a Disability Culture Gathering, bringing together representatives from several organizations to each give a three-minute presentation about what they did. Networking and working on joint projects is an excellent way to use resources to do bigger and better things, but we can't work together if we don't know about each other. The organizations CDT brought to the event were not only those directly connected to art and disability, but also mainstream art organizations that did a good job of including people with disabilities.

2. Ever Widening Circle Since 1999, CDT and the World Institute on Disability has hosted an annual performance event at the Yerba Buena Center for the Arts in San Francisco. This joint event is a fundraiser for both organizations and showcases some of the most talented professional performers with disabilities in the country. I talk more about Ever Widening Circle in Chapter Thirteen, but I wanted to mention it here as one of the major activities and accomplishments of CDT.

3. Living Room Festival CDT worked on the Living Room Festival project with several other media organizations. It was four years in the planning before the public saw the results on their tube. (People often don't realize how much work it takes to launch a great idea.) CDT was given a sixty- or ninety-minute time slot to program every year for three years on the local PBS station, KQED.

CDT/Superfest has done many wonderful things over the years, but these things have happened because of the time, energy and resources of many people, usually volunteers. Only planners know how much time it takes to pull together even a one day event. Those folks who do the work of making important events happen and helping valuable organizations thrive need to be commended BIG TIME, because without them, many changes wouldn't happen. Yet, these planners are usually so busy that they go unnoticed. Just like in theatre, the actor on the stage gets kudos, but all the people behind-the-scenes who were on the production team usually walk through the crowd after the play unnoticed, while well-wishers rush to compliment the actors.

Change takes time. This is something I learned in the trenches. Many organizations grow fast and do great and wonderful things for a few years, but die as suddenly as they were born. When I first started to do activist work, I wanted everything to change overnight. I felt that I was a failure because things moved so slowly. Now I realize that every organization and every project has a pace of its own. The trick is finding that pace!

The pace of CDT and Superfest has been like that of a long distance runner, sometimes slow, sometimes fast. Now, it seems to have found its stride, and is growing slowly, but steadily.

I have seen many major changes with CDT and Superfest over the years. I already mentioned how the nature of the works submitted for the festivals has changed; the demographics of the makers has changed too. In the early years of Superfest, the videos and films submitted for judging tended to be made by non-disabled people talking about disability related subjects; now 30 to 40 percent of the works submitted each year are produced or directed by a person with a disability.

This trend makes me very happy, because people with disabilities need to be involved in the making of the images that represent us in order to ensure accuracy. Otherwise, the works we see are from the fish bowl perspective – as if people with disabilities are goldfish, removed from the rest of society, looked at from outside their bowl.

Another reason this trend makes me happy is because it reflects people following their Dreams. My story started with talking about Dreams and how I and many other people with disabilities gave up our creative Dreams or hid them away. People with disabilities are beginning to reclaim their Dreams! This is clearly demonstrated by today's entries in Superfest.

Another major change I've seen in CDT over the years is related to the internal power of the organization. CDT was started by a non-disabled man and many of the people who helped in the development of the organization were non-disabled. Today, almost all of the Board of Directors are people with disabilities, the Executive Director is disabled and most of the people hired on a contract basis have disabilities.

This is not a criticism of the founders of CDT, but rather a reflection of the times. There were many wonderful non-disabled allies, who started organizations and programs that benefit people with disabilities. However, the '90s brought power struggles to the heart of many of those organizations as people with disabilities began using the motto "Nothing about us without us."

As required in the CDT bylaws, over 51 percent of the board members of CDT have always been people with disabilities. However, it has often been challenging to find consistent board members who are not only personally familiar with disability, but also knowledgeable about media and/or art.

There are different takes on how to structure a board, but most consultants will say that board members should be rich and influential. This approach considers a board's primary function to be bringing money to the organization. In theory, I acknowledge the wisdom of this approach, but it has the potential to foster a patronizing attitude toward the population being served if that population lacks money and influence.

This applies not only to disability organizations, but to any organization representing a disenfranchised group. How do the leaders of an organization make sure that it is run by the people it represents and at the same time have a Board of Directors made up of rich and influential people?

Balance is one answer, and CDT has struggled with making and keeping a balance over the years. The leaders of CDT take the issue of diversity seriously and want board representation that truly reflects our society. This means aiming for a board that represents people of color, women/men, youth/elders, and gays/lesbians/bi-sexuals. (Did I leave anyone out? Oh, heaven forbid if I left anyone out!) Additionally, CDT wants to represent a variety of art forms and disability types, so you see how challenging just putting a board together can be!

One issue at the core of all this is that of allies vs. people who think they are allies. Cribbing from a one-page declaration called "On the Question of Allies" by Aprille Annette, I will present some thoughts on the subject below, while ducking.

There are three kinds of psuedo-allies among us: the Missionaries, the Vultures, and the Do-Gooders. Many people who are running programs defined as helping people with disabilities are one, two or all three of these. This is not exclusive to non-disabled folk; psuedo-allies can be people with disabilities also. However, most psuedo-allies are people who are not disabled getting mileage out of "helping the handicapped."

The Missionary gets points for helping us, but the trick is they are often helping us their way. I can't even remember how often I've been embarrassed by having things given to me that I didn't need or want and had to accept them with feigned gratitude (e.g. stuffed toys from carnival vendors, money from strangers on the street when I was with a group of friends).

The Vulture exploits us and often makes money off of our needs, our art or our lack of power. When a Vulture makes money off of our art, it is often more money than we make off of it. The Vulture started multiplying at an incredibly fast rate after the passage of the Americans with Disabilities Act (ADA).

The Do-Gooder is motivated by a conscious desire to help the less fortunate and a sub-conscious desire that is patronizing, condescending and demeaning.

Below are more telling signs of a possible pseudo-ally:

- They use terms like "courageous" and "inspirational."
- They get lots of publicity, with theirself in the photo.
- They make all the artistic decisions without consulting people with disabilities.
- They don't encourage or develop people to move beyond their program.
- They don't worry about or think about whether or not they are an ally or a missionary/vulture/do-gooder; they get defensive when the issue is brought up.
- They use terms like "these people."
- They use the terms "us" and "them" more than the term "we." (An exception is "we" as in "What are WE painting today?")
- They give extreme praise when it is not justified or earned.
- They get impressed by the wrong things.

However, we need allies and are grateful for the true allies. Some of our best allies started out as psuedo-allies, but came to be true allies as they got to know people as individuals. People don't need to know everything about disabilities to be allies, but they need to know when they don't know and ask questions. I think most people are comfortable being approached with questions and don't want allies to feel anxious about bringing up issues. Of course, there are appropriate times and places – Don't ask me to explain why I don't like the word "special" when I'm about to go out on stage!

Invariably, talk of this type produces the question of "How do you tell the allies from the non-allies?" Often, it is a true ally asking this question, because the psuedo-ally usually does not even have a clue that this problem exists.

The answer is rooted in power dynamics. If someone appreciates your work and leaves you feeling powerful, they are probably an ally; if they leave you feeling mainly grateful, they may be a psuedo-ally.

Here is a question that leaders can ask about the power in an organization representing artists with disabilities: Is the power in the hands of non-disabled folks or are there board members, staff, and advisors with disabilities within the power structure of the organization? To me it seems like a logical conclusion that an organization whose mission is to serve people of an oppressed group should be led by people from that group. True allies understand that it is disempowering for oppressed groups to be led by people who don't experience the oppression.

Now that I have probably ruined my chance of getting a grant or assistance of any kind ever again from any funder who reads this book, let me continue talking about the changes I've seen in CDT…

Another change I've seen is related to a shift in the definition of disability within the organization and around the country. Initially, many of the works submitted to Superfest were about people with Developmental Disabilities (DD) and many of the people who gave time and energy to CDT worked in the DD field (e.g. special education teachers, case-managers). Yet, it has always been the mission of CDT to include people with all types of disabilities.

More and more, as Superfest grew, entry topics began to reflect a wider and more diverse population. Works that are submitted now are from/about people with a wide variety of disabilities as well as lesser known disabilities, such as environmental illnesses or tricholillomania (compulsive hair pulling).

Today, CDT has a high percentage of people with disabilities involved in the structure of the organization – as Superfest judges, on the Board of Directors, as contractors and volunteers. Many of these folks are people with physical disabilities; people with Developmental Disabilities are not as involved with CDT as they originally were.

Factioning happens a lot in disability organizations, sometimes for financial and practical reasons, sometimes for discriminatory reasons. People with Developmental Disabilities are often not independent in the area of transportation. To include them means putting time, energy and money into finding a way to assist people with transportation to get to and from meetings and events.

Inclusion of Deaf people means finding ways to pay for interpreters or to provide real-time captioning. Both of these things are usually cost prohibitive for small budget, non-profit organizations.

These are examples of real issues that can get in the way of people with different types of disabilities supporting each other, but these things can also be used as excuses for not including people. We grew up with societal conditioning too – having a disability doesn't wipe away learned prejudices.

Many people with physical disabilities are uncomfortable around people with Developmental Disabilities. I have often heard wheelchair users comment how they hate it that people think they are retarded because they use a wheelchair? This "Better Than Thou" attitude causes a person with one type of disability to feel higher on a hierarchy than a person with another type of disability.

Another attitudinal wall is Survivor's Guilt. I have been guilty of this one many times… meeting a person with a disability that I feel is worse than mine and feeling guilty about it… so guilty that I avoid that person.

Many Deaf people don't consider their not hearing to be a disability. They do not align with people with disabilities because they see nothing in common with wheelchair users. In one sense, they are right, because they can function within Deaf Culture without hearing. But, if a Deaf person wants to also function within the hearing world, I see them as having a disability.

What about Little People? Are they disabled or just short? Some identify with the disability community, some don't.

With these walls among individuals, it is a challenge for an organization to welcome all types of disabilities. CDT does a good job of it and I am proud to have been involved during its teenage years.

We can change all the laws we want, but if people don't see accurate images of people with disabilities, the laws don't really change our social status. This includes the attitudes of the people who are making laws in our legislature… if they watch "Heidi," what do they learn about the true reality of living with a disability?

Superfest is the longest running international media festival on disabilities and provides a benchmark for positive and realistic portrayals of people with disabilities. Thank you to every one who helped raise CDT/Superfest from infancy to adulthood!

NOTE *I dedicate this chapter to my friend, Sue Glover, who died in her sleep the night I finished writing the first draft of this chapter. She had lived several years with multiple sclerosis. Sue was a faithful member of CDT and one of the best audience members you could ask for. Although some artists are only concerned about their relationship with Creativity, most artists I know would say that they are nothing without an audience to observe their creation. Thank you, Sue, and all art appreciators, for helping us to be artists.*

Postscript By Liane Chie Yasumoto

Some may think that my triple minority status – being female, Asian, and disabled — is a curse. I believe these characteristics enhance who I am rather than limit me. When I was introduced to the media field, I had a desire to change negative portrayals of Asian women and people with disabilities. Identity is vital to building one's self-esteem, but the images on screen, in print and on stage did not reflect the reality of who I was. I am not the stereotypical subservient, passive, or exotic Asian woman. Nor am I the heroic person with a disability who miraculously becomes cured or "overcomes" her disability on the movie-of-the-week. I am a strong, independent, optimistic woman who happens to experience the world sitting in a wheelchair. I desire to see accurate representation of individuals with disabilities. Often, this means that we ourselves must work to create positive change by writing, selecting, and/or promoting roles where inner talents are recognized and gender, ethnicity, and disability are not emphasized or mocked in any way. CDT has created a home for artists of all sizes, shapes, and colors to be represented and heard and continues to educate, empower and entertain the community.

Chapter Nine Wry Crips Disabled Women's Theater Group

HONEST, RAW AND INVENTIVE are the adjectives I would use to describe the innovative bunch of artists known as Wry Crips Disabled Women's Theater Group. This radical group was founded by Patty Overland, Laura Rifkin, and Judith Smith in 1985. Wanting to do theater work, but finding that traditional theater did not provide opportunities for people with disabilities, these women created their own opportunities.

Several women worked on pieces about their lives, mostly short poems. The group also wrote parodies of familiar songs and created skits developed from improvisations. Although most of the pieces were about disability related subjects, some were about love, sex, and the ordinary things of life that everyone experiences, disabled or not. Satiric humor and justified anger were the prominent expressions in their shows.

Membership in Wry Crips was fluid, though many women remained consistently involved for years. During more active periods the age range was 21 to 50, and ideologies spanned the spectrum from separatist-feminist to born-again Christians. Most members had low incomes and over half were lesbians.

Most of the women who came together to work as Wry Crips had no previous experience onstage or going public with their writings. Some preferred writing, some enjoyed performing, and some liked to do both. Enough were prolific writers that it was quite a task to wade through hundreds of poems to select those to be included in their first performance.

Women with disabilities found Wry Crips to be a safe place to express thoughts and feelings that had been bottled up for many years. Empowerment issues were constantly acknowledged, including the realization that talking and writing about a lack of power is empowering.

Right from the start it was important to the members of Wry Crips that the group reflect diversity and that no one be discriminated against. They were committed to representing people with various types of disabilities, ethnicities, and sexual orientations. Women with communication disabilities were included, as well as women with environmental illnesses, chronic illnesses, and mental disabilities – groups that are often left out, even in programs designed for people with disabilities. This led to many challenges for the group, but they dealt with them tenaciously. I respect and admire the women who stayed with that process, creating a strong model for inclusion.

I was involved in the first performance of Wry Crips, but I did not have the patience to stick with the processing. I applaud the women who persisted. The result of their work is commendable, not only creatively, but also for representing strong and new inclusionary practices.

The material and the ways women with disabilities were enabled to participate in the performances made for powerful shows. Wry Crips used creativity to adapt to individual needs. Their solutions towards inclusion often developed slowly and were painfully discovered. However, they stuck to it, driven by the belief that their theatre experiment would work. They invented access assistant roles such as page turners for women who were physically unable to turn their pages, and voice interpreters for women who had speech that was difficult to understand. One performer was bed-bound and unable to physically attend performances, so a chair with her photograph was placed on the stage while she recited her poems over a speakerphone.

Six months after the birth of Wry Crips, they performed their first show, a ninety-minute script called "Hors d'Oeuvres" – the concept being that this was just a sampler of "dishes" to be offered in future shows. This first show was for an audience of women only in order to accommodate some of the lesbians in the group who did not feel comfortable performing and sharing their intimate stories in front of men. Wry Crips was greeted with great enthusiasm by a full house of 200 supportive women who had come to the event despite a major rain storm.

"I thought there'd be twenty people and we'd all be miserable together, but the house was packed," recalls Peni Hall, one of the performers that night. "Looking out at the sea of drenched women made it so clear to me how hungry people were for what we had to offer."

Audiences in San Francisco and Berkeley venues are accustomed to unconventional performances and to art that pushes the envelope, but the first Wry Crips show opened up new territory on the radical frontier. For one, much of the material reflected anger, an emotion that is often considered dysfunctional or unappreciative when coming from a person with a disability. Since this was the first time that some of the women had given voice to their feelings, many expressed frustration about how they were treated in the world. Selecting the final pieces for the show, Wry Crippers scrambled for works that would create more balance, but the end result still reflected a prominent negative tone. Even so, the honesty of the cathartic pieces was respectfully received by the women-only audience.

The fact that it was a women-only audience was a point of contention for some people within the disability community. Subsequently, Wry Crips scheduled a second performance and the women who did not want to perform in front of men were not in that show. This type of problem-solving created the modular way that Wry Crips approached shows. Each performance was different, not only in material, but also in the make-up of the group. Some shows had several performers, like "Hors d'oeuvres" which had twelve. Others had as few as three. It depended on the type of event, and on who was interested and available.

Wry Crips shows were advertised to be perfume-free and smoke-free, to enable people with Environmental Illnesses (EI) or allergies to attend and perform. They went as far as having "sniffers" at the door for their first two performances to determine whether a person was scent free. In front of the ticket box was the sniffer table. If a sniffer smelled perfume on an individual, the person was asked to go wash up in the bathroom where scent free soap had been placed. If cigarette smoke was the offender, they were asked to remove their coat or to turn their shirt inside out. In both cases they were asked to sit as far away from the EI section as possible.

Most people were cooperative, if not curious, but the sniffer concept ruffled feathers and also became cumbersome. Ultimately, it was discontinued. Some people were so unaware of the issue that they didn't understand the sniffer's purpose. Instead of smelling people at the door, Wry Crips distributed informational handouts and samples of safe products. The issue stayed alive, but differently, and people were approached only if the ticket sellers noticed that they reeked of perfume or smoke.

Wry Crips remained proactive about allergy issues, advertising events to be scent free and choosing performance sites based on conditions related to smoke, perfume and cleaning products. Often, they would have people go to a venue the day before an event and use safe cleaning products. They replaced scented products in bathrooms and put air filters around the room.

Even with all of these efforts, problems came up. For example, one time they checked out a facility and it seemed fine. The day of the performance many people were having severe reactions to something. They questioned the manager and learned that the night before there had been a dance in the space with several people wearing perfume or cologne, and many being smokers.

Accommodating several types of disabilities can create interesting challenges. A blind audience member with a seeing-eye dog may cause problems for a person who has an allergy to dogs. Wry Crips' solution was to seat people with dogs and people with environmental allergies in two different sections. A similar situation had to be worked out for seating those who needed to be near an air filter and those who were sensitive to noise. There wasn't always a perfect solution, but they tried hard to work these things out.

All of this may seem extreme to someone who doesn't know much about environmental illnesses. Some people roll their eyes when they see "No Scented Products or Perfume" on a meeting announcement. I'm not going to go into a long diatribe, but I do want to point out that toxins affect many people, including some who aren't even aware of their own reactions. The introduction of synthetic materials (e.g. polyesters that give off a gas) and toxic solvents (e.g. strong cleaners) into our environment has compromised our immune systems. People often leave meetings with headaches, fatigue, moodiness and/or disorientation; they don't realize that they may be experiencing an allergic reaction, perhaps to the carpet, perfume, air freshener, etc.

Wry Crips educated many people about the need for environmentally safe spaces. As a result of their influence, many Bay Area venues are now less toxic. Managers changed cleaning products and order less toxic materials when remodeling. Many organizations list "Please, No Strong Scents" on their event promotional materials. EI seating was a radical concept when Wry Crips first did it, but their example paved the way for this type of accommodation to be included as common practice when thinking of disability access.

While we're on the subject of EI, I'll give you an example of an audience favorite from Wry Crips' repertoire. Peni Hall wrote her poem "Environmental Tiptoe" to be sung to the tune of "Tiptoe Through the Tulips":

Tiptoe
through the Mine Field
of the Lysol
and the Carpet Fresh…
Come breathe in
 cigarette smoke
with me.
Tiptoe
through the benzene
in the car fumes
on the city street
and soak up
all the tar fumes
 with me.
Relax…
And take it all in your lungs
Or else through your skin,
As you go

Splashing
on the toxins
    in your perfume
and your Right Guard too…
Just soak in
all the harm done
to you

— *Copyright © 1990 Peni Hall*

Two of my poems were in their first show, but I didn't read them. I was the Mistress of Ceremonies. That was the only Wry Crips show I was in, though my poems have been in several. Wry Crips has ebbed and flowed over many years. Most of their activities are not public. They are gatherings of women with disabilities who share their writings with each other. When they are invited to do a show, those who are interested pull together some material and make an appearance. Once in awhile, Wry Crips organizes and produces a show. The emphasis has always been on sharing writings, with performances being an occasional by-product. In fact, there was a five year period where they met twice a month with no goal of performing.

When Wry Crips does perform, whether invited or producing their own show, they are always greeted with a full and appreciative audience. Their material is revolutionary in that it gives voice to many thoughts that have been kept private for too long. They perform material that few have the courage to cover, subjects that are considered taboo or unmentionable in regards to disability. They encourage a celebrating of disabilities and not making apologies for them. In fact, one of their shows is called "No Apologies."

Wry Crips uses a reading style in performing, modeled after the style used by Mother Tongue Reader's Theatre and Fat Lip Reader's Theatre. Sometimes a single voice is used; sometimes they say things in unison. Sometimes they share lines; sometimes they alternate lines. Sometimes one person says a whole piece. Some of the pieces are short; some are long. Some are simple, some are dramatic. Their method of sharing and alternating lines reinforces the words in one of their pieces: "…me and my disabled sisters…"

ANNIE F. VALVA

Sascha Bittner, Pandoura Carpenter and Jan Levine of Wry Crips

Several women have been longtime Wry Crippers in important ways and I can't possibly mention all of them, partly because I don't know all of them. I would like to mention Diane Hugaert who was the first coordinator and the woman who gave the group it's sassy name. Though she spent most of her time in bed with chronic illness, she organized, facilitated and kept records for Wry Crips, enabling them to function.

Cheryl Marie Wade was the second coordinator and further helped to flesh out guidelines, policies and other behind-the-scenes stuff. Meanwhile, Wry Crips produced its' second public performance, "Just Desserts." The performance hall was crammed with 350 women, men, and children… word had gotten around about this new in-your-face theater group. The two-hour show featured the group's first venture into sketch comedy, which included "Crip Jeopardy," a parody of a popular TV game show.

In the Wry Crips version of the contest that gives the answers and contestants have to guess the questions, categories included Crip History, Meds and Feds, Crip Etiquette and Red Tape. Here is a taste of what the audience was treated to:

GAME SHOW HOST:
He was known as the closet crip president.
SMART CONTESTANT:
Who was President Franklin Delano Roosevelt?
GAME SHOW HOST:
The answer is yellow tape.
SMART CONTESTANT:
What do bureaucracies use when they run out of red tape?
GAME SHOW HOST:
Sneezy, Grumpy, Sleepy, Dopey, and Bashful.
SMART ALEC CONTESTANT:
Sounds like the nurses on the graveyard shift.
SMART CONTESTANT:
What are just a few of the symptoms of Environmental Illness?

As Wry Crips productions became bigger and more involved, the group grew to need a Technical Coordinator and Peni Hall picked up the baton. Peni has a Masters degree in technical theater and worked as an instructor at Oberlin College. She had left her art on a side street for many years after developing a chronic illness. When Wry Crips formed, she found a place she could again be an active artist. In addition to performing, she worked on the sound equipment, lights and props. She also video-taped many of their shows, and eventually edited together a documentary about the group. This award-winning video interviews Wry Crips women and features clips of some of their performances.

The third coordinator was Pandoura Carpenter, who served for several years. During this time there were many performances, including one done specifically for a group of psychiatrists. It benefits both professionals and their disabled patients when they get first-hand education from performers like Wry Crips. [If the psychiatrist who did couple counseling for me had gotten a dose of Wry Crips, he would not have dared to tell me that my five year marriage was failing because I hadn't "accepted my handicap."]

In 1993, Wry Crips did its only performance outside the Bay Area at a Women's Conference in Los Angeles. The group found a way for all who wanted to perform to be able to go, including Jan Levine. Jan was a long-time Wry Cripper, but travel isn't easy for someone who uses a large power wheel-chair and needs lots of attendant assistance. Pandoura took the Wry Crips concept of inclusion seriously and did not take the easy way out.

Patty Overland, one of the Wry Crips founders, has filled many roles over the years. One of the groups hallmark pieces, "Super Crip Girl," is performed with fervor by Patty at most of their performances. She is the only Wry Cripper who has remained involved since the birth of this ground-breaking collective.

Part of the power of Wry Crips comes from the fact that their work is written, produced and directed by women with disabilities. Through group performance and involvement, Wry Crips women develop skills and gain confidence. Through their accomplishments as writers, performers, technicians, directors, task doers, meeting organizers, facilitators, and support persons they have the opportunity to view themselves as contributors rather than dependents. The shows and tapes produced by Wry Crips contributed not only to the enrichment of each member's life, but to Art. They represent the power and potential of women with disabilities.

Wry Crips is not only edgy on stage, but in process too. All decisions are made by consensus, often through hours of intense processing over several days. They have sometimes tried to be so politically correct that they've backed themselves into corners. They could have long debates over issues like what color to wear on stage or the usage of one word.

Wry Crips learned that it is not possible to find a solution to all conflicts, but that talking about the issues educates and makes people more sensitive to and appreciative of each other. To demonstrate, some of the women were allergic to perfume, but wearing perfume is a cultural aspect for some ethnic groups. How do you find a compromise to that type of situation when you are trying to be politically correct in matters of disability and ethnicity? Can you? Sometimes. Sometimes not. Wry Crips tried hard to model respect for the opinions, needs, feelings and differences of all the members – even when it took hours of processing.

Sometimes, despite all their effort, Wry Crips failed to resolve an issue. At one tense meeting, one Wry Cripper asked another what she could do to ease the friction caused by their class differences. The response was "There's nothing you can do. Your mere existence on this planet offends me!" Wry Crips certainly gave women a place to speak their truth.

I realize that as I write about Wry Crips, I find myself struggling with tenses. Sometimes I speak in present tense, sometimes I speak in the past. It may confuse the reader and make you wonder whether Wry Crips still exists. That is a question that many of us ask.

Often a couple of friends will be talking about the old days, about how much we miss the Wry Crips shows, and how we wish the group was still around. Then, seemingly out of nowhere, they appear and a performance happens. The general public is never really sure whether Wry Crips still exists or not until we see them onstage. As I said, a lot of their work is about women sharing their writings with each other. We, the audience members, are honored when they choose to share them with us.

Additionally, the ebb and flow of the Wry Crips organization depends on the women currently putting energy into it. Sometimes it is made up of women who have no desire or energy to perform publicly; at other times it is made up of women who love the stage. Sometimes the women involved have strong organizational skills and the knowledge to pull off a production; other times, the women only want to be writers and to share with each other.

Though I am friends with several of the women who created and raised the group, even I am usually uncertain of the current state of Wry Crips. Unfortunately, I think this demonstrates how undervalued the arts are in our country. Wry Crips is an excellent group that deserves ongoing funding, but it has had to play the nonprofit grant-writing game to keep afloat, taking energy away from creativity. It doesn't take a lot of money for women to gather together to share their writings, but it does take money and energy to produce shows from those writings. We are the ones who lose when outstanding artists have to fight for performance funding. Artists will still do their art, but the public won't see it.

The last time the group performed under the name of Wry Crips was in 2002. They had originally prepared the show for an event in Berkeley on disability and sexuality. When the organizers of that event became overwhelmed by the enormity and controversies surrounding what they had taken on, they reduced the event to fine arts only. Wry Crips was cancelled, along with all the other scheduled performers. Judy Finelli, the fourth Wry Crips coordinator, found an alternative venue and they performed their "Banned in Berkeley" show in San Francisco, opening for another show that was already scheduled. Shortly after, the members of the group changed the name to "Crip City Rollers" and put on a self-produced show in 2003, but has done nothing public since.

Has Wry Crips fallen off the map? Not hardly! Many women's creative lives were impacted through Wry Crips for over fifteen years. Some of those women still work creatively, but not in conjunction with Wry Crips. Some share writings through use of the internet. The video documentary mentioned earlier sits on the shelves in many libraries and homes.

One way or another, I am sure that most of the women who were ever involved with Wry Crips are still writing and that many of them are sharing their writings with each other, formally or informally.

One of my wishes is that Wry Crips will find a Funding Angel to enable them to continue the great work that only they can do. The creative energy and spunk that was Wry Crips still lives and is bound to reemerge sometime, somewhere. Perhaps as the original Wry Crippers go on to other creative ventures, younger women with disabilities will step up to take leadership roles and give the organization a shot in the arm.

The women of Wry Crips put voice to issues that people with disabilities have been taught to be passive about: medical abuse, health care monopolies, condescending relationships, stereotypes of asexuality, patronizing charity… And Wry Crips did it with sass! Regardless of the future of the organization, the voices have been heard and a ripple effect of speaking out has resulted.

Long live the sassy spirit of Wry Crips!

Postscript by Patty Overland:

Summer 1985, about twenty disabled women gathered to express ourselves, to speak our truths as disabled women.

We began to write our stories, we began to feel the energy of a group of us coming together and how the synergy of the group was more than just the sum of its parts.

I got to explore how to write about the sexuality of disabled women, disabled lesbians. The group was not only for lesbians. There was little opportunity for disabled women in general, so we didn't want to shut out straight women.

I was able to refine Super Crip Girl who does all kinds of extraordinary things. I got out some of my feelings about sexuality and anger in Crip Ramble and Crip Rage. I wrote for certain audiences, like a piece about anorexia for a gig we did for a Fall Gathering of Fat Women.

Wry Crips, and an offshoot group, Crip City Rollers, have given me an opportunity to work with other disabled women, and hone my crafts. Wry Crips gave me a chance to be a writer and an actor in a way that I could never have imagined.

IN THE MID-'80s, Thais Mazur taught a creative class for women with disabilities. This started the wheels turning that eventually formed a new dance company. One of the class members wrote a poem about becoming disabled. A performance piece resulted when group members decided to use movement to depict the poem. "In This Body" was performed in 1988, in Dance Brigade's "Furious Feet III" festival in Oakland, California. It included four women who use wheelchairs (Bonnie Lewkowicz, Corbett O'Toole, Judith Smith, and Cheryl Marie Wade) and three dancers who were not physically disabled (Leigh Lightfoot, Thais Mazur, and David Russell), and it was directed by Thais Mazur. AXIS dis/Abled Performance Group was the group's original name, but it evolved as they developed into a professional dance company.

After this first performance, the group realized that they were on to something and they wanted to continue. They not only saw value for themselves, but for the general public. Their focus became about presenting good art, not about making a political statement, though some might argue that just doing their break-through work is political.

Also in 1988, AXIS performed as a company in Dance Brigade's "Revolutionary Nutcracker Sweetie," sometimes called an anti-Nutcracker show. It was created by Dance Brigade's founders, Krissy Keefer and Nina Fichter. Their idea was to break boundaries of what the Nutcracker represents in regards to white, middle-class American culture. To do this, the show included performances from various groups and subcultures in society, including Latinos, Gays and Lesbians, women who had non-traditional dancer bodies, and other groups that were not usually seen in a professional dance performance. Disability is very apparent in Berkeley ("A crip on every corner!") and, therefore, they felt it was important to include performers with disabilities.

Dance Brigade did their first "Sweetie" in 1986 without involvement from the disability community, but they were continuously doing outreach to include "fringe" people. A meeting was held with people from the disability community who were beginning to take artistic risks. Many of the folks at the meeting began to work with Dance Brigade on future versions of this annual show.

The vision and result was fabulous! The 1987 version included a contact improvisation piece by Bruce Curtis and Patty Overland, both wheelchair users. AXIS became involved in "Sweetie" starting in 1988, adding a dynamic dimension to an already fantastic show.

"The Revolutionary Nutcracker Sweetie" played at Christmas time for ten years and AXIS performed in five of them (1988 – 1992). The first time they were involved, the group glided on stage as a Sea Dragon in an underwater world section, wheelchairs and dancers almost completely covered by a massive costume. In subsequent years AXIS performed their own creative and experimental pieces, sometimes as colorful sea creatures interacting in the underwater world. More important than the performance itself, working on this show and receiving positive public feedback gave AXIS a huge push forward.

AXIS quickly gained notoriety; they received many offers and began to perform in a variety of venues and styles, including work with Terry Sendgraff's low-flying trapeze to develop an aerial piece. As they began to clarify their goals and focus, their name evolved to AXIS Dis/Abled Dance Troupe. They had not originally intended to become a dance company, but things had snowballed. Before long they were getting non-profit status and putting together a repertoire.

The only co-founders of AXIS that are still with the group are Bonnie Lewkowicz and Judith Smith. Bonnie began dancing when she was five, studying for ten years prior to becoming disabled in a dune buggy accident. She got involved in wheelchair sports for movement expression until she rediscovered dance. With AXIS she has performed and taught nationally and internationally.

Judith Smith had no formal dancing experience prior to her spinal cord injury at age 17, but she had been a champion equestrian on the Colorado Hunter/Jumper circuit. Once exposed to the art of movement through contact improv, Judith almost instantly transferred her passion for riding to dancing. In 1997, Judith became the Artistic Director for the company.

Over the years I have watched the group evolve artistically and professionally. Their work is very different now from when they started. At first they played with how to create movement between dancers who used different methods of mobility. One of their early popular pieces, "Wheels," involved three dancers in wheelchairs, two dancers on roller skates and one dancer on foot. A later rendition also included a skateboard.

The dance that AXIS creates allows for maximum use of what a dancer brings to the floor, without relying on traditional ideas of what is allowed as dance. Some dancers use manual wheelchairs, some power wheelchairs. Some dancers who are disabled can get out of their wheelchairs unassisted, onto the floor or an aerial apparatus such as a trapeze, rope or ladder. New aesthetics were and are created by the flexible thinking of the dancers in the company.

Early on, it became clear that the members of AXIS were developing a new, innovative movement vocabulary. Traditional dance terminology was not broad enough to include their creative and experimental applications for movement. Terminology is always an interesting animal to watch. AXIS uses "physically integrated dance" to describe movement and dance that includes disabled and non-disabled dancers. Others call it "mixed ability dance" or "sit down/stand up dance." The issue of defining the disability aspect of an integrated dance company has been chewed on from many directions. AXIS is now known as "AXIS Dance Company" and has dropped the disability reference in their name, thus emphasizing that they are about dance.

AXIS moved well beyond a group of people with and without disabilities getting together to experiment with dance and movement. They performed in many shows within the disability community and they also began to work with other professional dancers and companies. And now, they have "arrived."

I say they have arrived, meaning in regards to their professionalism and their emergence in the dance arena. They are still struggling financially, like most art groups in our country, despite corporate sponsorship and grants/assistance from California Art Council and National Endowment for the Arts.

The success of AXIS is happening by leaps and bounds these days. I won't try to tell you what their latest achievement has been because, by the time this book is printed, they will have gone on to their next accomplishment. A recent success was to have a piece choreographed by the renowned dancer/choreographer Bill T. Jones. Also, two of the AXIS dancers, Nadia Adame and Jacques Poulin-Denis, performed with Mikhail Baryshnikov at the Kennedy Center for the Performing Arts in Washington DC.

One thing that helped AXIS was that Jeremy Alliger of The Dance Umbrella saw their work and recognized them as true artists. In collaboration with Dance Umbrella, AXIS co-curated the International Festival of Wheelchair Dance in Boston in 1997, the first event of this magnitude and prestige in the history of this new contemporary dance form. This began an international dialogue about the quality, aesthetics and philosophy of physically integrated dance, with high artistic standards being paramount in the Vision.

Thanks to allies like Jeremy Alliger, integrative dance is beginning to crossover into the dance world at-large. The dance community views the work of AXIS as a new dance form, rather than an imitation or interpretation of dance. They participate with other dance companies in mainstream forums, as well as forums specifically for integrated dance companies and for the arts and disability field. Their work is

MARGOT HARTFORD

Renee Waters, Judith Smith, Stephanie Bastos and Alisa Rasera of AXIS Dance Company rehearsing 'Flesh' choreographed by Ann Carlson

impressive and exciting. There is no doubt that they have reached a level of professional excellence.

Though I still very much enjoy watching AXIS perform, to my unsophisticated eye, they have lost some of the early playfulness that I enjoyed during their experimental days. This is not a criticism, but a reflection of my tastes. The only contemporary dance company that I thoroughly enjoy is the one created and choreographed by Pina Bausch, but to keep perspective on my opinion, it's only fair that I remind you that I don't like Picasso. There are others who feel just the opposite, who enjoy the work AXIS is doing now, as an accomplished, skilled dance company.

That's the beauty of art – something for everyone! I have never been to a ballet or an opera, but I have cried from the front row watching and listening to Eric Johnson do a guitar riff.

One thing I don't want to do in this book is to get into a "What is art?" discussion. My opinion is that if creativity is involved and emotions are being elicited, then it is most likely art. I realize that this covers a lot of territory.

Artists cannot stay stagnant; the process of creativity is one of fluidity. Just as a shark must continually swim or die, an artist who enjoys the creative process will not be happy doing the same thing over and over. As much as I wish that Jethro Tull would only play his old songs at concerts, he needs to move on to new things in order to be fulfilled as an artist. Likewise, we need to let the artists in the disability movement flow to wherever their creative juices take them.

AXIS participated in creating a new form of art. It is beautiful and moving to watch. They have done this while students with disabilities were denied access to dance classes in universities because the instructors could not see the point of including people with disabilities in a physically-driven art.

The world of art and dance is fortunate to have groups like AXIS pushing into new directions. Their performances are fascinating!

Postscript by Judith Smith:

AXIS' primary goal has always been to create good dance and the Company has evolved and changed over the years to keep reaching beyond this goal. When we started, we didn't know what would happen but it was obvious from the beginning that AXIS' work had a profound effect on audiences. This form of dance gives all of us the opportunity to expand our ideas about disability, dance and maybe even human potential in general. AXIS is creating a dance vocabulary that can only happen because of the way our dancers move together — be it in wheelchairs, with crutches, with spasticity, on one foot or two — and the potential is unlimited. I'm proud that AXIS has contributed greatly to having the dance world take this dance form seriously as the artistic innovation that it is. As a Company, we've felt a tremendous responsibility to create and teach dance that will speak for itself and not be applauded just because it's "special" art. We want to make work that audiences, presenters, choreographers, dancers and teachers — disabled and non-disabled — will want to be involved in because it's innovative, exciting and good.

Chapter Eleven   *M*oving Over the Edge (MOE)

IT IS DIFFICULT TO TELL THESE STORIES in a chronological way, because so many things were happening at the same time. If a social and cultural movement could be documented on video it might look like several dancers starting around the base of a hill, slowly working their way to the top.

Some move faster than others.

Some move forward and then backward and then forward again.

Some fall along the way, with others picking up their veils to continue their journey for them.

Some have to negotiate around trees and stumps.

Some dance with pleasure while others would dance with anger.

Some create their own dances while others imitate those of the people next to them.

… and eventually they wind up together at the peak, forming a Movement.

That is the best way I can describe what happened. Just like many pockets of artists or radical thinkers in history (e.g. Beatniks, Keat's group, the Soho bunch, the Surrealists), we were not aware at the time that we were a Movement. We knew that what we were doing was important to us and, after a while, we also knew that others were finding our work important.

Bruce Curtis is a man I consider one of the major leaders of this Artistic Movement, yet his impact has almost gone unnoticed. One of the things that drives me to write this book is a desire to put credit where credit is due. Many artists with disabilities have benefited from the work that Bruce started doing in the early '80s and continues to do today.

I met Bruce in Berkeley in the spring of 1984. I found myself needing an apartment and I wandered into the Housing Department at CIL during my lunch break. I stopped in my tracks. I don't stun easily and I rarely lose my cool, but my jaw dropped as I gaped at one of the most gorgeous men I'd ever seen.

There, in CIL's Housing Department, was an Adonis in a manual wheelchair, one of those sporty ones. He had luscious long, blond hair and deep, rich eyes that reflected the colorful poncho from Peru that he wore. Luckily, he was so busy looking at apartment ads that he hadn't noticed my staring.

I regained consciousness and backed out of the room unnoticed. My gut told me that this man was going to change my life! I was right, but not in the way I was thinking at the moment.

Within an hour I had spoken to several co-workers at CIL about this man named Bruce Curtis and I had collected various bits of information. I learned that he had been around during the 504 demonstrations and that he had been one of the people who had gone to D.C. to march on H.E.W. He left California after that, got married, got divorced, and was now moving back to Berkeley.

I found that people had mixed opinions about Bruce – people spoke highly of him as a strong voice in the Disability Rights Movement, but he was considered arrogant. Several people warned me that he wasn't an easy man to get to know. That didn't stop me. My gut is usually right and it told me to charge into that room and introduce myself. I took several deep breaths and went into the Housing Department.

He had left already. Wouldn't you know it.

He was back the next day, looking at the ads again. (Apartments are very hard to find in Berkeley, and needing wheelchair access makes it nearly impossible.) The next time Bruce came in, I introduced myself and we decided to look for a place together. The cost of renting in Berkeley is outrageously high and if two of us were looking, it increased our chances of finding something.

Bruce and I never shared an apartment, but we spent a lot of time together looking for one and hanging out when we got tired of looking. I enjoyed the depth of the conversations we shared. I didn't find him arrogant… aloof, perhaps, but not arrogant.

He is masked by the armor of his aloofness. Some people misinterpret his manner of saying things as arrogance. Those who take the time to listen to what he has to say find him an extremely intelligent man, with incredible vision and insight. He is also caring and sensitive.

I am glad that I pushed past my insecurities and did not allow myself to be intimidated by the surface of Bruce Curtis, because beneath lies a jewel.

However, I did get quite mad at him the first time we talked about dancing. We both like to go dancing at public events, but we have different tastes. I need a good old-fashioned rock 'n roll song in order to cut loose; Bruce likes to move to music with exotic drum beats or intriguing sounds from other countries. I like that type of music also, but I can't dance to it. Give me a loud version of "Shout" and you cannot keep me off the dance floor no matter how bad my back hurts.

Needless to say, Bruce and I usually traveled in different dance circles, but we'd talk about our experiences when we got together. Dancing was an important part of both of our lives. There came a point for Bruce where dance became his life. At first I didn't understand what he was talking about.

"I went to Ashkenaz the other night," he said in a state of ecstasy, "and something happened that's hard to describe, but I moved into a whole different place with dancing."

"I went out dancing this weekend also," I responded, "I went to a Sock Hop at the Hyatt Regency in San Francisco. It was a blast!"

"I'm talking about something different," Bruce retorted. "The music shifted and I found myself moving with it, more internal movement than dance actually."

I was getting the impression that he felt his experience had somehow been better than mine.

"I was dancing. I was moving." I said defensively. "Just because you don't enjoy dancing to rock 'n roll doesn't mean that it has less meaning than the music you dance to."

"There's nothing wrong with dancing to rock and roll, but it's recreational dancing," he countered. "I'm talking about moving in a creative way, finding the energy inside that matches what's happening outside and expressing it with my body. This is the first time since I became disabled that I've had this kind of experience."

"How can you say that the way I dance is not creative when you have never even seen me dance?!" I huffed away, thinking maybe Bruce was an arrogant jerk after all, a self-centered guy who only thought that the stuff he did was valid or important.

But the first time I saw Bruce dance, I realized he was right. I began to see the difference between recreational art and artistry. His dance was true art.

Bruce explored the new creative movements that were coming from within him, not really sure where he was going with it, but trusting that he was headed in the right direction. Eventually he discovered forms of dance called "contact improv" and "authentic movement."

The first time he explained it to me, my eyes glazed over; I had no frame of reference for the things he was talking about. Esoteric babble. New Age bull pucky. I tried to pay attention, but I just couldn't get it. I had to see it.

My lay person's explanation of authentic movement is that the dancer or dancers use their gut to dictate their spontaneous movements. You may ask, as I asked, how this is any different than dancing to rock 'n roll. Usually, my dancing was responding to a beat or sound in the music, with some of my movements based on how my partner was acting. But, all in all, that was where it stopped.

Authentic movement reaches deep inside and responds to the feelings that come from being present, in the moment, grounded, centered… as I see it, it's a very Zen thing. An external noise might affect an inner reaction, but it doesn't cause it. Instead of dance coming from bringing the outside inside, authentic movement is taking the inside and expressing it outwardly.

Contact Improv, as I understand it, is sort of the plural of authentic movement, meaning that two or more people engage in the authentic movement together. Their bodies and energies come in contact with each other and they react instinctually. Often, it results in a slow graceful exchange, though it can become an energetic tumbling of bounding and rebounding bodies.

If you haven't seen authentic movement, this may not make any sense to you, and my explanations may be causing many of the people who practice authentic movement to cringe, including Bruce. I cannot remember the exact words he used to try to explain it to me and I have never taken a workshop on authentic movement. (However, I will admit that I have secretly experimented with it in the privacy of my home, with the blinds shut.)

Since I've mainly been an observer, it may be presumptuous of me to try to explain what it is. However, this book is about how things happened for me and for others around me as we started to reclaim our right to be creative. Bruce was getting involved in something that he was excited about and most of us thought he was out of his gourd. That is, until we witnessed what he was doing.

Bruce was entering uncharted territory, trying to get experience in an art form that was extremely body-based. A quad in a wheelchair trying to get involved in dance and movement! On top of that, he didn't have any schooling or training in dance, even prior to his injury. I figured he was either the most impractical man I knew, or the most adventurous. There is no doubt in my mind anymore – he is definitely the most adventurous.

Whoops! I used a term in that last paragraph that some of you might not be familiar with. "Quad" is short for quadriplegic. It means that four limbs are affected by a person's disability. Usually it refers to a person who has become disabled because of a spinal cord injury, but not always. Logistically, I am a quad, because all four of my limbs are weak. But, among disabled folk, if we call someone a quad, we are usually referring to someone with a spinal cord injury.

Spinal cord injury means that the spine was damaged, usually broken. If the break is high, it can leave the person a quad; if the break is low, the person becomes a paraplegic, or "para" (two limbs affected).

Bruce is what we call a low quad, meaning that all four of his limbs are affected, but he still has use of his shoulders. He can push himself in a manual wheelchair and drive a car. The hands of a quad often tighten into a semi-fist. Bruce had cords cut so that his hands are flat and opened, but he has no finger dexterity. At the time that Bruce began doing authentic movement, he had been disabled for several years.

…Now let me get back to talking about something more interesting than definitions. I know Disability 101 explanations are important and necessary, but I've been doing it for so many years that it gets boring. I'd rather talk about art!

The first time I saw Bruce perform in public was at an event called "Leaders" in November of 1986. "Leaders" was part of two days of activities sponsored by Very Special Arts, an organization that I will talk about in a later chapter. The disability community was mixed on how it felt about Very Special Arts, so Bruce toned down the visibility of the sponsoring organization.

Bruce engaged in contact improv with Alan Ptashek, his partner for several of his performances. At one point, Alan lifted Bruce out of his chair and spun him around several times. For a fleeting moment, it reminded me of children playing airplane with their parents. With Bruce and Alan it was part of their graceful, beautiful dance. The visuals of it will remain in my mind forever.

When he started dancing publicly, Bruce explained to me that he didn't really move to music, but that it was usually played during performances for the sake of the audience. Spectators who were unfamiliar with authentic movement often had trouble making the leap to watching bodies move without an apparent trigger or audio flow.

Actually, Bruce said it didn't really matter to him whether there was an audience, though it was a common part of the process of authentic movement to have a "witness" present to watch. It was the experience of doing the movement, not entertaining people, that was the purpose. I still have issues with Bruce over this, though I think today he would acknowledge that he has used his dance to educate, if not to entertain.

Many performers come up against this issue – who is the performance for? If the performer is truly centered in doing their art, then one could argue that they do the performance for their own benefit. But, if a performer wants to impact people through their art, then one could argue that they do the performance for the audience. I consider great artists to be the ones who find the elegant balance between the two.

I have seen many performance artists use their art as a catharsis, with little attention being given to making it work for the audience. One of my biggest pet peeves about artists is the issue of timing. To drag an audience through a solo performance of more than an hour-and-a-half is usually self-indulgent and cruel, especially if there's no break. There are exceptions, but some artists are not self-critical enough to make a valid judgment. One of the most useful skills of an artist is being able to be judicious about choosing what to keep and what to let go of AT THIS TIME. I stress "at this time" because a piece eliminated from a current work can often find a place in a future work. It doesn't all have to be done at once – an artist who finds this out usually crosses the boundary from Average to Good, or even Great.

The audience issue is a tough one for many artists, regardless of art form. A painter enjoys painting, but often not the process of selling their work. A video maker enjoys making video, but usually not the distribution process. Yet most artists need to reach audiences in order to survive financially. Self-promotion and commercialization is a real dilemma for any independent artist.

Many artists also thrive on having audience feedback, inspiring them to continue their work and many need audience validation to prove to themselves that they are artists. For some this means an audience of peers, others doing the same art form. For some it means reaching people in a shared healing way, such as an incest survivor performing to other incest survivors about their process of healing. Some artists prefer to perform to others who share their issues as a way of connecting; in this regard, some performers with disabilities are primarily focused on sharing their work with other people with disabilities. However, some prefer to do just the opposite, taking their works to people who have never heard their stories before, educating people about issues that are new to them. Regardless of whether preaching to the choir is one's focus or reaching the uninitiated is the aim, many artists have someone that they want to touch with their art. The trick is to touch enough people to be able to be a working artist.

Bruce wanted to be a working artist. He had found a way of expressing himself that he wanted to delve into full-time. His creative juices started flowing strong enough that nothing was going to hold him back, and he infected many others with the creative virus.

He ran into difficulties, but he kept at it. Hardly anyone, disabled or not, could understand what he was trying to do. He had friends who weren't disabled that he danced with and some of them sort-of got it, but this "authentic movement" thing mystified them also.

The closest Bruce could get to finding allies or co-conspirators was within the authentic movement and contact improv circles. The difficulty there was that he was coming from a place of using a wheelchair, trying for inclusion among people who were creative athletes. He kept at it, and gradually Bruce made friends who could see the potential in his vision. He began to practice more and to learn about his body in space, in movement. He'd do it alone, in duets, and as part of a group. He'd do it every time he got a chance, sometimes traveling to other states and countries just for the opportunity.

What was the "it" he was doing? Bruce's descriptions of their gatherings sounded like physical jam sessions. Some describe it as being like two dogs romping – jumping and falling all over each other, getting up and running away from each other, and then jumping towards each other some more. Everyone gets in touch with their breath, their feelings, the state of their inner self, and then they move in whatever way they feel compelled. If more than one person is involved, they respond to the energy of others. Spontaneity, creativity, staying in the moment, floating through energy, rebounding, reacting…

The art is in the doing, but an observer can share in the art by tuning in to the energy as a witness. The publicity for "The Exposed to Gravity Project," Bruce's dance and movement company, describes him as dancing in his chair, on the ground and in the air. Watching Bruce engage in contact improv was artistically and personally stimulating because it was new territory – his quad muscle tone and the way he moves is something that had not been seen in a creative movement form before.

I can't say much more to explain it to you. Either you know what I'm talking about or you're just as lost as I was when Bruce first tried to explain it to me. If this intrigues you, the best way to understand it is to witness it yourself, by attending a contact improv performance that includes people with disabilities.

Bruce was excited about his discoveries in the world of Creativity. He wanted to show the disability community what he was doing and he needed performance opportunities. He also recognized similar seedlings in many of us, though not only in the area of dance and movement. He became evange-listic in his push to get some of us to take the leap into expressing ourselves artistically. These motivations led Bruce to create the Moving Over the Edge (MOE) shows.

Obviously, this is a defining moment in my story. I've named my book after these shows and I've named this chapter after these shows, so they must have been important, eh? You betcha!

Bruce pulled together the first show in 1988. He chose the Fool card from a Tarot deck as the icon for publicity flyers, because it symbolizes a risk taker. The Fool walks along the edge of the cliff blissfully enjoying life, full of innocence and adventure. He is close to the edge, with his foot raised for his next step, too busy enjoying the sky and the music to notice that he's about to step off into the unknown. He has no cares and is totally in the experience of the moment. Nearby, a dog barks a warning, reminding the traveler that there is an edge to the cliff. Caution. Risk. Caution. Risk. Trust. Risk… All part of being creative. Many artists are said to take their work to "the edge." Bruce encouraged us to take our work over the edge.

He challenged many of us to be Fools, to move over the edge, to trust that we would find flight rather than falling. He encouraged us to explore creativity without boundaries, to approach both our art and our disabilities without limits.

Like a Pied Piper, Bruce pulled together a group of performers with and without disabilities to put on the first Moving Over the Edge show. It was a potluck of art forms and experience levels.

Many artists took flight after this or other MOE shows, whether they were in the shows or audience members who became inspired by the risk-taking demonstrated in the shows. Thank you, Bruce, for blazing the trail.

Bruce reserves his laughter for moments that his heart is tickled; when he laughs, it's like a gift from the gods. His heart opens and his eyes burst with delight. I hope he laughs when he reads this chapter, because it was written in the spirit of friendship and love… and to honor a true Fool.

Postscript by Bruce Curtis

Almost 20 years after starting my journey of exploring the possibilities for a severely disabled man to participate in Dance and Performance Art, I feel great satisfaction knowing that many disabled men, women and children have joined me in Moving over the Edge. Of course, everyone comments about the courage it takes for anyone with a disability to be seen publicly dancing. But what is truly amazing to me is the personal decision that other disabled artists have made to let the beauty and joy of our unique bodies become a public celebration!

Now, I am trying to create a bigger audience to watch us as we explore and perform. A growing number of countries are hosting international disability film festivals. Through powerful images of persons with disabilities choosing to Move over the Edge, we are succeeding in surprising the minds and touching the hearts of the citizens of other countries.

The Moving over the Edge Festivals were created 20 years ago by a handful of disabled artists in order to provide an opportunity to show the public our artistic explorations and adventures. We succeeded then in our desire to inspire and provide support for each other. We have succeeded in revealing ourselves. Now we are surprising the World!

THERE WERE ONLY FOUR SHOWS that I call MOE productions, though there were other events that happened around the same time, many as a result of people's involvement with MOE, as an artist or audience member. I describe these events in significant detail in this chapter because they are historically important. I cannot recreate them, but I can document what I observed. These shows and performers are valuable legacies of the Disability Art Movement.

For the shows, Bruce pulled together artists who shared a common vision about taking the experiences of their lives as human beings and as disabled people and working those experiences through their art. He created the MOE shows with the belief that sharing our experiences this way would change perceptions and ideas about what is possible, not only for people with disabilities, but for everyone. The artists wanted to dispense with old myths about disability and create new definitions, stretching the concepts of art and of disability.

At the first MOE show I was a spectator, an audience member. I was so blown away with what I saw on stage that I wanted to get involved, and I offered Bruce my help for the next show. That's how I wound up being the Mistress of Ceremonies for MOE II. By MOE III and MOE IV, I had become inspired to perform myself and joined the artists on the stage.

MOE was not a recreation program for the handicapped. It was professional art. Even if we had to create our own opportunities for cutting our
performance chops, we expected everyone to do their best. Anyone who did
sloppy work would have been letting down the other artists by lowering the
quality of the show. We were trying to get taken serious as artists and there was
a lot on the line. Each show we took more risks and pushed ourselves further.
We were doing ground breaking work and we wanted to knock some socks off.

It was a seminal and exhilarating moment the first time MOE artists got
together; the individuals represented cross disabilities, cross forms, and cross
life styles. Part of the importance of what we were all doing was how we connected with each other, sometimes just being influenced by each others work,
sometimes going as far as working together on other projects. Our work set
off sparks for each other. For example, when we saw the movement work that
Bruce was doing, it stimulated an artist like Cheryl Marie Wade to say "That's
what I'm trying to do with my poetry to give it that kind of depth."

And now, on with the shows!

MOE I (January 31, 1988) At the beginning of MOE I Bruce welcomed
the audience. Dressed in white, his long blonde hair pulled up into a bun on
the top of his head, he made a striking impression. He said that what we were
about to see was the realization of a vision of a few people who wanted to find
a way "…to make it possible to share our talents and our visions of ourselves as
we create them, and how we see society and our place in it and in the world."

The show opened with performance art pieces by Claire Blotter, Jay Yarnall
and Richard Sales. Their art used spoken word, body rhythms, sound effects,
computer generated audio, electronic sounds, and drum beats. I found myself
captivated, yet unable to logically follow the surreal travels of the words
themselves. No recognizable train of thought was there on their meandering
path, yet my sub-conscious grabbed at pieces of phrases and the highs and
lows of sounds. Just when I thought I had a clue as to what they were babbling
about, they'd leap the track and go off on a strange tangent. I traveled through
several layers of emotion as they twisted words and sounds into unrecognizable
shapes… joy, anger, sadness, love. At the end of their set I had no rational
idea of what I had just observed, but my heart felt stronger and my soul felt
touched.

After the opening esoteric trip, the audience was turned 360 degrees by Wry Crips reading an original collection of writings. "The Miss Normal Pageant" is a satiric look at the idea of people with disabilities striving to be as "normal" as they can. Four "crippled girls" compete for a crown, the winner to be the one who comes closest to achieving "normalness" in spite of her disability. Iris Crider played the part of the contest judge, A.B. Normal (A.B. = Able Bodied). Jan Levine's role was that of an over-achieving "Yuppie-Crip" who rises at 4:30 am to be at work by 8 am, has three volunteer jobs on the weekend to help those less fortunate than herself, never accepts "reasonable accommodations" from her workplace and is involved with a strong yet, of course, gentle man. Peni Hall, Patty Overland and Cheryl Marie Wade played contestants who weren't as placatory as Jan. Through pieces like "Sassy Girls," "SuperCrip Girl" and "Woman With Juice," the trio turn Jan around to seeing that she isn't the problem. The pageant ends in a rebellion, the competitors deciding to throw out the word "normal."

After intermission, Jay and Richard reminded me of jazz instruments as they played off of each other free-style on a computer-linked keyboard (Jay) and guitar (Richard). Claire returned to the stage to do a personal work and then was rejoined by Jay and Richard. The electronic chimes mesmerized, the beats intoxicated, and the spoken word performance was, once again, mind-bending.

Following this mix, Bruce performed a contact improv duet with Patty Overland while Kathy Martinez drummed. Both Bruce and Patty stayed in their wheelchairs except for the few moments that Patty raised herself to cover Bruce as he bent forward. Bruce and Patty had never performed together before, yet their movements harmonized as if they'd done it for years. It was the first time Patty had performed contact improv on stage.

Today, many years later, we have seen integrated dancers (dancers with and without disabilities) take movement and dance to many fascinating places. But, back in 1988, it was just beginning. The creativity that Bruce and Patty presented was edge-work… two people in wheelchairs moving around each other, contacting each other physically, taking the space of their bodies into the world with an attitude of gracefulness and a right to flow…

…while a blind woman beat out a rhythm on the drums. Kathy's excellent drumming provided the perfect accent for the movements.

This dramatic performance ended the show, but people would not leave! The video of the event runs for several minutes after the finale. It is obvious that MOE I had a strong impact on people because of the way they rushed Bruce and the other performers afterwards. People were in awe and wanted to know when the next show would be. The show was a performance success. The camera caught a thumbs up from Wavy Gravy (of 60's Woodstock fame) as he exclaimed, "Great show! Great show!"

I was especially transformed by the work of Jay Yarnall and timidly approached him afterwards. At that time, I was in the process of putting together a team of artists with disabilities to work on a creative video piece (more on this in Chapter Fourteen). I wanted Jay on the team, but I was hesitant. Why would a man of his artistic caliber be interested in li'l ole me and my amateur video? He greeted me enthusiastically, making me feel instantly at ease. His warmth and gentleness enabled me to ask and he instantly agreed to be part of my creative team. I felt (and still feel) very fortunate about this turn of events.

MOE II (December 22, 1989) I helped Bruce pull together MOE II and I was the MC. There was a moment when this became an interesting exercise in group leadership, because we had a mild earthquake tremor in the middle of the show. Though I was prepared to take charge of an emergency, I looked around the audience and became aware that no one was reacting. Either people were so engrossed in the program that they did not notice the shakes, or people in California have become desensitized to an occasional shifting of the ground. In any event, the audience seemed calm, so I continued with the show.

MOE II was a Holiday show, taking place in December. Anyone who knows Berkeley knows that this means a mixture of Christmas, Chanukah, Kwanzaa, Winter Solstice and any other bringing-of-the-light celebration that happens at that time of the year. But, no one would DARE call it a Christmas show, though we did have a Santa in a wheelchair.

Jennifer Jacobs was a regular MOE interpreter. She was excellent as a platform interpreter and very patient about last-minute scripts changes and sudden shifts. Artists, being constantly creative, will sometimes ad-lib or decide to change things on the fly. Jennifer's calm nature went with the flow gracefully.

I was all decked out for the show. It's a goal of mine to approach artistic events in the disability community with a Hollywood flair, dressing like the celebrities we are. (After all, many of us have performed several times, in doctor's offices or in hospitals, right?) I encouraged people to come to the MOE shows elegant or weird, or both. I worked hard to set the standard, though it never really caught on. I'm still trying.

For MOE II, I wore a sparkly black, low-cut top and black slacks with white horizontal stripes down each side. I had a long, dangly, beaded red earring in one ear. I wore my hair striped and frizzed.

I don't know what I said that night, but I sure did talk a long time. I have a video of the show, but the sound is blank except for one dance performance and the party after the show. We were cutting our technical teeth at the same time that we cut our artistic teeth and someone forgot to plug in the camera microphones.

The show opened with comedian and mime, C. J. Jones. I first saw C. J. at a Berkeley Disability Art Fair event. He was a young man with a significant hearing loss. Much of his routine was related to his deafness, such as a hilarious skit he did about a hearing-impaired musician. C.J. is skilled at communicating non-verbally with both hearing and Deaf audiences. He is a master at complementing his use of Sign Language with body language, facial expressions, and timing. He is a real crowd pleaser!

The second performance that night was by Charlene Curtiss, a petite but muscular woman. Charlene came out of the woodwork – no one had seen her perform before. She amazed the crowd with a choreographed, aerobic dance done in her fancy sports wheelchair. She spun, did back flips, and danced on her back wheels. She took over the floor, moving to the rapid music that blared in the large auditorium. Charlene was a public defender in a nearby town who had created the dance piece for a commercial video she produced in exchange for getting a free chair.

Jay Yarnall and five of his play buddies performed next, as Melodius Thunk. They did something totally different than what they did at MOE I, though it was still in the realm of the "unusual." Rather than jamming with spoken word, they jammed with instruments; one woman added vocal sounds. The room filled with the music from electronic instruments side-by-side with instruments made from nature. The mesmerizing cyber-sounds were mixed with those from gourds, drums, bells, and other odd shaped instruments, many from Tibet. They referred to their group as an improvisational ensemble made up of trained and self-taught musicians who melodiously thunk towards a musical snapshot of the moment they are playing in.

The "Exposed to Gravity Project" presented Bruce Curtis and Alan Ptashek after intermission. While the audience heard a drum and a flute, Bruce and Alan engaged with each other in a playful, innovative contact improvisational dance. They gracefully moved from one position to another – Alan laying on Bruce, then climbing on him and over him. Bruce lowered himself from his wheelchair to the ground and Alan did a headstand on him. At another moment Alan picked Bruce up and spun him around. The piece reflected lots of energetic touching, acting and reacting, spinning, turning and rolling.

The improv duet was followed by a Wry Crips reading, represented by Jan Levine and Alana Theriault. Both of these spunky women look sweet and innocent at first glance, but have the ability to cause the sound of what Wry Crips calls "a bunch of stereotypes hitting the ground." They read selections from the fast-growing collection of Wry Crips pieces and called their presentation, "A Conversation Between Friends."

The last act of the evening was a performance by AXIS Dance Company. At the start, a slow flute played while Judith Smith and Bonnie Lewkowicz did a beautiful duet together. As they finished the piece and exited the stage, the mood shifted. The wheel from a manual wheelchair flew from stage left to stage right. The wheel disappeared and Thais Mazur entered on roller skates with a spinning wheel in her hand; she crouched down to glide to the other side of the stage. David Russell entered on roller skates holding a manual wheelchair on his head. He skated around as Judith entered with Laura Rifkin standing backwards on the back of her wheelchair. Nina Haft entered, holding a wheel that was eventually snapped onto the chair that had been on David's head. Laura left Judith's chair, got into the now assembled manual wheelchair, and more of the dancers entered. Eventually, the stage featured six dancers; five women, one man. Three were in wheelchairs, two were on skates.

The artistry and elegance of movement was outstanding. Many things went on at once. The graceful patterned piece unfolded in fluctuating combinations. Three pairs of people interacting became two groups of threesomes interacting. There was a constant move and flow that wove dancers in and out of relationships with each other. When the piece ended, the audience applauded delightfully for "Wheels," one of the popular pieces in the AXIS repertoire.

The energy was high at curtain call and the audience was cheerful, ready to party. Dance music played and, dressed as Santa and Mrs. Claus, Michael Winter (then the Director of Berkeley's Center for Independent Living) and his wife Atsuko rolled around passing out candy.

MOE III (April 27, 1990) By the third MOE show, artists were ready to take even further risks, and Bruce decided to do a show on the theme of Sensuality. He wanted to push the envelope as far as it could be pushed, but not so far as to alienate people. We spent a lot of time talking over whether he should present the program as a program on sexuality, eroticism, or sensuality.

It was time to go past the subject of relationships and to approach the subject of sex, but this would be new territory for many of the performers and spectators. Although many people were hungry for material on the subject of sexuality, there were many degrees of experience.

Not too long ago, here in Berkeley, a fine arts exhibit on the subject of disability and sexuality was considered controversial, even though there were no overt displays of sex in any of the pieces and nothing approaching pornography.

Much of the hesitance that we have around discussing and displaying disability and sexuality themes stems from an overprotection of people with disabilities. We want to be considered sexual beings, but we don't want to be exploited because of our disabilities. It can be a fine line between the two. We approached MOE III cautiously, but committed ourselves to push the envelope in the area of sexuality.

The materials advertising the show presented it as "A Community Performance on Sensuality by Disabled Artists and Friends." The Center for Independent Living and other disability organizations helped to fund the event and some of the sponsors became nervous about what would be shown. As I look back at the show, it seems tame, but at the time it was risk-taking for most of us on the stage or in the audience.

I was the MC and I also performed. It was the first time I performed my poetry in public. This was quite a move for me because I'd kept my poems pretty much hidden until I was 30 years old and I met a woman who was also a poet. We would get together once a week to share our writings with each other. It was scary for me to take the pieces of paper that I had collected since my early teens and expose them to another individual. It was even more frightening to share these poems out loud to a whole crowd of people.

As MC, I felt it was important to dress to the theme. I first came on stage in a bathrobe. The second time I wore a dark blue, silk negligee that was suggestive but not too revealing. During the second half of the show I was wrapped in a beautiful piece of sky blue material with bright flowers, shoulders bare, a jade choker around my neck. I had long silky hair with a flower behind one ear, and I went barefoot through the whole show. I positioned myself in my wheelchair so that one foot rested down and the other one was tucked under my knee in a semi-relaxed position. I tried to adapt an air of seductive composure as I gave the introduction:

"Tonight's show is on sensuality and those of us who will be on stage today have accepted a challenge to perform something that has to do with that theme. Those of you who are out there in the audience have also accepted a challenge, because you have come here and you don't really know what you are going to see tonight. You probably also don't know how you're going to feel about what you'll see... Sensuality is a very individual thing. What might be sensual for one person is another persons' pornography or exploitation. So it's really tricky. Eroticism is somewhere in between the two. But, one thing that we do know about sensuality is that it's something that's a part of our culture. We are disabled but we are sensual beings, and hopefully tonight's show will be able to chip away at that stereotype that says we're not. The other thing that I wanted to say was that some of you might feel delighted by a lot that you see tonight, but you might also be offended by some of it, and some of it might make you feel uneasy, but hopefully most of it will entertain you."

A teaser? An enticer? A disclaimer? A seduction? Permission? All of the above? I was trying to help everyone feel safe and comfortable with the material that was to be presented, to prod gently.

Unfortunately the performance space was not very intimate. We were performing at the Veterans Memorial Building, in a very large room with a stage that was not wheelchair accessible. Ignoring the stage, we performed on the main floor, so performers and audience members were on the same level. We had needed to bring in lights to "create" the stage. The ceiling was high, necessitating our using microphones; this created an echoing sound quality which does not equate with a sensual show. The room was hollow, the floors were wooden and some people had brought children to the show. All of these conditions made it hard for the performers and the audience to feel a sense of eroticism and sexuality, but we gave it a good try.

The line-up for the evening was a real potluck. It included poetry, performance art, dance, comedy, song, and contact improv. The interpreters for the program were Jennifer Jacobs and Judith Lerner. There were many jokes (not new) about people watching the interpreters whenever four letter words were said in order to see how they signed them. There was a lot of nervous energy and giggles before the show began.

With pleasure I made the first introduction, "The first performer tonight is a woman that I think is quite sexy. She has a real way with words, not only writing them, but also speaking them. Her name is Cheryl Marie Wade."

Cheryl came out dressed in a silky blue blouse (casually slipped off her left shoulder), a pink scarf draped around her neck. Her brown hair was full bodied at shoulder length. Bangs tickled her eyebrows. She laughed and giggled and really enjoyed herself. Her joking helped to relax the audience and they became playful. They especially liked her shyly admitting that, as a teen, she'd had a crush on Paul McCartney.

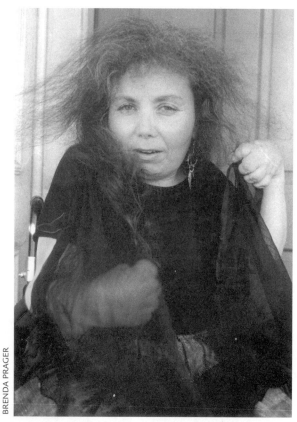

BRENDA PRAGER

Cheryl Marie Wade, "Queen Mother of Gnarly"

Cheryl traveled through her collection of "Poems of Love and Lust," describing her evolution to womanhood. She began one powerful poem with the following statement:

"This is the very first poem I ever wrote. I wrote it in 1985 and I don't think it's any shock, certainly to me, that the first attempt at understanding my disability begins with a study of some body parts; and, in my case, certainly the most stunning difference, that's most noticeable, are my hands. They are the most eloquent expression of my disability reality and so my first poem was a poem to them."

Cheryl has graciously allowed me to include that poem here. It jumps out at you when she performs it. In print, it's still a grabber:

Mine are the hands of your bad dreams   Booga Booga
from behind the black curtain
Claw hands
The Ivory Girl's hands
  after a decade of roughing it
crinkled   puckered
sweaty and scarred
A young woman's dwarfed knobby hands
that ache for moonlight
that tremble
and struggle
Hands that make your eyes tear
My hands
My hands
My hands that grace
your brow
your thigh
My hands
Yes

— Copyright © 1986 Cheryl Marie Wade

Some of Cheryl's poems are full of whimsy, some are full of disability reality, and all of them weave in layers of interesting words and thoughts. Probably most of the people in the audience had seen Cheryl on stage before, but regardless of whether they had or not, they enjoyed every minute of her performance. Cheryl is the type of performer that one can watch over and over. She quotes her grandmother who said, "No matter how oppressed you are, you can still create magic."

My luck of the draw was following Cheryl, but Bruce Curtis made the transition smooth by giving me a great introduction. Five of us performed three of my poems as a medley that I called "Montage a Trois." Our makeshift props and furniture had rested invitingly "on stage" since the top of the show; it included a bed with red sheets, a blue pillow, and a hanging wicker lamp. I entered wearing a dark blue satin negligee with my bare legs exposed, while Kathy Rote played the guitar and sang the Beatles' "Something."

I slowly scooted from my wheelchair onto the bed and arranged myself into a comfortable position. Getting out of my wheelchair onto a bed is a nervous moment with new lovers because my legs and movements are atypical. I wanted to do a piece where a woman with a physical disability moves to her own body's version of grace as the words "something in the way she moves attracts me like no other lover" are heard. Beauty is in the eye of the projector; if I project beauty, it is beauty. The song helped me project confidence about my sensuality, and the sense that I found my movements graceful.

Once settled on the bed, I turned on the lamp and looked lovingly at a framed photo as I read the first poem about waiting for my lover, trying to decide how to present myself. What mood would I be in, how would I dress? Would I be a temptress or would I be shy? I decide that I'll lay nude, feigning sleep as my lover enters. I let my negligee slip off my shoulder.

After the first poem, Kathy played another refrain as Julie Nesnansky entered and sat on the bed next to me. We chatted and giggled cozily, occasionally touching each other in a way that showed closeness. The song tapered off and I read the second poem, about my unrequited love for a woman. At the point in the poem where the woman left town, Julie rose and backed out of view.

Kathy played another refrain while a free-standing curtain was removed. Behind it, on the floor, sat Norma Scheurkogel. Norma and I both had long dark hair, and our faces and body types look similar, yet she is many years younger than me. Norma played the part of me, as a teenager, lying on the beach.

Larry Collins, a former Mr. Oakland body builder, entered to exchange with Norma as I read a poem about one of my adolescent fantasies: Tanning on the beach, I'd cover my legs with sand and someone would come by and fall madly in love with me, not knowing that I was disabled. Norma and Larry acted out the fantasy. At the end, I was carried off into the sunset, my admirer so smitten with me that exposing my short, skinny legs didn't change anything. Larry picked Norma up from the ground and carried her off, into the sunset.

Kathy played the end of the song as Larry entered my "bedroom" space and sat on the bed beside me. He flirtatiously put one of his legs on my legs that were hanging over the edge of the bed by this time. We laughed and flirted on the bed as the song came to an end. Larry picked me up the way that he had picked up Norma and carried me to my wheelchair.

After the five of us took a bow, I returned to my job as Mistress of Ceremonies and had my hands full. It was necessary to do a bit of rearranging, not only of the stage area, but of the audience. Props and furniture had to be cleared from the stage and the audience needed a traffic controller. It had gotten very crowded and people who had come late were bottlenecked at the entrance. Seating can be quite interesting when you have over twenty wheelchairs in one room. Several chair users' views were blocked by people in larger wheelchairs. We had to take a few moments to rearrange both on and off stage.

The next performance was by AXIS Dance Company, a piece called "Ellipsis." I interpret it as being about the push and pull of relationships. Bonnie Lewkowicz gracefully pushed herself onto the stage in her manual wheelchair and David Russell entered on his feet; they moved with each other to slow music. It was a very sweet and sensual dance. In one movement, David pulled Bonnie's chair over backwards and held her in his arms from the floor. It was so graceful that it didn't look like a struggle even when he raised her chair back up.

David gave Bonnie's chair a backwards push so that she glided off, into the wings. He was left prone on the floor, arms outstretched. The music shifted and Thais Mazur danced in, laying on top of David momentarily. They rose and moved as a duet until their relationship dissolved, triggering Thais to exit and Judith Smith to enter.

Judith dashed in as David grabbed hold, to almost fly across the stage, pulled by her in her motorized chair. They played a bit of peek-a-boo, him behind her chair, peeking at her from one side to the other. David exited and Bonnie came back.

Judith and Bonnie moved together, manual chair and motor chair, in a powerful combination of turns and moves. Bonnie left as Thais entered to dance with Judith. At one point in the dance Thais stood on Judith's footrest, at another point she rode on the back of the chair. The whole piece was chasing and teasing, ending with Thais curled on Judith's lap as they slowly turned in circles to mellow music.

In each vignette that AXIS did, whether using a manual chair or a power chair, the movements were graceful and incorporated seamlessly into the dance. Rather than standing out as extraneous, the wheelchairs added to the dance. At the end, the four dancers came on stage in their black and shiny blue attire and took a professional bow.

After a ten-minute break, I introduced Ben Stuart. I believe it was the first time he was performing in front of a disability crowd. He approached the microphone with erratic driving as if he was drunk, crashing into the microphone with his wheelchair.

Dressed casually, Ben wore his hair long and sported a slight beard. He had an average size head, no neck, and bony hands. His trunk dominated his body and flipper leg-feet were shoeless, but stood out in bright socks. During his routine he often used wild hand flying gestures and tapped his feet to make a point. He sat yoga style, his feet short enough that the heels touched each other.

Groupies of the MOE shows and other disability art events had not seen Ben perform before. His jokes were crude, racist, and politically incorrect. He didn't hold back. People were unsure about the OK-ness of laughing at some of Ben's jokes, so he wasn't getting much audience response. He was great at quickly reacting to an atmosphere – "Nice to be here at the Wax Museum."

Ben told the audience that he made jokes not just about disabled people but also about non-disabled people. He then started to tell a joke with "These two ambulatory guys walk into a bar…" Some of the people in the audience got it and others just scratched their heads.

Ben made no apologies for being the bad boy that he was. He talked about going to a nuclear power demonstration in a Styrofoam wheelchair with elephant skins on the sides. Although the audience warmed up toward the end of Ben's performance, they weren't quite ready for his disregard of political correctness. After all, many people in Berkeley and in the disability activist community try hard to always be PC. Ben would perform in the next MOE show, but by that time, people had realized that, yes, they could laugh at his jokes.

Ben was followed by Ron Washington singing a Gershwin tune. He had planned to sing several songs by Gershwin, but he had dislocated his shoulder and said that one song was all he could manage. Dislocated shoulder and all, Ron was at least able to treat us to one short and sweet song. His being a quadriplegic affected the volume he could sing, but the microphone compensated. The deep, rich tones of his voice filled the hall.

The last act of the night was "Evening Play," a contact improvisation duet presented by The Exposed to Gravity Project. Bruce Curtis and Charlene Curtiss tumbled and crawled over and around each other, sometimes in their chairs, sometimes on the floor. They were occasionally clumsy, but there were many dramatic and beautiful moments. They did things that made people gasp (Bruce on the floor bent forward as Charlene leaned back from her wheelchair, got on his back, and pushed her chair away) and things that made people go "aah" (Charlene in her chair gracefully extending one leg to Bruce's hand). When it came time for the piece to end, Bruce teased Charlene with her wheelchair, moving it towards and away from her as she sat on the ground. Just before that, she had chased him as he had crawled away. It was a playful and lively contact improv and reminded me of the moments when two lovers need to get out of bed to go about the day, neither wanting to leave.

The evening ended with Jay Yarnall playing spontaneous music on an electronic keyboard. Vicki VanSteenberg (one of my high school classmates who I'd reconnected with) passed out donated flowers to the performers. Dancers with varied body types moved to Jay's meandering music, trying out free-floating movements while the tech crew cleared the equipment. The audience had been creatively stimulated by the show and many tried out new movements, some in a frenzy, some seemingly in a trance. The room filled with a surreal energy as people left their wheelchairs to get on the ground and people who weren't disabled took over the abandoned chairs. The combination of wheels included shopping carts and wheelbarrows for carrying dismantled equipment. A bicycle was added to the mix at some point. That's when I realized I was in the heart of a Salvador Dali painting.

MOE IV – October, 1990 MOE IV was performed in a mainstream San Francisco venue, with tickets sold through a large distributor. This was a first (and only) for the MOE shows. Bruce Curtis and Cheryl Marie Wade co-produced the event and it was advertised widely and presented as part of a larger set of activities called Festival 2000. There was a matinee and an evening show on the same day. The line up at both was the same. The matinee was superb, while the evening show was only good. This difference was mainly due to energy levels and technical difficulties.

At this MOE show the fine arts emerged. Jill Lessing and Jasmine Marah had put together a delightful three-part collage that doubled as a screen, blocking the side of the stage that performers entered from. On one panel, a large wheel from a manual wheelchair formed the focus for objects twirling on a velvet background. Another panel was of shimmering pastel texture, and a third had a charcoal drawing of three ghost-like figures. The work was done to compliment the piece that AXIS Dance Company performed in the show, but it was so beautiful that everyone agreed to keep it up for the whole time.

The hall was packed as Cheryl Marie Wade opened the show. She wore a shiny scarf and her long hair frizzed out dramatically, with a sprinkling of grey hairs. She introduced the show as a disability arts performance concert and listed those organizations which had helped fund it. She made the point that even with that, the performers were not going to get paid unless there were a few generous people in the audience who wanted to contribute towards the show. She gave disability access information, including that one side of the audience was set aside for people with environmental illnesses and that an air filter was there; she asked people who smoked to not sit in that section. She introduced the interpreter, Bobbi Skiles.

Cheryl went over the list of performers for the first half of the program, mentioning that she was doing this because there were no Braille programs. By the evening show, Cheryl joked "I'm gonna run through what's going to happen. I'm not sure we have enough programs for everyone and I'm not sure everybody could see the programs anyway." We had under-estimated the number of people who would attend – each performance played to a packed house!

After her introduction, Cheryl began the program with a set of her own poems. Many of the poems she recited are audience favorites, like "Sassy Girls," and "I am Not One of The." Her performance was outstanding, as she wrapped the fluctuations of her voice around the power of her words. At the end of each poem, she would duck her head shyly and not "take the moment" that time would teach her to bask in. Cheryl received an overwhelming applause of appreciation after her set of dynamic poems. She modestly left to be followed by AXIS Dance Company.

AXIS performed "Ellipsis," the same piece they had done in MOE III. There were minor changes here and there, though it was basically the same piece, honed and polished. They looked right at home in the professional performance space. They had caught their stride and would go on to perform on many such stages.

Afi-Tiombe Kambon was the next performer. She is a historian who studies the slavery movement and writes performance monologues based on historic fact. She researches oral and written histories to get the information that she uses in her stories. The piece she did in this show has become her hallmark, "Black Diamond."

Afi-Tiombe confidently strode to the microphone on her wooden under-the-arm crutches, wearing a white high heel on her one foot and dressed in brown with a blue scarf tied around her head. Except for the white high heel, she looked like she could have been a character from the story that she told. (For the evening performance she changed to a jeweled hat and matching earrings.)

Her story began with a group of people living in a village, working in the fields and singing songs. She describes their capture, their being brought to America as slaves, and life on a breeding plantation. The technique that Afi-Tiombe used was to speak in a monotone voice through the majority of the storytelling as if she were only relaying history, with no feelings or emotions. As she approached the end of her story she began to demonstrate emotions, pulling the audience in, making it a very powerful piece. The story ends with a woman on the breeding farm giving birth to a child who is disabled and the plantation owner killing the baby because he viewed it as defective cattle. Afi-Tiombe incorporated her beautiful singing voice in poignant spots, making it even more authentic. It ends with the mother's moans transforming into a hymn of healing.

Bruce Curtis and Charlene Curtiss did a movement duet, using the same music as they had in MOE III. They moved around each other sensuously and flirtatiously in their chairs. Bruce got on the floor first and Charlene remained in her chair for awhile, moving about teasingly. Eventually she left her chair and pushed it away in a very dramatic movement. I don't know if it was their intent, but there was a strong message to me of two people making the decision to push potential barriers between them away. They interacted in a delightful, playful way on the floor – two people enjoying each other, leaving their disabilities on the sideline. At the end of their piece they wheeled off the stage modestly, engaged charmingly with each other, shyly bowing towards the audience.

Next up was "Tasty Tidbits" by Wry Crips. Six women entered, two in power wheelchairs, one of them using oxygen, two in manual wheelchairs, a large woman with a cane, and a woman who had no visible disability. The woman who did not appear disabled was an access assistant, her job was to sit between two of the women and turn the pages of their script as they read. The Wry Crips performers who were in this production were Pandoura Carpenter, Peni Hall, Jan Levine, Patty Overland, and Alana Theriault.

"Tasty Tidbits," like all Wry Crips performances, reflected a sense of pride and a sense of disability culture. "Tips for Crips" are sprinkled throughout their set. An example of a tip is: Never express anger. However, it is followed by poems reflecting a reclaiming of the right to express anger.

One piece was an advertisement selling blinders to block the view for someone who doesn't want to see a disability. There are panels around a large pair of glasses, like the blinders put on a horse, to block out crutches, wheelchairs, or anyone who is not at eye level. The piece ends with the phone number on a large placard: 1-800-IM-A-JERK.

Their performance ends with them singing "The Wry Crips Family," a parody of the Adams Family theme song from television.

After Wry Crips performed there was an intermission while the stage crew set up electronic equipment on the stage. After the break, Cheryl welcomed everyone back and introduced the second half of the show. First up, she said was Ben Stuart, with his "poster-child-gone-awry-view-of-the-world."

Ben entered with a flair. Eyes opened wide, he bobbed his head like a knick knack on a dashboard, driving a power wheelchair with a miniature body. A colorful shirt and a Buster Keaton hat seemed fitting with his long hair, beard and mustache. The audience was quiet, not knowing what to expect. Ben mugged the camera and then exaggerated a struggle to reach the microphone. Slapstick humor. That explained the Buster Keaton hat.

"I feel like I'm opening for Pink Floyd," Ben commented, indicating the electronic equipment behind him that was for the next act. Then he took the audience on a wild ride through sex jokes, drug jokes, and jokes about mustard. (Two wheelchairs pull up next to each other and the one in the fancier rig asks the other, "Excuse me, do you have any Grey Poupon?") Many times he would jump from one subject to a completely unrelated subject, but his delivery style made it work. The audience was slow to warm up to him, barely chuckling at the beginning. He didn't seem to be impacted by this, but continued jauntily spewing out one-liners while he waved his arms and wiggled his toes. He spoke in a slightly raspy voice, but left one knowing that he was a brazen contradiction to the munchkins in Oz.

Within the first few minutes of his comedy routine, Ben made a joke using the F-word. He said he likes to open using the F-word just to break the ice. He replaced it with the term "messed up" in the evening show. I don't know if someone censored him or if he censored himself, realizing that the audience was at a different level than his usual comedy club audiences.

He interacted and responded to audiences so well that I wondered if he had planted people there. A child got excited and squealed. Ben said hello to the kid and asked "Hey, when you outgrow your clothes, can I have them?" By the end of his performance the audience had totally embraced his bad-boy style and gave him a huge applause.

After Ben left the stage, the lights were half dimmed, drawing attention to the equipment sitting on the stage: two keyboards, a computer, a video camera and a projection screen. One by one, our group called Hephaestus came out. Dave DeWeerd entered first, with a gold hard hat, vest, and a gold metal snake wrapped around one arm. I entered next with a pair of sunglasses covered with feathers, framing my face. Both Dave and I entered in power wheelchairs, though Dave eventually climbed out of his and sat on the back of his wheelchair, putting the video camera on his shoulder, with his back to the audience. Jay Yarnall entered last, in a manual wheelchair, pushing his wheels with hands that had little finger dexterity.

Through most of the piece Dave was closest to the audience and in front of him were two electronic keyboards where Jay and I sat. Behind us was a large screen. Dave videotaped Jay and me, and simultaneously the video footage was projected onto the large screen behind us. Dave used in-camera effects like strobe and freeze-screen. Jay and I played electronic sounds on our keyboards. The piece we performed was called "Wheels of Alchemy," but rather than describing the piece to you here, I will reprint the words later, in Chapter Sixteen.

The audience went wild after Hephaestus performed. I could try to be humble, but I have the video to prove that the audience did actually go wild. Afterwards, people referred to me as the Laurie Anderson of the Disability Rights Movement. The piece that Hephaestus performed was a break-through piece for artists with disabilities. It pushed art into some of the new forms and styles that were being used in the mainstream art community. People with disabilities hadn't seen something that cutting-edge performed by their peers before and it got people really excited. Dave and Jay were the electronic wizards who created the extravaganza; I was along for the ride as a pretty face that could rhyme.

After Hephaestus performed, we needed to clear the electronic equipment from the stage. To keep the audience occupied during this time, Cheryl led the audience in a song called "Body Parts," which was a Wry Crips number rewritten to the tune of "Lollipop." Cheryl ad-libbed and the audience seemed to enjoy the temporary opportunity to perform themselves.

Once the equipment was removed, AXIS Dance Company performed the final piece in MOE IV. They performed "Wheels," the same piece that they had done for MOE II. However, it was smoothed and refined. It was obvious that by this time they had committed to developing a professional company.

After bows and ending remarks, the audience drifted out. The cameras were kept running and comments were heard here and there, picked up by the unnoticed voyeur. It was clear that the audience had been left entertained, stunned, empowered, thrilled and illuminated. The show had reflected the degree of professionalism that many of the performers were beginning to develop.

Although the same pieces were done in both the matinee and the evening shows, the performances varied in little ways. Afi-Tiombe changed her hat, and Ben Stuart changed his material. The performers were less energetic in the evening. The multi-media piece that Hephaestus performed wasn't quite as multi-media because the projector and camera hit a glitch in the evening, significantly affecting the "WOW" factor of that performance. The audience in general was a tougher audience. They were not as responsive, although they did yell "bravo" at the end of the show when all the performers came out for a final bow.

It Wasn't All Roses Frequently, performers in MOE were given flowers at the end of the shows. These were received with pleasure and often with a touch of shyness. The flowers were nice, but the shows weren't all roses and kudos, and although some people moved on to fame, there certainly wasn't any fortune at the time.

There were behind-the-scene problems for the MOE shows right from the start. What do you expect from self-absorbed performers, eh? That IS a joke. Actually, if self-absorption had been the problem, it probably could have been overcome. The politics of the MOE shows ran much deeper than performers' egos, though we certainly had our share of those too.

Access is always an issue at events by and for people with disabilities. We insist that access be provided for us in the world at-large, so there is great pressure to have complete access at events that come from within the disability community. What constitutes access and to what lengths should people and groups spend money and energy to ensure that EVERYONE is accommodated?

The MOE shows were put together as grassroots ventures, with little or no funding for each one. Although tickets were sold, the door receipts rarely covered expenses. Usually no one was paid for the coordination of the events. Most ticket revenues barely covered the cost of space rentals and interpreter fees.

Wry Crips was a role model in providing access to people with environmental allergies and, because of their involvement, many things were done at MOE I that probably wouldn't have been done otherwise. A non-smoking site was selected and cleaned with safe products beforehand. Air filters were set up the night before the performance. Flyers advertising the show requested that people avoid wearing perfume and not have smoke scent on their clothes. However, access at MOE I wasn't perfect. I don't believe programs were put into large print or Braille, and the site location was in San Francisco and far from easy public transportation.

MOE II and III were held at the Veterans Memorial Building in downtown Berkeley. This made transportation much easier than it had been for MOE I. However, the trade-off was that there were problems with bathroom access. One restroom was in the basement with no elevator access, so the main floor bathroom was made unisex and even that one had narrow stall doors. For this reason two attendants were provided (one male and one female, each wearing an identifying arm band) to assist people in the restroom. When bathrooms are accessible, I feel this goes beyond the call of duty, but under the circumstances it was an important thing to do.

Another issue that reared its head at MOE I was censorship. It wasn't clear-cut censorship, however, or folks could have easily solved the issue by refusing to tolerate it. It was a more difficult kind of censorship, the kind that wears a cloak of Political Correctness. There were concerns about some of Jay Yarnall's script, because he was a white man discussing Native American issues. He was asked to make changes to his script. Though a compromise position was eventually found, there was a residual of discomfort left on the floor. Censorship, like access, is a tricky little coyote.

Diversity was another issue that was stirring at that first MOE show. Bruce had tried hard to find performers of color to be in the show. Kathy Martinez was the only one he had talked to who was available and felt ready to take the risks that were taken that night. Like access, we need to always work on improving in the area of diverse representation, but too often people make the assumption that it is not a priority of organizers. It WAS a priority to represent diversity in the MOE shows, both in ethnicity and disability type, but the most visible folks coming out to take creative risks were physically disabled white performers. The nature of oppression is that it keeps people down. Marginalized people are often less visible and have had less support to follow their Dreams; add to this the multiplication of issues when one is a member of more than one under-represented group. It takes time to find diverse representation and to build trust. Gradually, though, performers of color and those with other disabilities were identified and got involved in the MOE shows, but it took some scouting.

Finding affordable, accessible performance spaces and finding a diverse representation of performers were the main ongoing challenges for the MOE events, but certainly not the only challenges. Since the shows used a variety of people who didn't always know each other, disputes occurred behind the scenes and no one was taking the role of Producer or Director to help prevent or settle these disputes. Sometimes they were access issues, such as the time a woman used hairspray in the dressing room, causing another performer to have a severe allergic reaction.

Money, of course, is often a source of contention. When there was a profit from the ticket sales, how should it be divided – by performer or by act? People gave their best for their individual performances, but there was a lack of group commitment and responsibility. I doubt we'll ever know which performer's wheelchair leaked grease on the dance floor, causing a deposit to be forfeited.

Time, money and energy are limited resources, particularly for people with disabilities. A grassroots effort cannot usually have everything done perfectly. We need to take access seriously, but realistically. We need to trust that the organizers of events will provide the access that is feasible to the degree possible. Granted, sometimes people need to learn what access is needed and how to provide it, but criticizing organizers is not the same as helping to educate them. When everyone is volunteering their time and taking money from their own pockets to make an event happen, we need to learn the delicate balance between compliment and criticism. If we don't, we only keep ourselves down, because organizers will become discouraged about producing future events.

The MOE shows were a great door opener. Performers tested out their talents in a safe environment, many of them moving on to bigger things later. Audiences were entertained and educated. The community (both people with and without disabilities) was enriched. Every show improved on the production mistakes made at the previous events and each one got better, both on stage and behind stage. However, the internal and external disputes took a toll on the organizers.

I debated how much detail to give you about the difficulties that were going on through the MOE years. I have copies of memos and notes that people sent to each other, some in anger, and some in jest. I decided to save you the melodrama. I don't see much productivity in airing our dirty laundry, but I would like to say that there was so much pressure on the MOE shows to be completely politically correct, that it became frustrating to continue producing them. I might go as far as saying they were PC to the point of extinction. Others may have a different view, but that is mine.

In all fairness though, I'll add that another reason the MOE shows ended is because other opportunities opened up for many of the artists. Success led to there no longer being as much of a need for the MOE venue.

Regardless of the problems, the MOE shows played an extremely important role during their short lived reign. They launched many people onto artistic paths. Some of the people would have eventually found their way onto these paths on their own, but the MOE events were like a match, setting off many bonfires.

Kudos to everyone who made these shows possible. This goes not only to the performers who were rarely paid, but also to the technicians who were never paid, and to the audience members who usually paid. There were also people who volunteered as access assistants, ushers, stage hands, and many others who gave time and energy to enable these shows to happen. I don't have room to mention everyone even if I did have all the names, but you know who you are. Thank you for being part of these powerful, creative productions.

Postscript by Peni Hall:

I spent most of my life doing theatre, and planned a career teaching it. Becoming disabled put a stop to that, so I looked for new ways to keep theatre in my life.

I began working with Wry Crips, performing and coordinating technical elements. Audience response was enthusiastic; it was clear people were hungry to see disabled people telling our own stories, instead of the "inspiring" stories by nondisabled medical professionals. When we performed at MOE I, I realized there were more disabled people doing innovative performance work. I was hooked.

It was great to work with Dave DeWeerd. We created the environment for Pamela's infamous seduction fantasy, taped gels to lights, and ran miles of cable for Hephaestus. I learned a lot of video stuff from him and Pamela. It was wonderful working in the arts again, even if figuring out how to do things from a wheelchair was as challenging as developing material and rehearsing.

We didn't know where these humble beginnings would lead - the International Disability Film Festivals, Integrated Performance Groups, art exhibits on Disability and Sexuality, to name a few. Now that the genie is out of the bottle, there's no way it's going back.

Chapter Thirteen   Springboarding

ONE OF THE GREAT THINGS that came out of the MOE shows was a sense
of a creative community among people with disabilities and our allies. We got
to know each other as artists. People in both the disability community and in
the general population began to recognize that there was an emerging artistic
movement. The result was a springboard effect.

A springboard allows one to go higher, to do more. That is exactly what
happened as a result of the collaborative artistic activities that occurred
during the time of the MOE shows. Motivation and encouragement gave
artists the impetus to continue and to expand their craft, and audience
members wanted more of what they'd seen. Word-of-mouth began to pack
houses when artists with disabilities were presented.

There were only four MOE shows, but there have been similar events
in the years since then. Some of the MOE artists began to weave in and
out of each others projects. Some took their skills to higher levels of
professionalism. Wry Crips and AXIS went on to do full shows. Disability
organizations started inviting performers with disabilities to appear at their
functions. Finally, the arts begin to be included when activism is the issue,
slowly filtering into the political movement.

The Bay Area gave birth to the Independent Living Movement in the
'70's and became alive with a fast-growing disability Arts Movement in the
'80's. Artists with disabilities began to emerge as a creative force.

One example of the activists embracing the artists was a night of performances that happened shortly after MOE IV, at a conference sponsored by the World Institute on Disability (WID). This was an international conference bringing together people with disabilities from all over the world to discuss political issues. Local artists, many of them graduates of MOE, were asked to perform one evening for the conference goers.

Another example is a BBC documentary about the Independent Living Movement called "The Gospel According to Berkeley." Bruce and I were hired as the local coordinators. I had shown them footage of the MOE productions and they wanted to include a performance by Hephaestus in the video. The arts are represented as part of the Disability Rights Movement just by the fact that the documentary opens with footage of this performance.

WID continues to recognize the importance of the arts and collaborates with the Corporation on Disabilities and Telecommunication (CDT) to host an annual fundraiser of a new kind. Instead of using typical archaic fundraising methods, like having people pay $100 to eat a skimpy TV dinner, CDT and WID got creative. Starting in 1999 they began hosting fundraising performance events, bringing professional artists with disabilities from around the country to perform at a gala showcase.

The CDT/WID collaboration exemplifies recognition of Art as social change work. WID does public policy work; CDT works in the area of art and media. Combining the missions of these two organizations into an artistic event is a major move forward in acknowledging the contribution of artists to the Disability Rights Movement. As Deborah Kaplan (past Executive Director of WID) and Liane Yasumoto (Executive Director of CDT) explained in the program's first welcoming letter:

"We desire to demonstrate through this collaboration that art and public policy can successfully be brought together. WID's policy and advocacy work depends on broad social acceptance and requires a new understanding of disability as a cultural phenomenon. CDT's mission and activities, promoting new images of disability through artistic expression, are radical forms of advocacy because we move people through the arts. Public policy that advances disability rights and independent living is strengthened by direct linkage to the arts. The broader disability movement also deepens new advances in artistic expression that reflect the disability experience."

The event was named "Ever Widening Circle: An Evening of Entertainment Celebrating Art & Disability," – EWC for short. The name was inspired by a discussion with playwright Charles Mee, Jr. The concept of the ever widening circle refers to how art has progressed historically, gradually including more and more people throughout the ages. Now, the circle widens enough to include artists with disabilities.

The first EWC was a gala event with a silent auction prior to the show. Many of the performing artists featured in the show came out of the time and place that I've been talking about, the San Francisco Bay Area in the 1980s. Five of the artists were from the Bay Area, three being graduates of the MOE shows that had been held ten years previously. These artists have achieved widespread recognition, some staying in the Bay Area and some moving on.

Danny Glover and Ysabel Duron hosted the show.

Most of you probably know of Danny Glover, but you might not know that he is a native of San Francisco and that he has a learning disability. But that is not why he co-hosted the CDT/WID benefit; he did it because he's a good guy. In addition to his film career, he has worked for many human rights causes.

Ysabel Duron is a reporter and anchor for KRON-TV in San Francisco. She produced a highly acclaimed series, "Life with Cancer," chronicling her winning battle against Hodgkin's Disease. The topics and the depth of her stories help to make social change.

They made a great team to introduce and comment on the incredible performances that we saw. On stage and off, the room was filled with people who did political work, people who did artistic work, and people who did both.

Cheryl Marie Wade started off the show, performing some of her delightful poetry. She is an amazing bundle of sass! Next, C. J. Jones, The Living Cartoon, had the audience in stitches with his comedy routines. After C.J., AXIS Dance Company WOWed the audience, followed by David Roche who captivated everyone's attention with his wit and charm.

Diane Schuur was the headliner that night. She has been awarded two Grammies for Best Jazz Vocalist and her recordings have topped the charts. She was the imported performer of the bunch – the only one not to come out of the Bay Area. She was an extremely shy child, blind since birth, who used her voice as a bridge to the world. She has crossed that bridge with such greats as Dizzy Gillespie and B.B. King. Needless to say, her performance was impressive!

This entertaining and enriching evening ended with original poetry recited by Guy Johnson, son of Dr. Maya Angelou. His words added the perfect touch to bring us back to issues of humanity, where creativity and life walk hand-in-hand.

As I left the event, I asked myself a question that I have asked many times: Why is it so hard for Art to be seen as social change work? In my mind, the event that I had just attended was definitely social change work. Yet, many groups of disability activists still do not recognize the artists among them and do not support the organizations assisting those artists. When activists with disabilities write new legislation, careers in the arts are not included in the thinking. For example, the Americans with Disabilities Act is a wonderful piece of legislation defining the rights of people with disabilities, including the right to attend artistic events, but it doesn't address issues of backstage access for artists with disabilities.

An artist who is disabled does not get support in the mainstream art world either. Organizations and facilities that provide support to artists are often not accessible to people with disabilities; but, because arts are viewed as a luxury in our country, enforcement of access laws for art facilities are not seen as a priority. If the theme of an art work is disability related, it is difficult to get art funding, because it is not considered a topic of general interest. Yet, it is difficult to get "disability" funding because of competition with housing, attendant care, and other vital services.

The artist with a disability is the neglected child of the Disability Rights Movement and the abandoned child of the artistic community. Slowly, this is turning around and I think it will turn around even faster as people recognize that the art coming from the disability community is not only about disability, but it conveys messages on issues that all people can benefit from, such as self-image, adapting to a hostile environment, and combating societal stereotypes.

Themes that artists with disabilities wrestle with are often more universal than one might initially think. For example, the occurrence of sexual abuse among children with disabilities is shockingly high. In some of my solo performance pieces, I have used material about my being an incest survivor. Many times I have had non-disabled audience members approach me after the show to thank me for bringing these issues into the open; they will often disclose that they too are an incest survivor and that it is the first time they've told anyone.

I return to my question: Why is it so hard for Art to be seen as social change work? The sociologist in me has come up with one theory: Many people with disabilities developed workaholic tendencies during their struggle for independence. If you combine that with the fact that our society, in general, does not respect Artists as workers, a wall is built between activists and artists. To reconcile with this division, I've called myself a disability arts activist.

EWC events might be said to be segregated productions in that all the performers (or at least one in a group) are people with disabilities; however, they are professionals who do their art in the mainstream and they are acknowledged publicly for their art, not for their disabilities. EWC gives acknowledgement to their accomplishments and raises money for two very important organizations.

The annual EWC events are similar to the MOE events, except that the MOE events were coming from a grassroots place and EWC events are artistic professionals who have honed their craft to a high level of quality. In a recent year EWC featured the Blind Boys of Alabama to a near sell-out crowd!

EWC gives two awards each year, one recipient picked by WID and one by CDT. CDT presents to people who have worked to encourage representation of people with disabilities in the arts. Some of the recipients have been Paula Terry from the National Endowment for the Arts, Olivia Raynor from the National Art and Disability Center, and Greg Smith for his nationally syndicated "On A Roll" radio show that pushed disability issues into mainstream radio.

There are other examples of how the artists are beginning to get the recognition they deserve. Another non-art based organization that has reached out to the creative disability community is the Society for Disability Studies. This is an academic group working for the inclusion of Disability Studies curriculum at universities, similar to how women's groups had to work for the development of Women's Studies departments. SDS holds an annual conference and arranges for performers with disabilities to present at some of its activities.

Independent Living Centers host art exhibits and performances by people with disabilities for publicity, fundraising, or both. Other groups break artists with disabilities into even more layers of subculture, such as a Queer Disability

Conference, and the Disability Arts and Minority Organization (DAMO); both greatly honored artists through performances and video screenings.

College and University classes for people who will be working with students with disabilities (i.e. special education majors) have also begun to recognize the importance of hearing the truths that come from the artists with disabilities. Several Bay Area schools of higher education encourage field trips to video screenings and performances at Disability Culture events.

Many of these things have evolved since the MOE shows, sometimes directly because of an audience member or performer who was at one of the shows, sometimes simply because "the times they are a changin'." MOE was just one of the springboards that accelerated the emergence of artists with disabilities. Similar things were popping up around the world at about the same time. Springboard, trampoline, boomerang... Whatever metaphor works best... the point is there have been many after-effects of these cultural events... for individuals, groups, and society. And it just keeps on BOINGING...!

Postscript by Vicki VanSteenberg

The MOE shows were indeed a springboard for the artists with disabilities. AND for their audiences. I watched social change happen in front and inside me. The shows bridged the first-person expressions of artists with disabilities and the shifting perspectives of onlookers.

As a Special Education teacher, I had learned to see a person first, over their disability, and I was familiar with various disabilities. The creativity of the artists in the MOE shows still had a profound effect on me, personally and professionally. The shows touched artistic perceptions that spoke to all of human abilities and experiences. A door opened to form lifelong friendships with some of the artists, deep respect for their work, and a fuller reality of connectedness for us all.

The performances took me past professional definitions of disability and plunked me into sensibilities of spirit and passion. I was a teacher being taught, getting higher training in the heart of living. The shows helped us imagine, question, and create with fresh eyes.

I took art lover friends to performances. One friend from Mexico was a woman in a wheelchair. Another was a high school teacher who had had little exposure to people with disabilities. The night had a strong impact on both of them! The friend from Mexico returned to her country as an invigorated, disability rights activist. The teacher became a solid voice for inclusion of Special Education students in regular classes. She became one of MOE's best Public Relations representatives, giving rave reviews of the joi de vivre she had experienced in action – a break through in the edges of thinking and feeling. I could not agree with her more!

Chapter Fourteen   Into the Echo Chamber (1990)

WHEN THE MOE SHOWS BEGAN, I was working as a video producer and editor. In addition to a fifteen-minute video called "Strong, United and Proud" about people with disabilities demonstrating for access to public transportation, I had also made a few artsy videos. They were a bit too on the edge for my friends and family. What do I mean by "on the edge?" That's a hard question to answer, and one that even artists grapple with. It's a question that can ruffle hairs because some people think of it as an elitist division.

When I say my work was on the edge, I mean that it wasn't following the general format that was used in videos at the time. If you stand on the edge, you have part of you facing the known, and part of you facing the unknown. In many ways my work followed the rules, but in a lot of ways it didn't. Only a small number of people appreciated my art videos.

When I saw MOE I, I was in the planning stage for a video that was more conventional than some of the art videos I had been doing. I wanted to do a video that presented artists with disabilities working together on a project. Dave DeWeerd and I had collaborated on some projects. I wanted to bring more people together to experiment and create with each other so that we could grow our artistic feathers.

Before he gave birth to the MOE shows, Bruce talked about wanting to find a way for people to come together to practice their art, to exercise their creativity. We talked about something he tentatively called the

"Experimental Laboratory for Visionary Disabled Artists." At first I thought he was talking about a facility, but eventually I figured out that people could get together for a "lab" even if there wasn't a consistent facility. This idea was germinating at the time that I saw the first MOE show.

The person that impressed me the most at MOE I was Jay Yarnall. I was awed by his performance that took me on a surreal journey of spoken word, drum beats and electronic sounds. After the show, the performers came out to engage with the audience members. I tenuously approached Jay and introduced myself. I told him that I was planning a video project that would bring artists together to collaborate on a piece. I asked him if he would be willing to be one of those artists. I was surprised when he instantly agreed. I felt like I was talking to a rock star who had just said "yes" to playing at my high school prom.

Inspired by MOE I, it didn't take me long to pull together five artists to work on the collaborative project. They were Bruce Curtis, Dave DeWeerd, Kathy Martinez, Cheryl Marie Wade, and Jay Yarnall. Adina Frieden was my support person and there were many times I was glad I had set up that arrangement. Avril Harris was the primary camera operator for the project.

This mix of artists made up an interesting group. Dave and Jay were both disabled, but had not connected much with the disability community. Cheryl's artistic expression came out of her experiences in the disability community, kick-started with her involvement with Wry Crips. Kathy had been wearing the cloak of an artist off and on since early childhood, but most of her time and energy was spent working in disability politics and for disability organizations. Bruce played and worked in both the disability and the non-disability worlds.

Adina was my best friend and a woman with Cystic Fibrosis, a condition that gradually decreased her lung capacity. She later became a published writer, but at this time she wasn't calling herself an artist. She coordinated the Independent Living Skills department at the Center for Independent Living in Berkeley, teaching people with disabilities how to live independently in the community.

Avril is the only person in this bunch who was not disabled, but her life partner used a wheelchair. Avril had become involved in the disability community during the 504 demonstrations and was working for the Disabled Students' Program at UC Berkeley.

This eclectic mix of political and artistic experiences created a deep well to draw from, but it had its drawback. The video I originally thought would take six months to do took a year and a half to complete. I had estimated it would cost me $500, and in the end it cost me $1500 out of my pocket; it would have cost even more if East Bay Media Center hadn't donated editing time to me.

The documentation of the collaboration involved videotaping every meeting between the five collaborators. I had told them I would not direct what the final project would be, but that I would fund it. It was up to them to come up with the concept for a seven-minute video. After a year of their bouncing around ideas, I retracted that statement and took a more directive role.

Part of the difficulty in their coming to any concrete decisions was that, in addition to being eclectic in their art, they were also eclectic in their approaches to making art. At one extreme was Jay who likes to do things extemporaneously, and on the other extreme was Cheryl who was used to editing, and re-editing things. Some people in the group wanted to know exactly what the piece was going to look like before they did it, others wanted to just do it and then see what they wound up with.

The addition of Jay to the mix had a big impact on the direction that the final piece took, not only because of his artistic input and his zen approach to creativity, but also because of his resources. I did not know at the time that I invited him to join the bunch that Jay had a professional sound studio. We would gather to talk about some themes, then go into Jay's studio and play around with some of the ideas. His studio was filled with lots of electronic toys as well as instruments made from natural objects such as bamboo and gourds.

Avril videotaped our meetings and jam sessions. (I had the camera turned off if I called "break," though, so I could decompress with Adina when things weren't going well.) She also taped each of the five artists doing their art. She videotaped Cheryl performing with Wry Crips, Kathy Martinez drumming in a parade with Sistah Boom, and Jay exploring eastern traditions on his keyboard in a "new age" performance. To represent Dave's art, I used footage from his video, "Phoenix Rising." I used video footage from the "Leaders" performance to represent Bruce's artistic expression.

I was too busy being the parent to realize that we were on a playground having fun. None of the people had worked together before, though most of them knew each other. Jay was the only wild card, the new face.

The final product was a half hour video called "Into the Echo Chamber." The last seven minutes of it was the artistic short that the collaborators created, called "Dreamweave." In "Echo" I show the artists coming together for the first time as I present the collaboration idea to them. Jay invites us to play in his studio, and from there it took off. The video goes back and forth from meetings to jamming to highlighting each of the five artists. At the end we see the collaborative work that came out of the long pregnancy.

Besides Jay's studio, we did three location shoots; two made it into the final product. The shoot that was cut showed beautiful footage taken from Mount Tamalpais, a peak above the Pacific Ocean. Kathy brought her drums and Jay brought several wind instruments. We played in the wind by the sea. Though none of the footage made it into "Echo," it was a wonderful experience to play in nature, making sounds and laughter. This is one of my favorite memories from that project and I find it fitting that it is the one that is not seen by the public, as it represents the process, not the product.

We also videotaped playing in the Sculpture Garden in Berkeley. This is an interesting place Cheryl found near her home. A weed field grows around several metal sculptures rusted with age. Some of the sculptures are several feet high, some are short and long. An improvisational dancer instructed the artists in "letting go" and moving freely among the sculptures. At one point, the five artists crawled on top of one of the sculptures and played the instruments we had brought, the same ones that we had taken to Mount Tam. At this shoot I was present in the background wearing masks, symbolizing my role as the producer, always in the background but not one of the artists.

We did an indoor shoot at the Veteran's Memorial Building, the same building that had been used for a couple of the MOE shows. This was a shoot where we used a fog machine to create an other-world atmosphere. Each of the artists entered as if they were being drawn together into the unknown. They carried candles to symbolize the bringing of light. Kathy played her drums and pulled the artists towards her.

The shoot at the Veteran's Memorial Building had initially been scheduled for another location, but we had to cancel because Dave wound up in the hospital. Dave's diabetes often caused complications and he was hospitalized six times that year. Working on this video meant being zen, because people had disabilities that sometimes interfered with plans we had made. In this case, we changed locations for the shoot because the original location had not been available later. However, in our Berkeley way, we felt that the place we wound up shooting was where it was "meant to be."

Even though we sometimes had to make adjustments in our schedules or activities to accommodate people's disabilities, we didn't let that stop us from moving forward. I still get teased about being a producer with a whip, because of how I even made Dave work while he was in the hospital. We had not figured out exactly how to do the lighting for the indoor shoot and where to position the cameras. I scooped up several Lego dolls to represent each of the people to be in the scene and took them to Dave in the hospital. Using his hospital tray-on-wheels, we plotted the lighting arrangements using Legos and paper cones.

When we passed the one year mark in the collaboration, I decided to take some control. Several ideas had been brought up over and over again, but the artists hadn't made a single final decision. I presented what I'd seen as reoccurring themes and said that these elements were going to be in the piece. Rather than resenting my taking control, everyone seemed relieved that there were some parameters being set.

The themes that had emerged frequently were the bringing of light, braiding, weaving, fire, hair, and hands. Once we discussed these themes, Cheryl took them away and wrote a poem. In "Dreamweave" Cheryl recites the poem amidst the fog:

She is a young woman
    or old
seated in front of a mirror
she is watching a lover's hands
    brushing her hair
watching hands weave
    small tentative braids
watching hands.

they could be anyone's hands
all the hands that have held her
        harmed her

and as she watches the hands
slide from hair
to shoulders
to breast
she dreams of flight
to be the hawk
know Mojave by skyward view
fly the length of Snake Canyon
    over and over again

but it is not to be the hawk
that is her dream
it is to be air in the bones of the hawk
to be that thin braid of air
in the bones
air

— Copyright © 1990 Cheryl Marie Wade

Once all the footage was shot, Dave and I went into the editing studio.
I made the decisions on the documentary part of the work and Dave
(with input from the other artists) made the decisions for "Dreamweave."

Looking through the hours and hours of footage that had been shot over the 18 months, it was so clear that we were in the laboratory that Bruce had envisioned. This is what influenced the title of the work – Dave and I decided we had been in a chamber, echoing off of each other.

There were many times during the production of this video that I figuratively pulled my hair out; but now, many years removed, I look back on it as a fond experience. We came together and fed the artistic animal inside of us on a regular basis. My frustration at the time came from my being more focused on the product than the process. I often pulled Adina aside during a shoot and vented my frustrations at how slow things were moving. Listening was the major part of her job as my support person and she did it very well.

Peni Hall was another support person who played a major role in the process. Peni was quite involved with Wry Crips at the time that we were working on the collaboration, but she was still able to assist me in many ways. She was not only a wealth of technical knowledge, but she was a great cheerleader. The only time that she actually worked on site was when we had an indoor shoot and needed her lighting expertise to help us with some major issues. One time we were considering having a shoot in a mansion with the artists all sitting at a feast. Peni even offered to cook our turkey and other goodies to make it look authentic. What a trooper!

Peni has a severe reaction to perfumes and smoke. The shoot that Peni assisted with involved candles, fog, and lighting gels for unusual light effects and coloring. We joke about how absurd it was that a person with chemical sensitivities was operating the fog machine, but sometimes that's what happens when you get lost in art. You forget to eat, you forget to sleep, and you forget that you're allergic to chemicals.

I had many expectations for what I wanted to happen with the finished work. I entered it in several film festivals and sold individual copies. I wanted it to be a crossover work that would win awards in festivals that were not about the theme of disability. I wanted the piece to win because it was an interesting story about five artists who happened to be disabled, with disability as a secondary subject. It was received very well in the disability community, but not in the mainstream world. It failed to make the big bang that I had hoped for.

People who knew little about disability found the work to be lacking because it did not talk about each individual's disability. I would reply by saying that the work was about their being artists, not about them being disabled. I'm tired of patiently waiting for the mainstream world to get past our disabilities to see other aspect of our lives.

[Ironically, a short work that I made to prepare everyone to work on "Echo" did become a crossover success. In my video work, I use what I call a "layed-back" approach. By that I mean that I don't want people to push themselves too hard or to ignore basic needs. I encourage people to rest when exhausted and eat when hungry. I shot a video of me talking to the camera explaining this philosophy to the artists. Dave did the camera work and we staged my talk in various relaxed settings. I addressed them from a cot in a barn with a chicken on my belly, from a bathtub in the woods, and from a bed with my morning coffee. This work was called "Notes on a Layed-Back Production." Though it was only intended for use in-house, one of the artists shared it with someone who knew someone who knew someone and I was approached by someone who wanted to broadcast it on an independent television satellite program. As a result, "Notes" was seen across the United States and I was paid for airtime. It had more success than "Echo."]

Looking at "Echo" now, after years of distance, I can see why it did not win at festivals. It is not an excellent piece of work, but historically it is very important. It documents some of the work of the artists coming out of that period of time. It was also important because it gave a boost to the artists who were involved. Most of them would go on to develop their art further and to take advantage of the things they had learned during the time they worked on this piece. The echoes of that project are still being heard.

Postscript by Avril Harris:

Fifteen years after the journey "Into the Echo Chamber," I remember the experience as if it happened yesterday. Maybe not all the details, but certainly the feelings of excitement and exhilaration about the "great experiment."

I was a novice when Pamela Walker invited me to join the project with a group of talented, political activists in the disability community. I was deeply honored to be a part of it, and fortunate to have the opportunity to apprentice with Dave DeWeerd and learn more about his craft.

My role as one of the camera operators was to capture the flow of artistry without getting in the way. It was critical to capture the essence of each artist in their boundless creativity and not their obvious physical limitations. A most memorable session for me was at Jay Yarnall's studio when the artists jammed the first time. I was truly awe-inspired as I weaved my way through and around the various artists. This first session highlighted the synergy that was to emerge from this group. Pamela's ingenuity and vision for this piece reveal her natural ability to collaborate with others, and to foster and channel creativity which resulted in this dynamic cutting-edge work.

Chapter Fifteen

Talent Bridge Begat PEP

THE MOE SHOWS PROVED TO ME that we had a lot of talent in the disability community. I helped Bruce find people to perform in the shows. We were especially looking for people from a variety of ethnicities and disability types. At the same time, I had been working as an actress in industrials (CDs or videos done for a particular audience, usually educational or informative). I had come to know the local casting scene, I had taken several workshops, and I had become a union actress.

When "Echo" was finished, I was available to embark on another adventure. I took stock and decided to start a talent agency that would specialize in people with disabilities and from other disadvantaged and under-represented groups. I applied for and received a PASS to start my company "Talent Bridge." (PASS is a program through Social Security that enables a person to build a career or company for a designated time without being penalized for monies earned. All monies must be used as approved, thus the word "Plan." PASS = Plan for Achieving Self Support.)

I called my company Talent Bridge because I saw a need to bridge the gap between performers with disabilities and the mainstream casting community. It also seemed to be a good name because most of the jobs were in San Francisco and most of the people with disabilities were in Berkeley or Oakland. A long bridge connects the East Bay with San Francisco.

I operated Talent Bridge for six years and during that time I found roles for many performers with disabilities. In San Francisco most of the work that is easily available for people with disabilities and that pays well is industrial work. However, there are an increasing number of feature films shot in the Bay Area. Especially for beginning actors who were willing to do extra work, it was easy for me to get them on the set. I also found that it was sometimes possible to get people positions in theater productions.

It was fun and personally rewarding work. I placed clients as extras in several movies, including "Made In America" (Whoopie Goldberg), "Angels in the Outfield" (Danny Glover), and "Murder in the First" (Christian Slater and Kevin Bacon). I also placed extras on "Nash Bridges," the TV series starring Don Johnson.

Many times my work involved contacting a company that advertised they were looking for diverse talent for a CD ROM or an industrial video. Knowing that they usually meant ethnic diversity, I would call them to check out what they were looking for. If they were looking for a wide representation of society, I was often able to convince them that society included people with disabilities from a diverse range of ethnicities. After a "What-a-Concept!" moment they agreed to audition some of my clients. My most successful example of this was for a CD ROM to discourage smoking among teenagers. They wanted to represent many types of people and ended up casting six of my clients!

Casting directors and agents got to know me and frequently called when they were looking for an actor with a disability. At first these calls were clumsy, as the person at the other end tried to be politically correct. After they got to know that I rarely took offense when people didn't know how to talk about disabilities, the calls sometimes became quite surreal. For example, here is a loose rendition of the call for extras for "Murder in the First":

THEM: I'm looking for men to play specific types as extras in a movie.
ME: OK, what do you need?
THEM: We need three amputees who are of an age that they could play WWI Vets in the 1930's.
ME: How many missing limbs?
THEM: More than one would be good – two or three.

ME: Arms or legs?

THEM: Huh?

ME: Both legs missing, a leg and an arm, or would a mix be okay?

THEM: Well, I hadn't really thought about it, but I suppose each should have at least one missing leg, and beyond that maybe a variety of combinations.

ME: No problem. Where and when are the auditions?

Some of my work was educating the industry. One time a casting director wanted an actress who used a wheelchair. I asked her if it should be a manual chair or a power chair and she responded that the character was wealthy, so she imagined that she'd use a power chair. I diplomatically informed her that the type of chair a person uses is not usually a matter of economics, but of function, that a person with full usage of their arms would likely use a manual chair.

I was also educating my clients. Taking the information I'd gleaned from my own training as an actress, I helped them with their resumes and coached them for auditions. I helped many to get low-cost headshots and pick appropriate monologues for auditions. I coordinated workshops and used my industry contacts to lead them. Joe Paulino, one of the top ten voice actors in the Bay Area, gave a voice workshop that was outstanding. It was great for my clients and a good opportunity for non-disabled industry folks to get exposure to some of the great talent available in the disability community.

I was opening doors, but I needed people ready to go through the doors once they were open. My goal was not to create a separate agency where people with disabilities would cluster, but to create a bridge. The greatest success I could have, I felt, was if I could assist a performer to get enough experience and validity to enable them to find a franchised talent agency to take them on as a client. Franchised agencies are those which have met the standards required by the union and the labor commission.

I had success, but not enough to sustain myself financially once the PASS period ended. I didn't want to see all the work I had done dissolve into nothing. The industry needed to learn more about disability, and people with disabilities needed to learn more about the industry. When I notified my clients that I was no longer going to be running Talent Bridge as an agency, I transitioned many of them into situations where they promoted themselves or got another agent. There are several hotlines people can call to get casting leads and I made sure they all had that information.

Just as I was wrapping up my career as a talent agent, I was approached by the Magic Theatre. This is one of the most respected theaters in the Bay Area. They have a long history of providing a home for new works and were going to workshop a piece by Charles "Chuck" Mee, Jr. They wanted to cast people with unusual body types, people we don't normally see on the stage. They had called several casting agencies and kept getting referred to me, because I had become known as the source for "unusual" talent. Kenn Watt was the director for this project and he and I became good friends. I was hired as casting director and assistant on the project, although my credit in the program was as "sex symbol" (a story for another book). I not only helped with casting but I also went to most of the rehearsals and helped with communications and adapting roles to accommodate peoples' disabilities.

Chuck Mee is well respected in the theatre community and lives in New York. He had polio at a young age. I had not known that he was disabled until I began working on this project. The work did not have anything to do with disability but it was a goal of Chuck's to cast people with disabilities to add an interesting element to the project.

We approached casting with nothing set in stone, and we began to beat the bushes for people to audition. I called in several of the people who had been my clients who I felt were at a level to work on something this big. It would be difficult to work on this project because it was not completely written and actors would be helping in the development process. It would also demand an ability to work with a non-linear script.

We were looking for other atypical folks besides people with disabilities. For example, there was a scene where a woman would break into an opera song. We wanted to find someone who could sing opera but who had an atypical body. We were looking at people with tattoos or piercings all over their body. We looked at the Radical Faeries, men who dressed in skirts. Tall people, short people, fat people, extremely thin people… we were open to auditioning a wide spectrum of body types and appearances.

We held auditions for two days and at the end of the first day I was in tears. We had seen performers with and without disabilities and the difference in professionalism was so obvious between the two. Many of the performers that were disabled had talent, but they lacked a professional slickness. Finesse. Very few of the performers with disabilities had headshots, some didn't have resumes, and some had picked inappropriate pieces as monologues. Some came dressed as if they had just gotten out of bed. I was frustrated that after six years of working with actors with disabilities, the chasm between the professionals and the beginners was so wide.

We could have had as many as five people with disabilities, but some weren't right for the part and others didn't have the chops to do what it would take to work on the production. Not all of the actors with disabilities were unprofessional but most of them were. Eventually we hired three actors with disabilities for the workshop process. None of them had the degree of experience that the actors without disabilities had.

The workshop performance used only two of the actors with disabilities, Afi-Tiombe Kambon and David Roche. Both Afi and David were pushed greatly during the rehearsals for this production. Kenn had taken a risk on the two of them because they had talent and their personalities fit the casting needs. However, I underestimated how difficult it would be for them to stretch themselves as far as it would take. Though both had great success doing their solo performances, they had not had much work in ensemble productions, and none in experimental pieces.

"Summertime" was well received and played at the Magic for three weeks as a workshop production. Later it was developed and completed as a full show, but David Roche was the only performer with a disability cast in the final production.

The difficulties of the "Summertime" project inspired me to find ways to increase the professionalism of performers with disabilities. I attended a national conference of the Association for Theater and Accessibility. This organization has since dissolved, but for several years it met annually as a place for people who were involved in theatre and disability to come together for workshops, discussions, and networking. This particular year, California Arts Council had given grants to several non-profit organizations to send representatives to the conference. These were people from organizations that were not about disability, so it gave an excellent opportunity for the two worlds to learn about each other.

At this conference I met Rica Anderson from Theatre Bay Area and Deborah Cullinan from Intersection for the Arts. Both of these organizations

Mary Ann Tidwell, Christopher DeJong, Rica Anderson and Jeff Wincek in an Alchemy Works production.

are in San Francisco and serve the theatre community in a variety of ways. Rica and Deborah were motivated to begin to include people with disabilities in the work that each of them did at their organizations. The three of us formed a network and created the Professional Enrichment Program (PEP).

PEP has evolved and shifted since its inception, but primarily is still continuing some of the work that I started with Talent Bridge, bridging the gaps between the theatre community and the disability community. PEP produces theatre productions through its company Alchemy Works, casting performers with and without disabilities so that they can learn from each other. This has been an excellent opportunity for mainstream professionals to become familiar and comfortable with a population they may not have been exposed to before. At the same time, it provides many theater workers with disabilities the opportunity to develop their skills.

PEP is going through the growing pains of a young non-profit organization and it's possible that it might not survive to see the publication of this book. I hope it does, as it provides an excellent model for inclusion of artists with disabilities – not one that is a separate program or organization, sticking out like a leg in a cast, but rather a coalition approach of partners from the art world and disability community. If PEP is still around as you read this, they will have changed their name to ART: The Alliance for Representative Theatre.

Postscript by Rica Anderson

Drawn to Pamela's energy and vision, the PEP coalition was formed, and we produced quality theatre, featuring professional artists alongside emerging performers. I had the pleasure of performing on one production and the experience raised my consciousness in many ways.

The performance was at Julia Morgan theatre, a historic building that I assumed would be fairly disabled-friendly, though it might provide some challenges. Like many "accessible" spaces, there were unrecognized obstacles. The narrow dressing room caused wheelchair traffic jams; performers in wheelchairs had to cluster around one low mirror; and, while there was an accessible audience bathroom, there wasn't one backstage. Afterwards, Julia Morgan staff consulted an architect and will be building accessible bathrooms backstage.

Working with performers with disabilities taught me more about my craft than many professional productions I've worked on. I was inspired by their creativity, ingenuity, and imagination in expressing characters' needs and emotions, often using wheelchairs, crutches or canes to punctuate a moment. One time the director was struggling with how to portray a character going downstairs (Should we have the actor use her crutches? Should we use tape to show stairs?), when suddenly the actor "bumped" her wheelchair down an imaginary staircase, creating an evocative, funny moment that always drew a big audience reaction.

Watching Tristan Thunderbolt (a performer who is deaf) "listen" to another actor was another revelation. Listening to your scene partner (as though hearing it for the first time) is essential for a believable performance. Here was someone LISTENING with an intense focus and a spontaneous reaction. He wasn't displaying a carefully crafted reaction, but a magical moment of something real, happening now. Since then I consciously try to bring that kind of listening to every role I play.

1990 WAS A PROLIFIC YEAR for me. MOE III was in April, the final edit
for "Into the Echo Chamber" was finished in July, and MOE IV was held in
October. It was also the year that Hephaestus was formed by Dave Deweerd,
Jay Yarnall and me, to perform in MOE.

Arrangements for MOE IV to be part of Festival 2000 were made only
about six weeks before the event took place. Dave, Jay and I had worked
together on "Echo" and had enjoyed the collaborative process of jamming
with each other on the equipment. We decided to develop something having
to do with perceptions of disability related to our own self images and society's
images of us. We laughed together at the absurdity that we were going to be
performing something in six weeks and we had no idea what that was.

Jay and Dave appreciated the styles and techniques used by Laurie
Anderson, a premier performance artist known primarily for her multi-media
presentations. Jay and I were strongly influenced by many mythological
themes, so we added that to the mix.

Jay told us about Hephaestus, a Greek god with a disability. There are
various versions of Hephaestus' disability. One is that he had grotesque features. Another is that he had one leg shorter than the other and walked with
a limp. The most widely accepted version is that he was the ugliest child of
Zeus. When Zeus saw Hephaestus for the first time, he picked him up from his
crib and threw him, permanently injuring one of his legs.

Hephaestus was one of the two Greek gods involved in the arts. He was a blacksmith, working with fire. In addition to making weapons, he also made jewelry, candlesticks, and things to decorate the home. Hephaestus married Aphrodite, the goddess of love. Also known as Vulcan in Roman mythology, he became disabled because of his father's reaction to his looks. His story provided a great base for a performance about images of disability.

Hephaestus was the perfect name for our group because the combination of disability, art, and a marriage to the goddess of love was a natural fit for all of us. We had a name, but we still didn't know what we were going to do. For advance press purposes we had to define more than a name. We made up something about doing a multi-media performance based on images of disability. Then we set about to figuring out what that was.

Dave and I frequently made the two hour journey to Jay's studio to jam, talk, and explore our own feelings about our disabilities. We didn't do as much talking as we did free association, putting words into the computer keyboard and riffing off of those words. Eventually we came up with a performance, pretty much under the wire.

Our performance involved two keyboards, a video camera, a projection screen, a projector, and lots of other

Jay Yarnall in his studio

electronic gizmos that only Jay could explain. I moved the mouse to make chime sounds, using a computer program that enabled rotation of the mouse to vary pitch and tone. The program would not allow a person to play chords that were discordant. A variety of sounds were available, but I liked the way the chimes sounded. To the non-technical members of the audience I looked like a great musician. Smoke and mirrors.

Art is magical! When you put people together with artistic toys, and give them permission to explore, amazing things can result. We called the piece we created "Wheels of Alchemy" because each of us had our own style, but put together it created a whole piece. Hephaestus was an alchemist, and alchemy is the process of putting unlike substances together to make something totally different. We surprised ourselves with what our alchemy produced.

I will try to give you an idea of what the performance piece looked like:

The three of us wheel onto a dimly lit stage where several pieces of electronics wait, lights flickering. Jay and I, wearing masks, approach keyboards. Dave wheels to the front of the stage carrying a video camera, wearing a gold hard hat, a vest over a bare chest, and a piece of gold snake jewelry curling around one arm.

A projected image on a screen at the back of the stage shows a blacksmith striking his hammer on an anvil as a spotlight comes up on Dave. He tells about Hephaestus. His voice is manipulated to give the effect of him having a deep, vibrating voice. Subtle keyboard rhythms and wind effects add to the sound of the hammer. Speaking slowly, he tells the audience:

Hephaestus was the lame god
 Or he might have been a King.
But he might have just been a lame god.
Hephaestus was a blacksmith
 Or he might have been an artist.
But he might have been an artistic blacksmith.
From the forge of Hephaestus
 Came weapons, tools and treasures
That inspired myths and lore.
Hephaestus was the Alchemist
 And he married Aphrodite.
But did he ever make her   Gold?

When Dave finishes, he turns his back to the audience, raises the video camera and begins to project images of Jay and me onto the screen; these images pass through the camera where visual effects such as strobe and delay are added. The lights have been raised on the whole stage and a mixture of rhythms and chimes comes from the keyboards. Low male and female voices are heard with the chimes, saying pre-recorded "I am" and "I was" at varying pitches. Occasionally all music stops and either "I am" or "I was" is heard clearly, followed with a live descriptive statement of identity by each of us. Below is the list we draw from and we also throw out things extemporaneously.

I AM...	I WAS...
ancient ways	*alone*
two silver rods	*different*
my father's son	*sick and tired*
short-sleeved shirt	*unfeeling*
a video monitor	*High School Drum Major*
physical sensations	*denial*
bisexual	*homecoming queen*
many faces	*gypsy moon*
robin red breast	*rock 'n' roller*
my mother's burden	*hippie*
my father's plaything	*nervous breakdown*
a crooked olive branch	*reincarnation of Cleopatra*
apathy	*iron legs*
atrophy	*disabled*
invisible	*handicapped*
an empty well	*unimportant*
an empty nest	*invalid*
a blue shadow	*invisible*
an artist	*a cripple*
a creator	*switch hitter*
able to laugh	*cat lover*
able to cry	*Lego maniac*
able to play once	*an aging child*
a dream painter	*a hitchhiker*

After several rounds, the chimes end as each of us follows "I am" in turn with "a cripple!" Thunder is heard and the lights go down on all but me in a feather mask. I remove my mask. A beat begins and I rhythmically recite:

With a backdrop of rock 'n' roll
And a '50's way of knowing
Miss America was my dream
And the fantasy started growing
The crown would rest upon my head
Of this I had no doubt
Until a newspaper clipping
Turned my reality all about
"Miss Handicap America"
Is what the heading said
And all my dreams and hopes and joys
Were smashed and left for dead
And the wheels of alchemy started turning… turning… turning…
Wheels started turning… turning… turning…
Ten years later I took a toke
And watched as two streams of smoke
Rose to the sky, made me aware
Of how my life was in the air
One stream showed the truth of me
The other how I was expected to be
As I took my last hit… Only one stream rose
I asked myself which… but who really knows
And the wheels kept turning… turning… turning…
Now, having a disability
is part of my reality
But lovers, friends and family
Closed their eyes and wouldn't see.
Yet to all the strangers on the street
All of me was in my feet
And everything I would do, think or say

Was seen as being

   The crippled way

Well… what is having a disability really about?

Being disabled is being unable

Unable to what?

Unable to hang onto the myth of the indestructible human

It is to know that no matter

What cure,

What adaptive aid,

What cosmetic surgery,

What bottle of peroxide,

What brand of toothpaste,

No matter what wrinkle remover or vitamin,

What cosmetic surgery or cellulite plan…

…I still have a body

   That will age

      That will die…

But… Meanwhile…I'm a gypsy moon

I'm a golden tear

I am alive!

And I am here.

A second of silence is followed by the low howl of wind. Lights go down and come up on Jay. He removes his mask and begins the final piece about his passage from one life to another, speaking in a dream-like voice:

I remember walking, although it feels like floating now

I remember walking, although it feels like floating now

With legs like wings folded, with legs like wings folded

Hitchhiked across the country in 1967, from Florida to San Francisco,

   AWOL from the Navy, in flight from the killing machine,

A skinhead on Haight St. in the Summer of Love.

I wasn't a sailor, I wasn't a hippie,

I was stretched out between everything and nothing, till I could no longer
    hold myself in and I jumped through a window, shattering the glass.
I remember flying, although it feels like floating now
I remember flying, although it feels like floating now
With legs like wings folded, with legs like wings folded
one second I was running,
one second I was flying,
one second I was on the ground
    lying so still, trying to die, die, die with every breath, while three black children
    stared through a wrought iron fence. Finally, contained by my last breath, I felt like
    a cold stone in dark space. I would not remain this way forever. So I crawled back
    into my body, feet first, to possess myself, cool fire in moist carbon burning, cool
    fire in moist carbon burning.
I remember sitting, although it feels like floating now
I remember sitting, although it feels like floating now
With legs like wings folded, with legs like wings folded
[In a haunting singing voice] Let me move before they see me, the children's laughter
    feels like a dangerous wind, I'll sit behind the window curtain, no one's seen me
    lately, just the wind, WSSSSSSSH........
I remember standing, although it feels like floating now
I remember standing, although it feels like floating now
With legs like wings folded, with legs like wings folded
I woke up in a dream, in a circular white room, with a rose bush in a hole in the center
    of the room, next to it was an easel, on it a painting full of vivid colors.
I sat before the painting, bent forward in a torn dirty cloak.
A witch rushed into the room, I leaned forward as her thumbs pressed into my eyes.
    The pain was so intense my screams were silent, pouring out of me as color to
    spread across the canvas. My tears flowed down to water the roses.
I realized for the first time that I'm pressing forward, leaning into her thumbs. I gin-
    gerly pull back, expecting some kind of horrible retribution, but the old woman just
    asks, "Don't you want to paint with your pain any more"
Suddenly, I realize if I just stood up I'd be taller than she.

Hesitating a moment, terrified, I finally rise, the rough cloak falling from my shoul-
*   ders, underneath it I have on a white silk robe. I look down into her eyes as her face*
*   changes into my loving Grandmother and she backs slowly out of the room.*
I remember walking, flying, sitting, standing, even if only
within myself, although it all feels like floating now
With legs like wings folded, with legs like wings folded…
[pause]
This
is
*   my*
*   body*
*   now*
[With a beat, this phrase repeats several times as Jay taps various parts of his body.
    "This is my body now," becomes a chant repeated by all of us and the audience
    is encouraged to join in. The projected image on the screen changes to a mirror-
    within-a-mirror image. Words float up the screen to reflect the words of the chant,
    with "body" and "now" being accented. The piece ends with one final, strong
    exclamation.]
THIS IS!

—*Copyright © 1990 Jay Yarnall*

"Wheels of Alchemy" was the only performance piece that this incarnation of Hephaestus ever developed. It was amusing and flattering that people
assumed we were a regular company, with a repertoire of pieces.

We were invited to perform in Amsterdam, but the prospect was too overwhelming for three wheelchair-using artists with a show that used computers,
live-effected video, and sound equipment. The amount of help we would need
to get our electronic equipment there would be even more of a challenge than
to get our wheelchairs and ourselves there. We had only ourselves, no roadies
to help us to travel halfway around the world. Not to mention that they'd
expect us to play more than one number! We chuckled about the vision of us
hurriedly coming up with more pieces – several all nighters at Jay's and lots of
chocolate. Though we turned down the offer, it was exciting to have received
it, and we did seriously consider it… for about ten seconds.

One reason I feel our show was well received was because it integrated concepts of disability with concepts that could be understood by anyone having a body. Also, we presented our message in nonlinear and experimental ways. People were excited to see originality coming out of the disability community.

The first incarnation of Hephaestus did not last long: I got a grant from the NEA and started to work on a one-woman show; Jay became more involved in sound recording, chanting and breathing work; Dave died. For several years Hephaestus remained dormant. I resurrected it in the late 90s when I started working in theatre more as an artist and writer and less as a talent agent. Jay said he was fine with me using the name we had used for our trio for my theatre company, so I returned to the vision of Hephaestus with my work called "The Rise and Fall of the Us/Them Empire."

I think it is crucial that marginalized people be able to contribute their skills and knowledge to theatre productions. I design Hephaestus pieces in modular ways in order to involve actors who often cannot commit to a production for various reasons. Directors and playwrights can open doors for non-traditional cast and crew members by thinking outside the box on such things as contingency plans, staging, casting, rehearsal schedules, and character design.

My long-term plans for Hephaestus involve structuring shows creatively to allow for a performance to go on in the event of a cast member's temporary absence. Performers would not have to be cut if a disability related issue prevents them from performing for a few nights. Mothers could be in the show, but be excused if their child gets sick. Other examples of actors who might be able to participate in this type of performance system would be performers who occasionally experience migraines, homeless folks, or those who are providing support to a dying family member or friend.

The Hephaestus company is very fluid. The only regular thing Hephaestus ever did was to perform in the Superfest Annual Media Festival Awards Show. Every year, this takes place in Berkeley in June, the first full weekend of the month. The festival is international, but many of the winners cannot come to receive their awards. For several years I wrote skits that allowed the event to go back and forth between presenting awards and providing comic relief. The performance was billed as Hephaestus and Friends, because I usually pulled in a variety of regular and new folks to play on the Superfest stage.

Occasionally other opportunities come up for Hephaestus. I have big ideas about other things I would like to see the company do. Will I ever make those ideas concrete? I don't know. I guess it depends on which way the wind blows.

Will I ever make it Gold?

Postscript by Jay Yarnall

Solitary flames gathered together in the sunny crucible room, the winds of those fires touched each pyre, at first slightly,
     murmuring together the heat built up into a slow boiling burn, then the bonfire broke out in a wondrous roar
and a song was sung

Chapter Seventeen   The Bittersweet

WRITING ABOUT THESE ARTISTIC EVENTS AND ARTISTS fills me with a large helping of celebration and pride. There is also a twist of nostalgia for the past and a dollop of curious expectation about the future. However, some of the layers of this cake have a bittersweet taste.

Factioning The art world suffers from racism, classism, sexism, homophobia and other divisional diseases between peoples. Add to these the sense of elitism that exists between mediums and styles . For example, modern dance companies may feel insulted when they lose a grant competition against a textile art project, and traditional opera singers may snub their noses at hip hop. Into this mix, add a handful of artists with a variety of disabilities, stir in the word "professionalism," and be ready to dash to the nearest exit.

There are many quagmires of separatism within the disability community. Any discussion of artistic professionalism or quality can become a battlefield where defenses go up and people stop listening to each other. I'll list a few examples of factioning in the disability community, but keep in mind that none of these are absolute:

■ Not all blind people make cruel jokes about Deaf people (and vice versa), but enough do that the rivalry between these two populations has itself become the subject of jokes.

- Members of a theatre company doing outreach to wheelchair users cringe the first time a person with a speech-related disability rolls in the door.
- A person who has been disabled all their life may feel a sense of seniority and superiority over someone who is disabled later in life.
- Deaf people often don't think of themselves as disabled, because around people who know sign language they are not disadvantaged in communications.
- People with physical disabilities often don't want to participate in programs that also serve people with developmental disabilities because they don't want to be perceived as "retarded."
- Dating or marrying a non-disabled person is worth more "points" in some people's eyes; others feel that "crip love" is better.
- Some dwarf couples prefer to have dwarf children; others pray that their child is born of "normal" stature.

Now let's add "Art" into this mess... Some folks feel that artists with disabilities should address issues related to disability in their art. However, artists want to create from their own imagination, not have a theme dictated to them, overtly or covertly. There are artists with disabilities who wish they could move past disability themes, but who can't shake the sense of obligation to "make a difference." An artist who expresses an uplifting, inspirational message may be criticized by some and applauded by others. An artist who expresses negative sides of disability may be dismissed as angry and bitter by some, but as exposing unspoken truths by others.

How do we reconcile all of this? Strive for balance. Seek a spirit of openness. Avoid hierarchies and stratifications. Value differences, including differences of opinion. Respect ourselves. Respect others.

Then maybe we can approach discussions about professionalism and quality of art with integrity.

The Issue of Quality "What is Art?"

"Maybe it's art, but is it good art?"

"Is THAT what you'd call art?"

"It's interesting, but I don't think I'd call it Art."

Overheard comments at art museums/events/performances reveal that the "What is Art?" debate is not exclusive to any community. However, for the disability community there are additional concerns that overlap this philosophical realm. The terms "standards" and "professionalism" are being used now in the Disability Culture scene, in discussions and panel presentations, at conferences and among individuals.

We have inherited a history of Art Therapy, Occupational Therapy and being told that something was "Good!" just because we were able to do it. Call me Politically Incorrect, but I am not going to applaud a guy who plays a guitar with his feet if the music is lousy. On the other hand, I want to support him for doing it if he enjoys it.

We need opportunities for people with disabilities to explore art and creativity, but does that make them artists? Does a person have to have a degree from a professional school to be considered an artist? Can a person become an artist "through the backdoor?" If so, how do we distinguish artists from people who are dabbling in self-expression?

We need to have quality work at a competitive level in order to be taken seriously. We can expect and get excellent art from our disability community! However, I don't want to see us recreate the same elitism that has told many people they weren't artists because they don't have an art degree or they have never exhibited in a major gallery.

Not everyone who performed in the MOE shows was a professional, and they weren't presented as such. The MOE performances were promoted as creative voices coming from the disability community. Some of the MOE performers went on to become professionals, but at the time it would have been more accurate to call us emerging artists. A distinction needs to be made between artists (those with artistic goals who are doing the homework to reach their goals) and people who are exploring creativity. This is a fine line and a debated line, but wherever the line gets drawn, I hope it's a fluid line. In the non-disabled world, people take art classes just for fun, but a few emerge from those classes as beginning artists.

As more people with disabilities begin to work in art related fields, the issue of quality is going to come up in many ways. This may especially create problems for people who are true allies trying to open doors for professional artists with disabilities. Let me give you an example…

Recently I was contacted by a program back east that integrates skilled performers with and without disabilities in their theatre projects. A performer with a vision-related disability auditioned and they were considering casting her for one of the parts. They were seeking input about ways to accommodate her. It so happened that I knew the individual they had auditioned, and I had seen her perform on videotape. The person that they were trying to cast was a beginning actress, not a mid-career professional.

I asked the director his reasons for wanting to cast this actress and found that they were based on wanting to provide the actress an opportunity, not on her talents. I reminded the director that their organization was designed to further the careers of professional level performers with disabilities, not a program for beginners. The director realized that his main motivation to cast the actress was a desire to be inclusive. This would have been a disservice to the actress, giving her unrealistic expectations about her ability to get cast in mainstream productions.

The issue of quality is hotly discussed among artists with disabilities, especially since it is often a lack of opportunity, rather than a lack of skill, that keeps our talents undeveloped. I encourage presenters and directors to take a small risk on an artist who has obvious talent, but might need some extra guidance. However, overall, the idea is not to lower the bar, but to find ways to raise it while artists with disabilities are hanging on.

To VSA or Not to VSA, That is the Question VSA arts is an international non-profit organization founded by Jean Kennedy Smith in 1974. Originally called "Very Special Arts," the organization provides support to artists with disabilities in a variety of ways. Programs include training institutes, artist-in-residence projects, art camps and emerging artists award programs. It can be extremely beneficial for artists with disabilities to connect with VSA, yet many have not wanted to be associated with them.

The internet is full of postings by people with disabilities on how they feel about VSA. Some posts address experiencing a coddling "take care" attitude from VSA personnel and point out that this does little to inspire. One person felt that more importance was given to his disability than to his art. Many who posted said that they don't want to be seen as "special," but as "equal."

People give varied answers as to why they are uncomfortable with the organization, but a consistent one is the original name. Many people considered "Very Special Arts" to be a patronizing and demeaning name that does not reflect inclusion. When VSA was started, there wasn't the level of awareness that we have now about disability and about the trickiness of terminology. It was a name that provided instant recognition of the population being served.

The organization has evolved considerably since its inception over three decades ago. The momentum of this change increased rapidly when John Kemp was hired as the Executive Director of VSA at the national level in the 90's. John was the first Executive Director who had a disability and one of his major goals was to change the name. He fought an uphill battle, because many people who had been involved with VSA for years had a lot of ownership and investment in the original name and wanted to keep it for recognition.

John persisted, along with others at VSA who felt that changes needed to be made. The name was symbolic of a bigger picture, reflecting internal attitudes within the organization. A compromise was eventually made. The organization is still VSA but it is now called "VSA arts," standing for Vision, Strength, and Artistic Expression.

The national office of VSA arts oversees a diverse network of affiliates, but they do not control them. Experiences can be very different depending on which chapter a person contacts. Some state affiliates still use the name Very Special Arts and don't understand why there are people who consider this an insult. Other states embrace the new name and are strong allies for artists with disabilities.

Since the name change, there are mixed opinions on VSA arts. Current internet posts from artists with disabilities say they feel more comfortable approaching the organization, that the condescending attitude has been replaced by an empowering one. Some people are connecting with the organization in order to be a part of the transformation. Some still keep their distance because they consider the organization as patronizing at the core.

John left his job shortly after the name change, but he left many ripples within the organization. Other people at VSA arts helped propel changes also, and many there today keep moving the organization forward in a positive direction. The dialogues inside and outside the agency over the name helped to raise awareness considerably. The process was a difficult one, but it had many positive residual affects. It's now a wait-and-see period between VSA arts and the disability activist community.

If we give VSA arts the litmus test for allies, we look at the make up of the board of directors and advisory board to see if people with disabilities have power in the organization. We find that, in fact, there are people with disabilities serving actively on both boards.

I feel that the biggest problem with VSA arts at this time is that it tries to provide two completely different services and yet it does not draw a clear distinction between them. There are some people who want the opportunity to explore the arts, but who don't identify as artists. There are other people who consider themselves artists and would like support in advancing their careers. VSA provides experiential opportunities in the arts and supports professional artists with disabilities. However, by not drawing a distinction between the two, it causes confusion in the field, as well as among those served by VSA arts.

For example, VSA arts might support the production of a theatre performance by young people, as a learning and experiential opportunity. This is what I was looking for when I was a young girl, but the door wasn't open at that time. People have to start getting experience somewhere and VSA arts can provide these opportunities. However, this is not the same thing as supporting professional artists.

If there is not a distinction between people having art experiences and professional artists who have honed their craft, the issue of quality gets watered down. If a reviewer attends a theater production such as the one I described above, expecting to see quality theater, they may not return the next time VSA arts promotes a show, even if it is a professional production. AXIS Dance Company has demonstrated an excellent model in this regard, providing classes for children and adults who want to explore movement and dance, but without compromising their professional image. They do this through well designed marketing and publicity materials that clearly distinguish between exploration of movement and professional dance.

VSA arts has been designated by Congress as the coordinating organization for arts programming for persons with disabilities in our country. This mandate is extensive, covering all disabilities, all ages, and all art forms. The chosen support mechanism is education. VSA arts programming is primarily supported through the Department of Education, which is why so much of their efforts focus on young people and emerging artists and less on established or professional artists. VSA arts' funding to support established artists, outside of an educational mode, has to come from private fundraising. [An important positive note about the educational funding support is that it comes through the Arts in Education line of the Elementary and Secondary Education Act (and has for over 20 years), NOT through "special" education.]

Although VSA arts is not a presenting organization, some state affiliates maintain galleries and some sponsor showcases of artists with disabilities. VSA arts' presentations, even on a small scale, often appear in publicity as showcases of "professional" artists. This hurts the credibility of professional artists if it is not high quality. How do we distinguish between the two?

Some might argue that I am debating a fine line and that forcing this division could be harmful in the bigger picture of support for arts and arts education. Though the expected results may overlap, they are different: The outcomes of an educational event are learning, experience, and exposure; the outcome of a professional performance is the work itself. I'll acknowledge that some groups have a dual mission and that one outcome does not necessarily exclude the other. My point is that we need to begin a dialogue about how to avoid hurting the image of professional artists while providing educational and training opportunities.

The concept of "life-long learning" can further blur the line between learner and professional. The creative process is a unique and distinct educational function. Creating art is a teaching and learning experience, even if offered to no one but one's self.

Many artists with disabilities wind up stuck in one spot and don't evolve or develop further because they work in a bubble. Without access to art education or other artists, they aren't exposed to new ideas. In Chapter Five, I talked about how Dave DeWeerd taught me to appreciate Picasso. He passed on to me many of the things he'd learned through his training, schooling, and contact with the arts community. VSA arts is here to see that people with disabilities today don't need to get their art education second hand.

VSA arts has gone through rough water over the last several years. On paper it looks like everyone is in the same camp, especially if one looks at the four essential principles guiding the programming and initiatives of VSA arts:

- Every young person with a disability deserves access to appropriate arts learning experiences.
- All artists in schools and art educators should be adequately prepared to include students with disabilities in their instruction.
- All children, youth, and adults with disabilities should have complete access to community cultural facilities and activities.
- All individuals with disabilities who aspire to careers in the arts should have the opportunity to develop necessary skills.

Pseudo-allies or true allies? Right now this question can only be evaluated case by case, state by state, individual by individual.

I have two suggestions to help folks cross the existing chasm: One, if you are an artist with a disability, give the new VSA arts a chance; if they don't do everything completely right, diplomatically let them know what they can do to improve. Two, for those who work or volunteer at VSA arts, quit calling us "special" and NEVER call us "very special."

Now, does anyone have a suggestion for how to get the "special" out of special olympics and special education?

Art Centers (Sheltered Workshops?) Sheltered workshops are places that involve adults with disabilities, mostly developmental disabilities, in task-related day activities. Sometimes clients perform a task, like cleaning rental equipment or stuffing envelopes, and they are often paid piecework. It is not unusual for a person to work a full day and make less than five dollars. There are mixed feelings about whether sheltered workshops are good or bad. Some people call them exploitative or free babysitters. Others point out that clients gain self esteem by being employed, making money, and doing something useful.

In 1982, Florence Ludins-Katz and Dr. Elias Katz began a new approach to providing day activities for adults with developmental disabilities – they started an art center. Today, many art centers are based on their model of providing the materials and instructions for adults with disabilities to work as artists. Participants are called "artists" rather than "clients," and they produce works that are often sold at exhibitions. A new genre of art has been greatly influenced by these works, called Outsider Art. The artists receive pay based on a percentage of the sale of the work.

Dr. Katz and his wife wrote materials and produced videos demonstrating different methods for enabling people with a variety of disabilities to paint, sculpt, and do other artistic activities. They are recognized internationally for the groundbreaking work that they did.

Their original center became a non-profit in its own right and they moved on to start another center, the National Institute of Art and Disability (NIAD), based in Richmond, California. Though his wife died several years ago, Dr. Katz is still affiliated in an advisory capacity. The legacy they leave is a rich one, and they have assisted many people to be able to pursue careers as artists.

Are these art centers different than sheltered workshops? Certainly I feel that a person who is inclined toward artistic expression is much better off at an art center than they would be at a sheltered workshop doing menial labor. However, I ask the same questions that I ask of any organization having people with disabilities as the main consumers. Where is the power in the organization? Are there people with disabilities on staff, on the board of directors, in an advisory capacity to the organization? Are artists with disabilities being presented in an empowering way or in a patronizing way?

I am posing these questions, not making a statement. Programs of this type are vulnerable to being patronizing and it is important to keep a strong influence coming from the disability community to be sure that this does not happen. Again, we have the question of allies. This model needs to be constantly reviewed under the lens of empowerment to determine whether the programs are being provided by true allies or pseudo-allies.

Disincentives for Artists with Disabilities on Benefits My book would be incomplete if I didn't address a major issue that affects the lives of many artists with disabilities: Disincentives to making money if one is on benefits.

Imagine a room in the Senate Building full of people with a variety of disabilities, most of them artists of one type or another. They get up and speak, one by one, to members of the Legislature and high-up officials in the Social Security Administration. These brave people begin many of their statements with "I'm afraid that by telling you these things…" or similar openings. Many of the speakers shake as they speak. One cries.

The word "intimidated" describes how many of us feel as it comes our turn to speak. We had been unexpectedly searched upon entering the building, and that hadn't helped our nerves a bit. To admit publicly that we earn money as artists is a frightening prospect. However, it is important to let the officials know the problems that exist, the holes in the system, and the cracks that artists with disabilities fall through.

One woman speaks about how she obtained a computer through a rehabilitation program, but she has no resources for repairs or software upgrades. The computer enables her to work as a graphic artist, but it is useless because she can't afford to keep it up. If she obtains money doing graphic design, she could pay for computer upgrades and software, but she is terrified of the prospect of earning anything and losing all of her Social Security.

Another person tells about how she wrote a book and had several thousand copies of it printed a few years ago. However, she has no money for marketing, and she is afraid to sell even one book because she doesn't know how it will impact her social security benefits. The books sit in unopened boxes all over her home.

Shortly I will tell you about the years of work that led to this meeting actually happening, but first I will tell you more about some problems with the Social Security System.

In Chapter Six I told you I had written two grants for a performance piece that I wanted to create and produce. I just received the rejection letter for the smaller of the two grants. (The jury is still out on the one I want most.) Although I would have liked to have gotten the CA$H grant, it would have caused problems for me with my Social Security benefits.

For people receiving Social Security, especially SSI (Supplemental Security Income), monetary gains are calculated (using a complicated formula) and the SSI recipient will often be responsible for paying back some of the money they received from SSI. All monies received are to be reported, regardless of amount and regardless of whether they are earned, gifts, awards, etc. One is also supposed to report non-monetary gifts of value, as they may be considered resources. (One year I traveled to stay with my mother for a month; SSI found out and said I had to report the lodging in her home as a non-monetary gift, unless I'd paid rent!)

The total amount of resources that an individual can have at any given time (in order to continue receiving SSI) is low. Individuals who receive too much money from a one-time source (e.g. a small inheritance of $3,000) are forced, by the system, to spend the money carelessly in one month. I say "carelessly" because the individual cannot buy anything of value with the money, or invest it, because then it would count as a resource.

Many people do not fear losing their SSI as much as they fear losing other benefits, especially medical coverage, that are attached to receiving SSI. There have been recent improvements to the system and more legislation is being considered to remedy some of the problems, but political gears grind slowly.

Although financial stress on the whole Social Security system has kept the monthly benefit amounts low, the formula used to consider income could be adjusted without adding to the budget. The amount that one can earn without having to pay anything back has remained the same for thirty years. This applies whether your income is part-time and, therefore, counted monthly, or whether it is self-employment earnings averaged over twelve months.

All of these problems make it very difficult for people with disabilities to work in artistic careers. The art field could potentially employ people with most types of disabilities. It not only provides many opportunities for artists, but also art administrators and others who work in supportive positions within the field. The span of positions is large: public relations, writers, directors, grant writers, computer program designers, animators, sound engineers, graphics designers...

To work full-time in an artistic field usually means working up a ladder. People with disabilities on SSI could potentially groom careers in the arts that would eventually pay well enough that they could completely remove themselves from dependency on the government for financial support. This doesn't happen overnight. You have to climb the ladder, prove yourself, get to know people and get small gigs that eventually become medium gigs and then become big enough that you can be self-supporting. The current formula for calculating received monies stops many people with disabilities from being able to even accept the small gigs without either being caught in an overpayment or jeopardizing their eligibility for benefits out right (i.e. no longer "seeming" to be disabled).

The formula used to determine an overpayment is so complicated that many artists are afraid to accept any money. If one does nothing, one is usually left alone by Social Security representatives. However, if one does a staged reading of a play and is paid $100, they must report it to SSI. They will often be barraged with paperwork and may also need to go to the Social Security office for an interview to explain the income and to prove that they are still disabled.

A person may work for years on a painting that they sell. If they are viewed as part-time employed and sell the painting for more than $85, they will have to payback monies to SSI for the month that they sell the painting and they cannot deduct for supplies and materials used. If they file self-employed, they will be able to at least deduct expenses that they incurred the year that they sell the painting, but not previous years' expenses.

SSI's level of allowable resources is too low ($2,000 for an individual, $3,000 if you have a spouse). The equipment that an artist uses might be considered as resources. This could include computers, video cameras, pottery wheels, etc. They need these tools-of-the-trade to produce their work and to move towards being self-supporting someday. Many artists do not report these as resources, because they fear doing so would make them ineligible for SSI.

Moving up the ladder for artists includes receiving grants, stipends, fellowships, awards, honorariums, exhibition sales, and other one-time monetary gains. The amounts may often be high enough to create problems for a person on SSI, yet they are not reflective of one-month, but rather of a body of work that has taken years to develop. The current system does not recognize this.

This barely skims the surface, but I hope that this information, in combination with the things I talked about in Chapter Six, will present an awareness of some of the disincentives for artists with disabilities who receive benefits. The good news is that things are happening to remedy some of these problems.

In 1998, I served on a committee that organized a nationwide conference that was the first of its kind: A National Forum on Careers in the Arts for People with Disabilities. This was a gathering of around 300 people from across the nation, many of them artists with disabilities. This Forum was a couple of years in the planning, combining the efforts and support of five agencies and several artists with disabilities from a variety of art forms. The five sponsoring agencies were:

- National Endowment for the Arts
- The John F. Kennedy Center for Performing Arts
- US Department of Education
- US Department of Health and Human Services
- Social Security Administration

A goal of the Forum was to identify obstacles for people with disabilities pursuing careers in the arts. It was a launching pad for addressing these issues. A problem-solution format was stressed throughout the three-day gathering. Input also came via separately scheduled, live internet exchanges between conference presenters and folks unable to attend. Most problems discussed fell into financial, educational or vocational rehabilitation areas, so follow-up plans were made to continue discussing these topics post-forum.

The problems heard most frequently had to do with Social Security benefits and disincentives to earning "irregular monies." One of the solutions presented was to have the relevant people sit down together at a table and begin to strategize towards eliminating these disincentives. A year and a half after the Forum, such a meeting came about. This is the event I described at the beginning of this section. I and several other artists and activists with disabilities presented and discussed disincentive issues with legislators and high up representatives from the Social Security Administration. I didn't expect instant miracles to come from this meeting of minds, but I believe it motivated people to start down that long road to reform.

Many of us faced fears of personal retribution that day in telling our stories about the financial juggling and games that the system forces us to play as we try to become working artists. More than one speaker voiced a concern, despite reassurances from the Powerful People there, that they were drawing attention to themselves and would go home to find a letter calling them into Social Security for a review. (Fortunately no such letter waited for me when I got home, despite my sharing openly that I'd earned $7,000 one year, but with justifiable expenses.)

Where Am I? Where am I? I don't mean that in an existentialist way – I mean just what it asks. Other than in "Christina's World," I cannot remember ever seeing myself represented in galleries or museums.

During my art advocacy years I traveled extensively and frequently took time out to visit local art venues. Most places that I visited as a tourist had at least a medium level of access for spectators with disabilities, but people with disabilities were still almost completely invisible in the art itself, except for an occasional occurrence as bizarre subjects.

I saw a delightful exhibit at the Hirschhorn Museum in D.C. called "Regarding Beauty," a mix of older and contemporary works. The only "disability" representation that I saw was black and white photos of people of atypical body types. The description said that the artist liked to use grotesque models for subjects. A collection of videos accompanied the show and one of them was entitled "Sketch for 'Monster'" – a 7 ½-minute work that showed a man as he applied scotch tape to his face to pull it into different shapes.

One of my favorite art experiences was a photo exhibit by Annie Leibovitz at the Corcoran Gallery, also in D.C. A wonderful variety of photos represented the enormous diversity of women in our country. Yet, no women with obvious disabilities appeared among the coal miners, the high society women, the homeless, the athletes...

A White House tour went through rooms with beautifully decorated holiday trees. One tree reflected the history of our country with dolls made by artists, depicting many of the people and events that make up our American heritage. It's possible I missed it, as we were rushed along, but I did not see 504 or the ADA represented, or Roosevelt with crutches or in a wheelchair.

This absence of disability in the artistic landscape shows that our work is far from over. There are many positive changes happening behind the scenes, and some right out front, but we must not forget that lasting change takes time.

Does It Always Come Down to $$$? Many of the problems I've discussed in this chapter could be minimized, if not eliminated, by money. Providing access is easier for productions that aren't on a shoestring budget. The difference between works considered "Quality" and those that are not is sometimes related to the cost of materials used. Economics can play a big part in Art.

FACT: People with disabilities have a lower employment rate than people without disabilities; the percentage of people with disabilities employed during the 1990's was in the 30 percentile range, whereas that of people without disabilities was in the 80 percentile range.

FACT: Over the past fifteen years, the employment rate among people with disabilities has steadily dropped, while employment rates among people without disabilities has remained fairly consistent.

FACT: Programs for artists with disabilities have a hard time getting funding unless they present their art as employment or education related, and even then it's a hard sell.

FACT: The few Art funders and presenters who do accept disability related works often do so on a theme basis and that theme is usually disability, not art. ("I'm sorry, we already did a disability project two years ago.")

FACT: The projects in the disability art arena that have managed to get federal monies, corporate sponsorships and large foundation grants have usually been administered by people without disabilities.

In Conclusion We need to be sure to include people with disabilities in the power structure of organizations and in the planning of events. We need to realize that there's always room for improvement and not to ever feel that we have it all right. This applies not only to providing support and opportunities to artists with disabilities, but also in areas of diversity and quality. We need to build bridges, not walls.

One might ask why anyone would want to work in the disability art field with all of these problems. Many of us have learned how not to give up when the going gets rough. This is true of artists in general, and this is true of many people with disabilities. Artists have to develop thick skin and, for an artist with a disability, that skin might have to be even a little bit thicker. An artist has to face having works and grant proposals rejected, bad critiques, and other emotionally trying experiences that happen when a people expose themselves in the way an artist does. In addition to that, artists with disabilities have another layer of crap put on us because of our disabilities.

Whether a person is an artist or an observer of the arts, our world is more intriguing with creativity in it. Art stimulates interest and creates a way for people to engage with familiar and new concepts. The world is a richer place because of art. Artists create because we have to. If I am not creating, I don't feel alive. The joy of creating and sharing creations with others is the payoff for many artists. Fame, fortune and roses are the fringe benefits, though they are most welcome when they come.

Postscript By Tim Flannigan:

It has been a pattern through my career that I alternate between working for someone and working for myself – neither worked well. When I work for someone, I am stimulated by other people, I have somewhere outside my apartment to work, and I receive a steady paycheck. However, I am late and I work slower than others, making it difficult to be part of a team. When I work for myself, I am free to work at my pace and develop my ideas, but there is no one to push me, and I am back on Social Security. I have never found the right situation that allows me to fulfill what I believe to be my potential. I am happy with what I am doing now, even though I remain frustrated at my pace. In the past, I have been anxious about getting out of poverty. What I have to do now is to let that go and continue in the faith that when I get my projects produced, I will have the money to live the middle-class lifestyle I have wanted. This may be common among many disabled people who try to work, including the artists you write about.

Chapter Eighteen Briefer Intermission to Deal With Life

THE BAD NEWS IS that the judge ruled against me in the District Court, regarding my lawsuit against SSI that I discussed in Chapter Six. He upheld the ruling of the previous court, that according to employment definitions established by labor regulations, I am employed part-time (not self-employed) when I work as a union actress. Bottom Line: I lose my SSI every month I work as a union actress, even if I only work one hour. My next level of appeal would be the Eighth District, a federal court. The Supreme Court would be the final place to challenge the ruling.

A lawyer friend encouraged me to continue with the case. He gave me the name and number for a lawyer in San Francisco who deals with SSI cases. I called her and she said that she doesn't take cases as far as the federal court; she gave me the number of a lawyer in Oakland who might be able to help me.

For six years now, this has been how it has gone every time I had to take the next appeal step. Everyone I called had a reason they could not help me, but they had the name and number of a person who they thought could. Even Protection and Advocacy, an agency set up to protect the rights of people with disabilities, including the right to work, would not directly help me. Follow-up call after follow-up call never got me help, except for pieces of advice. Though most people agreed I had a legitimate case, it fell through the cracks of knowledge for those in the legal profession who work on Social Security or disability cases.

Common sense dictates that I am right, but common sense doesn't usually prevail as a valid argument in court. Outdated and generalized regulations are the tools used for decision-making; unusual situations are interpreted by regulations that don't really fit, but are the closest match in the eyes of the System. The Department of Labor's general definitions were applied to a unique situation that becomes discriminatory when Union regulations are added. SSI, AFTRA and the Department of Labor have built a Catch 22 and refuse to do anything about it.

After six years of legally fighting a cause that keeps many people with disabilities from being able to pursue careers as actors, I am calling it quits. I cannot continue the battle alone, because it gets harder every step of the way. It has taken six years to get to the federal courts, so I regret having to stop at this point. I have made no legal headway on the cause and the next person to fight this battle will have to start again at scratch, taking six years to get to the place I am at right now.

But, I just can't go on. I'm worn down. I cried for an hour when I made the decision to stop. The most painful part of it is feeling like I have spent a lot of time and energy for six years for nothing. The second most painful part is that I can no longer pursue a career that I enjoy. Any month that I work a union job, I lose my SSI. If I work a non-union acting job, I could be fined $600 by AFTRA.

So that was the bad news, now do you want to know the good news?

One year from now I will be throwing and giving away files related to doing arts administrative work and arts activist work. I will be getting ready to be only an artist.

Recently, I sold my first piece of fine art. One of my collages sold for $125 at a silent auction. The validation that comes with knowing that I created a piece of art that someone wanted to pay for is more important than the money.

Having these two events occur in my life side-by-side, a decision about a lawsuit (me as an activist) and selling my first piece of fine art (me as an artist), was an example of synchronicity at its finest.

The good news? *I am an artist.* (period)

Postscript by An Artist, Pamela Walker:

Do you remember that sweet moment
when something delightful caught your attention
so strongly
that the rest of the world disappeared
that you forgot you were hungry
that you forgot you had a test or an assignment or a presentation
in one week
Do you remember that gentle calm
when all the noises inside your head stopped
so completely
that sadness joined oblivion
as if it had never been there
as if there was no such thing as bills or answering machines or calendars
in your life
Do you remember that sweet moment
when something delightful caught your attention
so strongly
that the rest of the world disappeared
Do you remember being an artist

Chapter Nineteen   *? – Disability Culture – ?*

THIS BOOK IS PRIMARILY ABOUT THE SAN FRANCISCO BAY AREA, but in no way do I feel the Disability Rights Movement nor the emergence of artists with disabilities happened solely in Northern California. Those who live in Berkeley are sometimes accused of being Berkeley-centric or California-centric, and for good reason. A lot of important things did happen here, but we need to remember that good things were happening simultaneously in Boston, Houston, New York City, Canada, Finland, and many other places.

Some say Berkeley is the hub and other things pivot around Berkeley, happening in other areas but connecting back to Berkeley. This does happen sometimes (the first Independent Living Center was established in Berkeley), but there are many artists, groups and organizations that sprouted up and grew independent of the Bay Area.

One of the exceptional qualities of the Disability Rights Movement is that it provides an excellent model for different groups working together, achieving goals through cooperation. Not only have people with different types of disabilities learned about and supported each others right to a quality life, but groups from different countries have met and shared resources with each other. We have studied how things are done around the globe and learned from each other, not only survival techniques, but quality of life issues as well.

The political activists and those sharing knowledge on living independently have been connecting together at least as long as I've been in Berkeley.

When I worked at CIL, one of the fascinating parts of my job was chatting with people from Japan, Germany, and Sweden, comparing and contrasting support programs for people with disabilities.

This sharing is now happening in the arts arena. There are international showcases of films and videos by and about people with disabilities. There are huge international art conferences where several days of showcases reflect the wealth of talent coming from the people with disabilities of many countries. Furthermore, the areas of activism and art are not independent of each other. Bruce Curtis and Kathy Martinez are excellent examples of people who have worked worldwide in political AND artistic endeavors, often integrating the two.

With all that is happening artistically and internationally, the concept of a Disability Culture has emerged, prompting many questions. What makes a culture? Is there such a thing as a Disability Culture? Are activists with disabilities claiming a culture as a way of finding a niche for funding and validation? Or are there qualities that make people with disabilities unique to each other? Are non-disabled people who are involved in our lives part of the culture? Is one a member of a culture merely by claiming a culture?

When Judy Heumann and I co-hosted "Disability Rap" on Pacifica Radio in the mid '80's, one of our listeners asked us to do a show on "Disability Culture." My immediate response was, "What ARE they talking about?" This led to Judy and I discussing whether or not there was such a thing as a Disability Culture and, if there was, whether it had a political base or an artistic base. I went back and forth on the issue, but usually I was on the side that said that there was no such thing. My Sociology degree had taught me to define culture using parameters such as language, heritage, common rituals and customs. With a few exceptions, such as among the Deaf, there were none of these things among disabled communities. Therefore, how could we claim a culture?

Now, after working among artists with disabilities for over twenty-five years, I find myself smack dab in the middle of a culture that I didn't believe existed. I have seen artists with work that has been greatly affected by their disability, regardless of whether they chose to directly depict disability themes in it. We may not have a culture in a physical sense, but do we have one in an internal sense? We may not have been raised among generations of people who were physically like us, but we have certain characteristics in common. We know what it is like to be "the other," we develop great skills at adaptation, perhaps we grew up in a family where we were different than everyone else but no one talked about how we were different, we know that there are people who feel sorry for us, and we have the gift of being unique in a world of people who don't stand out in a crowd.

It can be validating and exhilarating to find yourself in a conversation with people who *really* understand. There is a "sameness" among people with disabilities, even with different disabilities, that means I can have a significant conversation without having to explain that "disability" is not my whole life and that I am not my disability.

Recently I met two disabled women and the conversation turned to personal frustrations about when to ask for help and when to struggle to do something independently because our invisible "quota" (of helpee points) had been used up that day. From there the conversation led to the subject of interactions with our relationship partners and how we have to keep a balance so that we don't use our partners as attendants, but at the same time being aware that couples where neither person has a disability frequently do things for each other. Am I being needy to ask my boyfriend to wash my back just because I have a disability? Don't non-disabled women ask their boyfriends to wash their backs?

The above paragraph is meant as an example of three women who barely knew each other, but who were from the same "culture" (Disability), being able to easily discuss an issue that would have taken more explaining to someone outside the Culture. Regardless of whether a person was main-streamed or went to special education schools or classes, whether raised at home or in an institution, whether they were disabled in early childhood or acquired it later, all people with disabilities have many things in common. These are some of the roots of what is being called Disability Culture. Other aspects of our roots are the history of how people with disabilities have been treated by different societies throughout time and how we've been depicted in the media and in art.

So, what is Disability Culture? It's still in its infancy and, as such, is in the process of being defined. Sociologists, academians and writers from the disability community are in the process of creating this definition. The issue that Judy Heumann and I visited in the 80's is still on the table: If there is a Disability Culture, does it have a political base, an artistic base, or both?

There are voices that say there is no such thing as a Disability Culture, and some that say maybe there is one, but we should avoid labeling ourselves and thus enabling us to be pigeon-holed and ghettoized.

Even if one assumes there is a Disability Culture and it has an artistic base, it is still difficult to define because it involves many types of disabilities and many mediums of artistic expression. Also, unlike most cultures, it develops from people who have often been partially or totally isolated from each other. Cultural identification based on ethnicity comes, in part, from living and growing up around others of the same ethnic group; as such, the culture is natural to the environment. People with disabilities often grow up in families where they are the only one with a disability. "Culture" in the disability sense is more internal and, in fact, can partly come out of the experiences of being physically different from one's family members.

The degree to which a disability affects one's life varies considerably and, likewise, the degree to which an artist uses disability as an aspect of their art varies. I consider an artist part of the Disability Culture if he or she identifies with the disability community and reflects or acknowledges disability as having affected his or her art, regardless of whether their art is directly about disability.

These personal observations about artists with disabilities and Disability Culture might be good for late-night debates. To that end, here's more fodder:

- We've tried for so long to show that we can do the same things that non-disabled people can do, but to be creative is to do something that no one else has done before. Artists with disabilities first had to prove that they could do what anyone else could do and now are trying to prove that they can do something unique. This is quite a challenge!

- The observer of disability art has an interesting challenge also. They can focus on the disability and think it's incredible that the person has done what they have done, they can focus on the art and see how the disability has flavored it, or they can become familiar enough with the disability that it becomes only background, with the art as the message. If one focuses too much on the disability, they may miss other messages that the artist is giving that may not have anything to do with disability.

- A person's art pulls from their experience, consciously or subconsciously. I met a successful novelist who used a wheelchair for most of her life, but had never written about disability. When she "came out of the closet" about her disability, she felt that her writing became more honest and

human. She said that letting herself be whole enriched all of the characters in her books.

If a Disability Culture does exist, it includes artists who are not trying to pass,
who don't buy into an unspoken social rule saying we should be ashamed of
our disabilities, and who often portray a self-acceptance and pride about who
they are, not in spite of, nor because of, but including their disability.

Artists are an important element of the disability movement. There is concern among disability activists that integration into society is not happening,
despite the laws and Disability Awareness events. People ask, "What is the
way to true integration?" I believe that Art is the way. A "movement" requires
political change AND a cultural revolution – these two things need to go
hand in hand.

Images and opinions are changed through many means, but there is
always a strong basis in art. Any one who remembers the 60's knows how
music, psychedelic posters, album covers and the performance of "Hair" played
a part in reaching the public with new messages about individualism, peace
and enjoying life in the present. As a result, our country went through a
dramatic facelift.

Likewise, if art with a disability flavor can make the leap into the mainstream, society will be transformed in a major way. American society has been
strongly influenced by a body beautiful image and failure to meet that image
is at the root of many social problems such as teenage suicides and anorexia.
Americans spend too much time and money trying to reach for the illusive
ideal of perfection, though most standards for what constitutes perfection and
beauty are arbitrary. We would be a much happier society if we could eliminate
this conditioning. Acceptance of people with disabilities helps everyone be
happier with their bodies and with themselves. Artists with disabilities can
help society move in that direction through photography, self-portraits, and
performances showing their own individual grace and self-acceptance. Society
can learn that "different" is not just "okay," but "Great!" – that variety adds
spice to the potluck of humanity!

In 1932, MGM produced a movie called "Freaks" about the people existing
as side show subjects in a carnival. The movie shows these "freaks" being
exploited, though within their own social circle they have normal daily experiences and have adapted to their lives. The film allows audience members to

be voyeurs, staring at what is considered abnormal. It opens with a script that includes the following:

"For the love of beauty is a deep-seated urge which dates back to the beginning of civilization. The revulsion with which we view the abnormal, the malformed, and the mutilated is the result of long conditioning by our forefathers."

I interpret this quote as validating and excusing the viewer for their (assumed) attitude towards what they will see; implied is that we have no choice but to be repulsed by people who are different. I disagree! We can change the standards of acceptance and I believe it is the artists that will enable society to do that.

People with disabilities no longer have to be victims of social opinion. We can actually shape it! I challenge artists with disabilities to push into the main-stream art world. This means outreach to the general public when advertising events and it also means getting involved in THEIR organizations. (I'm not saying people with disabilities should turn their back on the disability com-munity; organizations with a disability focus are important, but that's only one side of the coin and it leads to segregation, not inclusion.)

Part of the picture of inclusion in the art world-at-large means that people with disabilities need to join mainstream art organizations, attend meetings and events, go to the offices of art organizations and study their bulletin boards, serve on selection panels, grant panels and boards of directors of main-stream art groups. See and be seen! Changes are being made at the top, but people with disabilities need to start moving into the art community camps. It's time to bust through the doors, but remember that most changes that are done well take time. Rome wasn't built in a day (and it also wasn't built with access in mind).

I challenge people without disabilities to take the risk, go see the artists with disabilities, confront fears actively and then drag a friend along the next time. Join us in our push into mainstream culture.

If artists with disabilities can successfully move into public view and into the general art community, all of society will benefit. Developments in com-munication and transportation allow art to reach larger audiences than ever before. In the past, enjoyment of many forms of art was generally an elite experience, restricted to those who could meet economic and social standards;

but, nowadays in America, almost every home has a television and this is one easy avenue for access to art.

Art can aid in changing attitudes in a way that nothing else can, not even laws. People in the general public might not go to a lecture, but they will go to a movie. The Women's Movement was aided by singers like Holly Near, by reader's theaters, by feminist artists and poets and by women in the performing arts. Disability Culture has its Holly Nears, such as Elaine Kolb who sings songs with lyrics like, "We're no longer grateful for the handouts you have thrown us; we're no longer begging you and holding out a cup; we're no longer satisfied inside your institutions; together we are moving, moving out and moving up."

If there is a Disability Culture, it has photographers like Mary Duffy from Ireland who portrays her naked disabled body with beauty, strength and being. It has rock 'n roll singers like "Van Gogh," two brothers in wheelchairs that light up with their choreographed moves as they sing out with an intoxicating beat. It includes reader's theaters, media makers, poets, and performing artists. We have Cheryl Marie Wade waving her gnarly fists at audiences, shaking them up with her well-timed "Bogga bogga!" We have our radio hosts like Greg "On A Roll" Smith, our poets like Mark O'Brien, our movie actors like Marlee Matlin... I could go on like this all day. My point? – *The artists are here and they are getting louder and pushier.* I don't think the doors can be held shut much longer.

It is debated among art historians where art will go next. As our environment becomes more threatening, there is a greater need to appreciate our common bonds. Individuality, humanity, and the human condition are subjects we have seen in art in the past and that will be part of art in the future. Who better than artists with disabilities to teach about adaptation? And who better to play a role in humanity's need to reconcile itself to the condition of being mere mortals? I believe that if Disability Culture can make the leap into mainstream art, disability art will be the next major movement in the art world.

Laura Hershey, a well known disability rights activist and writer, has suggested that future generations might look back on the 1990's as the time of the "Disability Renaissance." The renaissance period in Europe marked the transition from medieval times to modern times. Whether we call it a

Disability Culture or not isn't as important as just the fact that something big is happening in the world of disability. The medieval attitudes are being challenged politically, legally and artistically. People with disabilities are saying to society, "We can do this the easy way or the hard way, but we *are* joining your club. After all, this is the 21st century – isn't it about time you admitted we are here?"

Postscript by Paul K. Longmore

Pamela Walker explores the complementary functions of disabled artists and disability rights political activists. I would elaborate on one thought. Whatever their primary work, whether artistic creation or public policy change, the artists and the activists all speak from and for the disability experience from the inside. By "disability" they do not mean defect and deficiency, or a series of medical or functional or social problems to be solved. Instead, they view that experience as humanly valid, an authentic if nonstandard way of being in the world. The cultural creators seek to represent the disability experience in their art. They write poetry and plays, short stories and novels, memoirs and autobiographies and essays. They paint, they photograph, they dance, they sing. Meanwhile, the advocates, spelling out alternative values derived from that experience, envision a different sort of community, one respectful and inclusive of all its members and therefore truly democratic. They seek to implement that vision through political agendas and policy initiatives. Both the activists and the artists draw upon "disability" as a source of value and values. All are agents in one of the most remarkable social transformations in human history: the disability rights revolution.

Chapter Twenty *Moving Up and Moving Out*

THE MOE SHOWS WERE COMPOSED of several artists working together on a theme, plus or minus Disability Culture. There were many other artists with disabilities in the Bay Area struggling to do their own thing around this same time period (1988-1990), often the hard way: alone in the non-disabled world before or about the time that the Americans with Disabilities Act was passed. Here is a list of some of those artists that I haven't mentioned, or barely mentioned, and a bit about them. My tenses jump from present to past sometimes, because some of these artists are still alive and some are not, some are still creating art and some aren't. (Please excuse me if I fail to mention someone who belongs on this list. It wasn't on purpose, but I ain't infallible.)

Tim Flannigan produced television programs, including a piece for "Nightline." He worked for two and a half years producing talk shows for "Bay-TV," a cable channel developed by San Francisco's KRON. Tim has worked behind the scenes to open doors for people with disabilities who want to work in broadcasting, including developing an internship program at ABC.

Adina Frieden's primary art for many years was listening. She loved counseling but eventually had to slow down as her Cystic Fibrosis progressed. She discovered herself to be a writer and some of her work was published during the last few years of her life. Her short story, "Bigger Than the Sky," was included in an anthology that selected her title for the book title. She lived long enough to know of this success, but not long enough to see the printed book.

Judith-Kate (formerly Judi) Friedman took her songbird voice and acoustic guitar into the Women's Community and to folk/acoustic venues during the '80s, singing hopeful songs about the ups and downs of life. She has received several grants from California and Marin Arts Councils. In 1997, she founded Songwriting Works, a nonprofit that gives elders and young people new opportunities to compose and perform music. She has two CDs of her own and has been featured on others.

Lydia Gans' photography captures the moment of relationship between people. Her book "To Live With Grace and Dignity" features photos and essays of individual attendant-consumer relationships. Another book features youth with disabilities with their siblings. She has documented other marginal populations such as homeless people. She has the ability to say 300 things with one click of the shutter.

Ricardo Gil studied at the California College of Arts and Crafts. His astounding photographs and bold fine art pieces gained him wide recognition, and he received a California Arts Council Grant for his photographic efforts. Lately he has been stepping up to the acting plate, cast in Baz Luhrmann's version of Puccini's "La Boheme," and touring internationally for three years in "Mabou Mines Dollhouse." He is working on his second indie film, "Read You Like A Book," featuring Karen Black and Danny Glover.

Redge Green starred in "Boyz 'N The Hood." This was one of the few times in movies at that time when a person who uses a wheelchair was actually cast for a role of a wheelchair user, rather than being hired to teach a non-disabled actor how to use a wheelchair. He is on the theatre faculty of East Bay Center for the Performing Arts and reaches out to youth through his own flavor of Rap, Gospel and Spoken Word performances.

Heidi Hennessy started performing with "Theatre Unlimited" in the Golden Gate Recreation Center for the Handicapped, and was cast to play Benny's girlfriend on the "L.A. Law" television series.

Jim LeBrecht left his wheelchair and crawled to the sound booth at Berkeley Repertory Theatre for several years. An incredible sound designer, he eventually started his own company, Berkeley Sound Artists, to do what he loves: sound design for Film and video games. His credits include numerous well known films and documentaries. A book he wrote with Deena Kaye, "Sound and Music for the Theatre," is used at many colleges.

Paul Longmore had his historical book on George Washington published, but it caused him so many problems with Social Security that he held a press conference where he burned his book. This led to the "Longmore Amendment" to the Social Security Act, allowing authors to define book royalties as earned income. One of the leading authorities on images of disability through history, he is a tenured history professor at San Francisco State University and received the 2004 Henry W. Betts Award, an annual award given to a person who improves the quality of life for people with disabilities.

Neil Marcus is a Berkeleyite, but he is most famous for a play produced by Access Theatre in Santa Barbara. "Storm Reading" is based on his poetry and prose, and toured internationally for several years. Neil was given the United Nations Medal of Excellence. Neil's acting career also includes a speaking part on "ER" and a performance in another play written by him, "The History of Sex." Neil's "Special Effects" newsletters tickled people's minds at the same time that the MOE shows pushed parallel boundaries of comfort around disability.

Peggy Martinez played drums in many bands, including a folk/country duo called "Poison Oakies" and a punk band, "Seven Healing Dolls." For six years she sang with an avant/surrealist/metal band, "Barking Dogma," and they released a CD. She also performed in plays and with a radio theater group called "Shoestring Radio Theater," and produced a public affairs radio program. She currently plays drums and sings with a rock band called "Iron Rain."

Mark O'Brien spent most of his life in an iron lung in his apartment in Berkeley, yet he was known widely for his powerful poetry. A documentary film about him, "Breathing Lessons" by Jessica Yu, won an Academy Award in

1997. Though he was rarely able to leave his home, his mastery of words had a profound effect on many people.

Jana Overbo was possibly the first wheelchair user to get a Television Production degree at a community college. She was placed in an internship at KPIX-TV in San Francisco and subsequently secured full-time employment there. She also did a great job as production assistant for our Disability Rap radio show.

Steve Potter was a tech geek starting in his early school years, one of the guys who run the projectors in class. For three years Steve was the recording engineer for Strings, a live performance and recording studio in Berkeley. He was doing painting and drawings at the time of the MOE shows; he continues working in fine arts today, adding erotic drawings to his portfolio.

David Roche was first mentioned in this book as a comedian. He has become much broader than that, both artistically and experientially. Today he is a seasoned dramatic performer, humorist, and inspirational speaker. His award-winning one-man show, "Church of 80% Sincerity," has played to enthusiastic audiences in 26 states, Canada, Australia and England.

Dr. Susan Rutherford, Deaf Media, produced many great videos that helped to spread understanding between Deaf and hearing communities. "Rainbows End" is a PBS series that still holds up today as a fine example of great work produced as part of this program.

Debbie Saunders, a woman with an intoxicating voice, sang jazz and blues on her album, "A Shot in the Dark," which has fed my spirit often… those times you need reminding that life is what it is, nothing more but nothing less.

Norma Scheurkogel plays flute beautifully, sometimes with a group of musicians, and often to benefit Native American causes. She has also been a host for Public Radio programs, including "Beat of a Different Drum," covering issues of disability, wellness and empowerment.

Patricia Schwartz is a photographer with an eye for beauty in overlooked places. She did a series of photos called "Women of Substance." Postcards of the series sell in several bookstores. Using costuming, positioning and atmospheric techniques, Patricia features the gorgeousness of fat women.

Alana Theriault found a home for some of her writings with Wry Crips and others have been published in anthologies. While performing with Wry Crips, her sly persona captivated many audiences. She didn't stop her creativity there, but went on to work in film, animation and graphic design. She even makes art statements with her style of dress and unpredictable hair color.

Julia "Dolphin" Trahan hit the performance art world wildly with her "Queen of the Girls" show and went on to do other shows demonstrating that having a "different" body is not something to be ashamed about. Using exotic phrases and flesh-showing performance techniques, she turned the stereotype of "asexual cripples" upside-down.

Julia Vinograd, "The Bubble Lady," has sold her poetry books on Telegraph Avenue since the revolutionary days of the Free Speech Movement. Wearing her distinctive multi-colored tam, she sells books and occasionally blows bubbles as she strolls among the street vendors and sits in coffee shops. She has published 48 books of poetry and many of her poems appear in magazines and publications. In 2004, she received the Lifetime Achievement Award at the Fifth Berkeley Poetry Festival.

Cecilia "CeCe" Weeks produced "Women in Gear," a film about women with disabilities studying automobile mechanics. She was the manager for a punk band called "Tripod Jimmie" and started her own company, All Ball Records, to produce and distribute the band's album. She also produced a number of performances in local venues, often as benefits for Big Mountain, a Navajo reservation in Arizona. She played with the fine arts, too, through art collages and later computer graphics. Though she is remembered more for her political work, CeCe seemed to always be involved in some type of artistic endeavor.

Celeste White was a San Francisco poet and singer who used her gorgeous voice to tell stories and sing about her life as an African-American mother with a disability. She performed in Disability Arts Fairs, at other Bay Area venues, and in some video shorts.

Wesla Whitfield was already an accomplished singer when a gunshot wound resulted in her needing to use a wheelchair. She continued with her singing career and has just finished cutting her 17th recording. She has appeared in many prestigious venues, including four times at Carnegie Hall and for Hilary Clinton and Senator's wives during the Clinton White House. She travels all over the country to perform, especially to New York.

Lee Williams met Cheryl Wade at a poetry slam where he took home the first place award. He became part of our growing community of artists and we came to find that he had many more artistic talents. He has done some incredible fine art paintings and his acting and singing talents have landed him almost every part he has auditioned for.

Liane Yasumoto was dreaming about becoming an actress as she sat in "Social Welfare" classes at UC Berkeley from 1988 to 1992. She had been in theatre in her younger years, but a serious car accident moved her artistic Dreams into the closet. She reclaimed them in the 90's and performed in many videos and on stage. Her most notable role was with the Asian American Theatre where she was cast in a leading role in "S.A.M. I Am," a play that had nothing to do with disability.

Redundant Disclaimer: The artists I've mentioned are not all the artists with disabilities that came out of the San Francisco Bay area during this time period. These are the artists that I am most familiar with, several of whom I knew personally. If I have left anyone out, I am sorry; it was a daunting task to remember this much.

*   *   *

And what of the artists that were in the MOE shows? I have given updates on some performers and groups as I discussed them, but a few could use an additional encore.

AXIS Dance Company has achieved the delicate balance of providing quality art and having a place for beginners or samplers. Today AXIS sponsors classes and workshops as part of its ongoing programming, taught by members of their professional dance company. Meanwhile, the troupe tours, yet also has an annual home season where those of us in the Bay Area can still enjoy them.

Bruce Curtis is currently promoting the inclusion of disability film and video festivals in human-rights public education activities and is bringing the best disability films to audiences in remote corners of the world such as Azerbaijani, Siberia and Uzbekistan.

Charlene Curtiss realized that dance was a professional direction that she wanted to pursue. Now she and JoAnne Petroff tour with their integrated dance company, Light Motion. Charlene is also cofounder of Whistlestop Dance, a Seattle based performance and instructional modern dance company.

Peni Hall primarily works in the fine arts now. She exhibits and sells originals and postcards of her works in shows and galleries around the Bay Area.

"CJ" Jones is touring his one-man show "What Are You ...Deaf?" With his unique styple of visual imagery and storytelling, he tells about growing up in a tough St. Louis neighborhood in the shadow of his Golden Gloves champion boxer Deaf dad. He also goes into working as an actor/comedian in Hollywood.

Afi-Tiombe Kambon continues writing and performing as a story teller and oral historian, touring nationally, especially at colleges and universities. She also performs off and on in productions by the Multi-Ethnic Theatre (Next Stage) in San Francisco.

Cheryl Marie Wade is working on a script for a play with the working title "Visiting Jack." It is the most non-linear work I've seen her write, yet it holds together as a strong statement about Jack Kevorkian mentality.

Jay Yarnall continues to fly electronically and spiritually, guiding himself and others to the beauty of music, chant, and song. A chapter in "It's Here Now, Are You?" by Bhagavan Das features a part of Jay's life during the time that we were doing the MOE shows. Through his company, GlassWing Productions, Jay makes CDs, DVDs, Video, and sound to fill the present moment.

* * *

And what of the little girl who sat in the basement, vicariously and enviously watching Barbara Sanderson spin on a barstool?

In one simple sentence: She's come a long way, baby!

You have read dabs here and there of the things that I have been involved in as an adult. Though it might surprise folks who know me now, I was a quiet and shy child, usually listening and observing, but rarely speaking up. Becoming a political activist in the Disability Rights Movement put me in a position where I often had to be a public speaker. At first, I was terrified, and I'd write all my speeches out, memorize and practice them for time and naturalness, to make it seem as if I was speaking off the top of my head. The thing that I was most terrified about was the question and answer period that usually followed any speech.

Gradually I became a seasoned speaker and I realized that no matter the specific subject or group, a majority of my speech was always the same. I also found that most of the questions at the end of a talk were ones I had been asked before. I began to relax about speaking and learned to enjoy it. In time, I became so comfortable that I frequently give speeches without writing, memorizing or rehearsing.

I do prepare in that I think about the group that I'll be speaking to and make a brief outline. I think about what they want to learn and what they are able to learn, considering where they are coming from. For example, speaking to a group of students who plan to be special education teachers is a completely different thing than testifying in front of legislators. Public speaking is one Art form that I have pursued and developed. I don't do public speaking very often any more, but when I do, I am usually paid very well and I speak to audiences of a thousand or more. (But please don't tell them that I don't rehearse!)

What does this have to do with art? Well, besides being an art in its own right, this laid the foundation for me to step into acting and performing. It also gave me a confidence that I used to host radio and television shows. Moving to Berkeley gave me the opportunity to become someone who talked about disability issues to a large number of people through radio and television. I was no longer only talking about images of disability, but I was helping to shape them.

It wasn't until the MOE shows that I actually began to see myself as a performer, even though I had been one as a speaker and a radio host for years. My involvement in the MOE shows started as an audience member and led to my finally being able to "spin on a barstool in front of a bunch of people."

Somewhere along the line in my evolution to becoming an artist I also developed skills as a leader and an organizational development person. I served on the boards of many organizations that supported artists. Some of these specifically supported artists with disabilities; others were for artists in general. I took a leadership role in many organizations, founding some, and the resulting visibility led me to many opportunities. If people wanted to know anything about disability and media, my name usually came up. I got calls for many things, including auditions for roles that called for a wheelchair user.

My list of video credits is long and eclectic; the topics vary widely and my production role varies. I've worked on documentaries, art pieces, interactive CD ROMs, interview shows, television series, and more. I've been on camera, behind camera, and at the editing decks.

I have done some fun jobs with the BBC. For one project, I was a local coordinator and appeared in it as a dinner guest amongst a group of the early disability rights leaders. In another BBC production, I sit on an island with the Golden Gate Bridge in the background, talking about the impact that the Americans with Disabilities Act has had in our country. The most rewarding and interesting BBC project that I was involved in was one segment of a series about disability and sexuality. I was featured in one of those segments.

In all of these years of working in different capacities in the arts, there are a few formats I haven't touched, at least not publicly. I enjoy recreational dancing, and I choreograph pieces in the privacy of my own home, but I have never publicly explored dancing professionally. I also sing frequently in the shower, but rarely in public. Playing music on stage was limited to the computerized keyboard that I played with Hephaestus in MOE IV and for the BBC.

The other art form that I have not exposed much is my dabbling in the fine arts. I primarily do collage work and I rather like many of the pieces I've done but they hang in my home and are rarely shared publicly. My fine art and my poetry are the most personal expressions of my creativity. It's not surprising to me that these are the forms I am most hesitant to display publicly. Criticism of these works would be harder to rebound from than criticism of a role I play on stage that has nothing to do with my life. I do plan to take a big risk soon, though, and publish a calendar of some of my work. And, of course, this book is quite a risk!

There are so many more things I could tell you about what I've done as an artist, but I don't want this to turn into too much of a brag session. However, I have given other artists their due, so it's only fair that I get to take a few moments. My most famous adventures included being on stage with Danny Glover as a host for one of the Ever Widening Circle shows, being a guest exerciser on a television talk show featuring Richard Simmons, working on a theatre production with the renowned playwright Charles Mee, and having the opportunity to squeeze Jackie Chan's biceps.

In recent years most of my work has been in theatre. I've been an actor, a playwright, a director, a stage manager, a costume designer, a stage mother, and a backstage hand. I've enjoyed working in theatre, though the most exciting part for me is seeing my own work performed.

In Chapter Six I said that I hoped to have good news by the end of this book about my theatre piece "The Rise and Fall of the us/them Empire." I did not make it to the final round of Creative Capital's funding. This didn't stop me, however, and the show has been produced two times in different formats. Mike Ward directed a twenty-minute version of it through the Alchemy Works theatre company and I directed a fifty-minute version of it for the San Francisco Fringe Festival. The piece has never reached the level that I envisioned, but I am satisfied enough for now and have set the project on the back burner. I am torn between applying for funding to develop it further or letting it be what it was and enjoying the memory. I have videotapes of both productions and wonderful moments to hold on to.

At this time in my life, my creative energies lean towards writing and fine arts. Working on a theatre production takes a lot of energy, stamina and time. I'm not sure I want to invest a major part of my oomph in that direction any more.

Sometimes I look at my life critically and I don't see any place where I have really accomplished great things such as having a bestselling book or appearing in an Oscar Award winning movie. Usually thinking of that type is quickly replaced with a softer, gentler evaluation of my life. I am truly a

Jane of many trades, Mistress of none. I have had the opportunity to experience so many fantastic creative exchanges with people and with myself. It would be hard for me to have picked one specific art form to excel at. I've enjoyed them all.

I feel satisfied that the child in me has had the chance to explore a variety of art forms and styles. I've done this playfully, yet professionally. And now, I return to where I started – writing! The art form that I began to indulge in as a teen is the one that has survived through years of creative experimentation.

Postscript by my Sister, Linda S. Stoltz

While working for people with disabilities for three years, I had the opportunity to meet and assist quite a few of these artists, performers, writers, and media personnel. The disability community has more get-up-and-go-for-it than a lot of the able bodied world. Some AB's are more concerned about their outer appearance than what they have to offer from within. Many people with disabilities have already dealt with the outer image issue and have moved on, having the guts to go for their dreams and goals. I have seen some real talent, though I was not aware at the time (mid-80s) how much was going on around me. It was a very busy time of working with and for many different people. To read this book, and to see how far everyone has come, overwhelms me. It shows me just how much people with artistic dreams can excel if they exert the effort. It takes a lot of hard work and endurance, but can be so rewarding. Hats off to those who go for it!

Behindword

ENDINGS ARE TOUGH.

In many ways, reading or writing a book is like a relationship. I usually read series, because the characters continue on in other books and I can postpone ending our relationship. As a writer of a book that will not be part of a series, I am sad that this relationship is coming to a close. This will be our last chapter together.

It took me several years to write this book. A lot happened in those years – personally, politically, and culturally. Many of these things temporarily diverted me from writing, but one pulled me completely off track.

The World Trade Center was attacked by terrorists. That event greatly affected people in many different ways. It reminded us of our vulnerability, that we live in an ever-changing world, and that we cannot take anything for granted.

Prior to 9/11 most Americans had little first-hand knowledge about war on their homeland. A sense of safety and security enabled people to pursue goals with an optimistic assumption that those goals would be attainable. The events of 9/11 shook up that sense of order. It became obvious to people that their goals could be suddenly disrupted by circumstances beyond their control.

I began to question everything I attempted to do. I realized that I did not have an unlimited time to do my art. I put pressure on myself to be sure that I was using my time on the right project. The outcome of this was that I couldn't decide which project was the right one, and so I froze.

I did manage to complete a screenplay sometime during the year that followed, but the majority of it had been written prior to 9/11. The screenplay, as well as many other things, became suspended in time until enough of my sense of balance came back that I could pick it up and work on it.

Many Americans are probably like me in that the year after 9/11 is foggy in their memory. I know we kept on doing things, I know we kept on moving forward in time, but it's difficult for me to look back and say what I did during that year. Some day sociologists will probably look back and point out a significant change in the art that came from Americans pre-9/11 compared to post-9/11.

Eventually I was able to return to writing this book and now I find myself bringing it to a close. It is very hard to come to this place in our journey.

There is a great pressure on writers to finish with a bang. The most frequently rewritten part of a screenplay is the end. In a book such as this, I feel an urgency to say something impressive or to make some conclusions that will be seen as words of wisdom.

Instead, I'll use this ending as an opportunity to say things that I want to be sure to say before our relationship comes to a natural close. My original draft for this book included sections that never seemed to develop into chapters. This is a good place to bring many of those important thoughts together.

The Importance of Networking One of the most important things that I hope any reader has gotten out of this book is the importance of networking. Getting together with other people sparks creativity and ideas. Gathering with like-minded people can be useful for sharing resources. Artists are often short on resources, so collective sharing can be beneficial to all involved.

A great method for networking is to assemble a group and give each person three minutes to introduce themselves, say one thing that they need help with to move forward, and one thing they have to offer others. I've seen amazing results come from this exercise.

Working together is a great way for networking to happen, whether one is an advisor, a committee member, a planner, or a creative partner. Many of the projects I've worked on created networking opportunities every step of the way. Serving on a grant panel is useful in letting me know what is available in the field and also helps me to meet other people. Likewise, being on a committee provides me opportunities to get to know people who will remember me and perhaps utilize what I have to offer down the road.

Networking can lead to great programs. One example that I personally witnessed involved the national Careers in the Arts Forum for People with Disabilities that happened in 1998. A group of about twenty people planned the forum. We met and/or talked on the phone several times over a period of a couple of years to plan the event. Most of us were artists with disabilities, working in a variety of forms. Subsequently, some of us worked on other projects together.

The Careers Forum event was a gathering of approximately 300 people, most of them artists with disabilities, over a three-day period. Anyone who has ever attended a conference of this type knows that networking happens naturally. People meet at lunch and in the halls, learn about each others' work, and exchange cards. It's important not just to make contacts, but to follow up on them, and if one does, each contact can lead to another. Before you know it, you have a large pool of opportunities and resources available to you.

In the years since the national Careers Forum, some of the entities that funded it have funded state Forums. Every year five grants are given to make it possible for statewide Careers in the Arts Forums to happen. Once again, networking happens in abundance, during the planning of the statewide forums and during the actual events that occur.

It has been exciting to observe the process that spread over many years: the National Forum led to statewide forums which have led to formal ongoing networks for artists with disabilities and their allies. Whether it's an individual trying to build on their career as an artist, an organization trying to build stability, or a movement trying to get recognition, it takes time. People need to not get discouraged and to recognize that networking becomes a foundation that will be built upon down the road.

One of the wonderful things about the community of artists with disabilities is an overwhelming support for each other. Sure, there are times that some of us go for the same grant or the same part in a show, but it's a supportive competition. In fact, one of us will call the other to suggest they apply for a grant that we are applying for. Many of us feel that the important thing is that performers and artists with disabilities start getting funding and recognition, not that it has to be ME that gets it all the time. Of course I hope that I get the grant, but I will be equally pleased (well, ALMOST equally pleased) if another artist with a disability gets the grant.

The Importance of Mentoring Mentoring is critical if disadvantaged people want to make long-term systemic changes. Over my many years as an activist and an artist, I have had many opportunities to mentor others, to pass on my knowledge. Sometimes I mentored people my own age who had not had opportunities that I had had, but usually it was younger people who were my mentees. Although I mentored a few males, most of those I've mentored have been female. The time period of my contact with them has varied from one month to over twenty years. All of the relationships have enriched me, regardless of duration or long-term effect.

Mentoring may be thought of as a selfless deed, but it is not. Teaching what I know to others helps me to clarify things better for myself. It helps me to consider new options and ways for doing things. However, for me, the most rewarding thing about mentoring is watching a mentee take flight, to soar, and to know that I had a part in that.

Not all mentoring relationships have outstanding results. Both participants may have a minor impact on each other's lives, but in the overall scheme of things, the lasting effect may be minimal. There is always a chance for an exception, however, especially if one watches for such an opportunity.

When I met Liane Yasumoto, my gut told me that I had been presented with such a gift. We met in a van that provides transportation to wheelchair users; they were running late, so they had doubled up on their passengers. Although the unreliability of paratransit services is on my list of "Things that Make me Real

CHITOSE YASUMOTO

Pamela and Liane

Mad," I am so grateful that they were running late that day. Mentoring Liane has been one of the greatest relationships of my life.

"You work in media?!" she exclaimed excitedly, when I told her I was on my way to a grant meeting for an organization that supported media makers and artists.

"Yep, I sort of do a bit of everything," I answered, trying to sound modest.

"Wow." was followed by a long pause while her wide-opened eyes absorbed the concept. "Have you done any acting?"

I told her about a few of the videos that I had been in and a little bit about the MOE shows. She said she had never attended any and then she became suddenly shy. I thought maybe she was struggling with wanting to ask me something about myself that she thought was too personal, but instead it was because she was debating revealing a secret about herself.

"I have had a secret Dream to be an actress for as long as I can remember," she said, barely loud enough for me to hear.

"Really?" I smiled widely and said, "Think before you answer this, because I *can* make it happen... Are you absolutely sure you want to get involved in acting and the media?"

I thought her eyes were big before, but they got even bigger and she gulped as she mulled over the question. Finally she answered loudly and clearly.

"Yes!" she said confidently, "I'm ready to do it!"

When she answered my question, Liane didn't know just how involved I was in media. She quickly learned that I wasn't talking about pipe dreams. I whipped out a CDT pamphlet and invited her to an upcoming meeting.

I became Liane's mentor as an actress, but also in many other ways. It quickly became apparent that she had lots of potential and I learned that she had just finished college. The world was ready for Liane and she was ready for it. I feel fortunate to have been there at that time, to have had such a wonderful relationship with her that has spanned over two decades.

Liane realized some of her Dreams as an actress, but she also recognized her abilities at art administration in the media advocacy field. I mentored her further as she took over my role with CDT.

I literally passed her a torch, giving her a candle with several words of wisdom that I had typed and taped around the candle holder. One that she found to be most useful was, "You don't have to do it all, and you don't have to do it alone." I had learned this advice for avoiding burnout the hard way. It was just as important to share my shortcomings as it was to share my strengths.

Today Liane flies on her own, but she still calls me often, to share accomplishments and fun stories, and sometimes to ask my advice. It has been thrilling to watch her move from asking me how to do something to planning it completely herself and then asking me for feedback.

Two people who find long-term romantic bliss with each other are very fortunate. Likewise, two people who find a long-term mentor-mentee relationship with each other have found something golden.

Passing on knowledge, skills, and ideas is a gift that comes back in triplicate. Mentoring others has sustained many trades through the centuries. It applies to both the art field and the disability field. We need to mentor others.

Now I'm a mentee granny! – Liane has found a creative young woman with a disability who she is beginning to mentor. It's like having children without the expense! I highly recommend mentoring or becoming a mentee, whichever fits the place you are currently at. It may be a buzz word these days, but it really is a fantastic thing.

The Importance of Allies The mechanics are in place, the wheels are turning, and any other metaphor you think fits to say that things are already happening. However, we need allies to make sure they continue to happen and that they are done in a way that leaves artists with disabilities empowered.

Allies don't always have everything right, but they can still be strong allies. There are many people who are potentially great allies, but if they are on the receiving end of a burst of anger for not using proper terminology, they may never become the ally they could have been. I think we have been militant long enough and now it's time to relax a little bit.

Before some of you jump at me, please hear me out. Yes, some people are badly in need of an attitude adjustment, and sometimes these are people who think they are helping us when they are actually harming us. The important issue is not whether they make mistakes, but whether they are receptive to hearing about their mistakes. Are they educable?

I'm having a lot of trouble putting words together here, because this is such a touchy subject. We need to give people some space. If a person who is not disabled plans an event showcasing artists with disabilities, it's time to quit immediately assuming they are doing it from a patronizing place. If an event provides for some access needs, feedback to them won't be constructive if it starts with complaints about the access features they didn't provide.

Usually true allies and potential allies are best identified over time. Even if they don't have everything right, are they improving?

1. Assess allies by observing what they do that's helpful and by how well they listen and learn about those things they don't have right.
2. If you are on the receiving end of criticism, take it. If it doesn't fit, throw it away; if it fits, learn from it.
3. Quit flying the PC banner the instant someone doesn't do everything exactly right. Give them a chance to learn.

Allies are a very important part of any movement. Most of the events described in this book happened because volunteers helped plan or worked at them. We need to be allies to each other as well as to find and appreciate allies who come into our lives.

A strong ally to artists with disabilities is Paula Terry at the National Endowment for the Arts. I mentioned in Chapter Three how I first heard of her through the fabulous materials that answer many of the questions that museum and theater personnel ask about accommodating people with disabilities. Paula did not stop there. Early on, she worked with the state and regional art agencies to have them appoint a staff person who serves as their 504/ADA accessibility coordinator. The coordinators' responsibilities include educating and assisting staff, board members and grantees on access issues and compliance with the laws. Her office has worked with the six regional arts groups to organize and support two series of regional conferences to better train state art agency personnel and art administrators about making the arts fully accessible to individuals with disabilities. Paula is one of the people who kept the work of the National Careers in the Arts Forum in motion and her office helps support the State Forums that are underway.

Whenever Paula is given credit for the great work she has done, she is quick to pass credit elsewhere. She is not disabled, but involves people with disabilities in everything she does that relates to disability. For example, she did not plan the National Careers in the Arts Forum; instead, she pulled together a committee of people with disabilities to plan it. Another example relates to a time that she was asked to speak at a national conference of the Department of Continuing Education, in St. Petersburg, Florida. The subject was art and accessibility. Paula asked conference organizers to hire me to present with her because "a person with a disability can best address this important subject." That's the way she works.

Thank you, Paula, and thank you to everyone who has been working behind the scenes to create opportunities and open doors for people with disabilities in the arts. And thank you to the people who work for, volunteer for, and serve on the boards of organizations like CDT and NADC. The people in the trenches aren't as visible as those in the spotlight, but many times they are as, if not more, important.

The Importance of Video Video played a very important role in the artistic movement that I have described in this book. Not only did it document many of the artists, but video by itself is a useful medium.

For example, many artists with disabilities have problems getting valid input about their work. Patronizing people will praise it merely because the person did it, with their view of the work primarily affected by their perceptions of the artist's disability. People with disabilities may give positive feedback as encouragement, happy that someone with a disability is making art. Either way, it's hard for an artist with a disability to know whether the feedback they are receiving about the quality of their work is valid. Video is one way to look at your work from a distance. This works especially well for performers, but it can also work for the fine arts. Artists can videotape their artwork and look at it over a series of months to see how they feel about it as time evolves.

Cheryl Marie Wade is someone who discovered how video can help artists see themselves and to realize how good they are. Cheryl knew she had talent, but it wasn't until she saw herself on video that she could acknowledge how good she was. "Wow, this really does hold up!" she exclaimed when she saw the final results of the first video of her that I shot and edited.

Performers can look at a video of a show and see what they did well and where they need improvement. When I was doing the "Disability Rap" radio show and the "Barrier Free TV" program, I would study the tapes afterwards. I was disturbed by the number of times I said "um," or "you know," or rolled my eyes upward and away from the camera. By seeing and hearing myself on tape, I was able to improve the quality of my work.

Video is also useful for getting grant monies or exhibition opportunities. As the art world has become more receptive to the work of artists with disabilities, applications that are accompanied by video have been well received. Video proves, to ourselves and to others, that we are doing quality work. Cheryl feels that the video she submitted with an NEA proposal was the most influential part of her application and instrumental in her receiving a grant from them.

Sometimes video can be used to take a performance elsewhere, geographically and artistically. Making a video enabled Cheryl to share her work with a wider audience, people who were unable to attend her performances. Artistically, I was able to show Cheryl how video could enhance her work. She thought it would be flat, but we worked together on her video "HERE" and the result was very powerful. She was especially delighted by how adding strobe effects to her performance of "Hospital Litany" enhanced the piece.

"You understood the importance of the work we were doing before anyone else did. Not enough people were seeing it so you knew it had to be captured. The only reason we have this documentation is because you had the foresight to tape it. Don't forget that!" – *Cheryl Marie Wade*

I taped several performances and encouraged other artists to use video not only to document their work but to help them to take it further.

The Importance of Collaboration The work Cheryl and I did together was an example of the type of collaborating that came by getting exposed to each other through the MOE shows. I videotaped and edited her performances; she helped me by editing my written work. Ours is a great example of collaborating, bringing the skills that each has to the table. Working together not only conserves resources and inspires new ideas, but it's fun too!

The Importance of Inclusion The reality is that we will always need specialized programs, but we should also aim for integrated programs as much as possible. We need our art organizations specifically set up to support artists with disabilities, but we also need disabled folks included in mainstream organizations. Most people dedicate themselves to one camp or the other, and time is wasted going at odds or competing with each other. We need more bridges so that people can easily flow between the camps.

Here are the first wave steps that organizations can take towards providing inclusion for people with disabilities:

- establish an advisory committee of people with disabilities
- do an evaluation of your program and facility access
- develop a transition plan (short term and long term) for providing full access
- begin including a monetary line item for access in all budget and grant applications

As art organizations open their doors wider, artists with disabilities need to seriously prepare themselves to go through those doors. I don't want to be presented because I am disabled, but because I'm a good artist.

Organizations may worry that opening the door is setting them up to be blasted if they don't do things 100% right. They may feel they are better off doing nothing at all than starting to reach out to the disability community.

Time will alleviate many of these bumps. Meanwhile, trust and nonjudgmental communications can move us to Inclusion.

The Importance of Optimism Several years ago, while I was still doing lots of speaking gigs on images of people with disabilities, we had an incredible year. The same year that Wheaties put a person in a wheelchair on their box, athletes who were disabled participated in the Olympics, and Playboy magazine portrayed its first noticeably disabled woman. I incorporated these things into my speeches and said that they were all good indicators that a shift was taking place regarding acceptance of people with disabilities as part of society.

"However," I would quickly point out, "I will not consider our work towards changing attitudes to be done until we see a disabled Barbie doll."

Well, now we've not only seen Barbie in a wheelchair, but we've had a Deaf Miss America. An artist with a disability was featured in a commercial during half-time for the Super Bowl. Kohl's department stores have been using mannequins with disabilities in displays for over ten years and now have at least one in most of its 500 stores. And, 2005 saw Playboy photograph its first centerfold who is an amputee.

Is our work done? I wish I could say it was so, but it's not. However, I think all of these things are good indicators that the business world has recognized us as consumers. Money isn't the only motivating factor for this recognition, but it's a major factor at play. That's ok – they may be competing for our spending money, but they are making us visible in doing so. We have a history of people with disabilities being institutionalized and back bed-roomed to keep them out of sight. We aren't invisible any more.

I look at all this in an optimistic way. Yes, we still need to be vigilant and watch for violations of our rights and misrepresentations of the truths of our lives. However, I chose to assume that things will be done right, yet not be womped upside the head by surprise when they aren't. I'm not ready to let go of "Plan B" in situations, but I'm willing to see how "Plan A" goes first. I'm a practical optimist.

The Importance of the Political Artists There are many people with disabilities who have devoted their lives to politics, social change work, or providing support services to others with disabilities. Many had artistic Dreams that they set aside. I want to give thanks to all those folks, like Judy Heumann, who have given many years to improve conditions for people with disabilities. Just as I don't want people to ignore the artists, I don't want us to forget those who made the world a better place for the artists.

Years of effort and time are spent behind the scenes to make changes that may seem to happen naturally. Several people with disabilities have been pushing into mainstream organizations and politics for many years. Some artists with disabilities receive grants today from agencies that were educated and lobbied over several years, by invisible individuals in the background.

The Americans with Disabilities Act did not happen because of the goodness and intelligence of legislators; it happened because many people worked for years to draft, write, and/or lobby. Likewise, the Work Incentives Improvement Act and the Ticket to Work Program happened because of the efforts of many people behind the scenes for many years. (For information on these programs you can call your local Independent Living Center, Department of Vocational Rehabilitation, or Social Security office.)

The Importance of Making Peace with the Dragons Art affects people in many ways. This doesn't just apply to audience members or the observers, but also to artists. Many of the ways we are impacted through art touch deep memories inside of us. Some of these are difficult. I call these memories Dragons.

As an artist I find that when I have what is commonly referred to as "writers block" it's because I'm wrestling with one of my Dragons. A person who is looking at a piece of art might also find that it elicits similar emotions and they will find themselves in the middle of the Dragons. Below is a writing that I put in my journal during the time that I was working on this book, an example of a dragon that I had to wrestle with:

Why is the rewrite business so hard for me? As I work on the final draft of any project, the strongest emotion rising to the surface is fear. I can barely eat or sleep; when I do sleep, it is tossed and turned snatches of nightmare activity while my body tries to rest between 4AM and whenever the first phone call of the day wakes me. Visions from my childhood begin to haunt me. I am ridden with anxiety, panic, fear… constant fear.

"OK," I say to myself, "this is bigger than this project or a few constructive criticisms wrapped inside bushels of support and compliments. This is something old, something haunting me. What is it?"

I open myself to whatever it is that drives the insecure, fearful part of my creative angst. And it finally comes to me… memories of years and years of physical therapy with the goal being to get me to walk.

Many steps were achieved along the way, but there was never recognition of a success, only of what I had to work towards next. Learning to sit by myself unsupported was not praised or celebrated. I was only told, "OK, now it's time to learn to stand by yourself."

For sixteen years I worked hard towards the goal of walking. I went to therapy five days a week and worked out at home at least once a day. Some of the work was extremely painful, stretching tight muscles so that I could strengthen them by turning a free-standing bike for two-hour periods.

In all this time, none of the steps I took towards walking were treated as achievements in their own right, not even the steps I took with braces and crutches. Because I still wasn't "walking."

I never walked. I have trouble finishing projects because that would be to walk. It feels like none of the steps along the way are good enough. I need to separate a time where I got no support and little positive feedback from the present, where I have both. I need to know that I can "walk."

The Importance of Letting Go I've lost track of how many times during the writing of this book I have talked about someone who died. Part of my motivation for writing MOE is so these artists would be remembered through time.

Creativity is birth.

Our creations are children, left behind when we die.

Creation. Birth.

Death. Beginning. Cycles.

I now release this book into a life of its own! . . .

Postscript to Thank

Thanks to my two feline muses, Coffie and BuckBuck; to Hannah Jo Karpilow for walking the path with me, my right arm in getting the book to completion; to Michael Horton who woke me with a cup of coffee and a kiss when I needed to work, and provided "Farscape" and "Buffy" distractions when I needed a break; to all the people who shared their Art, photos and memories with me and who read drafts to help correct or add to some of my details (to name you all individually would be a chapter of its own, but I do remember and appreciate you); to all those who wrote chapter postscripts; to Olivia Raynor who encouraged me to write this book; to Bruce Curtis, who started the "Moving Over the Edge" adventure; to California Arts Council and The National Arts and Disability Center for an Arts and Accessibility Technical Assistance grant; to my sis Mona Walker for a safe place to retreat to in order to clear my head and write; to my sis Linda Stoltz for her magnifier editing and her dictionary skills; to Al Byers for over 40 years of friendship and support, and for the long-distance calling card I used to check some of my facts; to Jane Berliss-Vincent for the answers to multitudes of obtuse questions; to Alissa Blackman and Marc Sutton for helping to keep my mind and body in shape; to guildmates in EverQuest who provided sufficient diversion to keep my writer's isolation from becoming too alone; to friends who let me know you cared about me even if I did disappear and didn't return phone calls (you know who you are!); to Jay Yarnall for providing music-to-write-by; to Bonnie Kahane for hearing it all; to Andrew Wyeth for "Christina's World;" and to Berkeley, for what she was.

Resources

Individuals

For current information about the activities of some of the artists that have been mentioned in this book, or to order their art works, see below.

JUDITH-KATE FRIEDMAN *Singer, Songwriter, Producer of Recordings, Events, Concerts*
- **WEBSITE** <www.judithkate.com>, <www.songwritingworks.org>, and <www.cdbaby/judithkate> (for song samples)
- **EMAIL** judithkate@aol.com
- **ADDRESS** PMB 606, 2625 Alcatraz Ave., Berkeley, CA 94705
- **PHONE** 510-548-3655

RICARDO GIL *Photographer, Actor, Fine Artist*
- **WEBSITE** <www.ricardogil.com>
- **EMAIL** ricgil@earthlink.net

REDGE GREEN *Motivational Speaker, Actor*
- **WEBSITE** <www.eastbaycenter.org>
- **ADDRESS** East Bay Center for the Performing Arts, 339 11th St., Richmond, CA 94801
- **PHONE** 510-234-5624

PENI HALL *Fine Artist, Video maker*
- **EMAIL** HeyPeni@webtv.net
- **PHONE** 510-548-1645

CJ JONES *Actor, Filmmaker, Speaker, Artist, Percussionist, Deaf Culture Consultation*
- **WEBSITE** <www.CJJonesLive.com>
- **EMAIL** SignWorldTV@aol.com

JIM LEBRECHT *Sound Designer*
- **WEBSITE** <www.berkeleysoundartists.com>
- **ADDRESS** Berkeley Sound Artists, 2600 Tenth St., Berkeley, CA 94710
- **PHONE** 510-486-2290

PEGGY MARTINEZ *Singer, Drummer*
    EMAIL   pegmar1@sbcglobal.net *(To get the "Barking Dogma" CD - $10)*

FRANK MOORE *Performer, Video maker, Fine Artist, Writer*
    WEBSITE   <www.eroplay.com>
    EMAIL   fmoore@eroplay.com

DAVID ROCHE *Performer, Motivational Speaker, Humorist*
    WEBSITE   <www.davidroche.com>
    PHONE   1-800-820-8971

ALANA THERIAULT, EXPRESS INDEPENDENCE *Writing, Training, and Advocacy services*
    EMAIL   expind@comcast.net
    PHONE   510-845-5387

TRISTAN THUNDERBOLT *Actor, Filmmaker*
    WEBSITE   <www.tristanthunderbolt.com> and
                 <www.brokenearsproductions.com>
    EMAIL   deafwarrior@yahoo.com
    PHONE   510-232-4070 (V,TDD), 415-290-0992 (cell)

CHERYL MARIE WADE Poet, Performer, Writer
    EMAIL   CMWade48@yahoo.com
    PHONE   510-525-7960
    NOTES   Contact her about her videos "Here" (1990) and "Body Talk" (co-produced with Diane Maroger, 2001)

PAMELA KAY WALKER *Artist*
    WEBSITE   <www.madknight.com/pamela>
    EMAIL   TalentBridge@aol.com

WESLA WHITFIELD *Singer*
    WEBSITE   <www.weslawhitfield.com>
    EMAIL   wesla@weslawhitfield.com

JAY YARNALL *Sound Wizard, Graphic Artist, Musician*
    WEBSITE   <http://www.wireonfire.com/jayyarnall>

Organizations

For information on organizations I've mentioned or that I think you might want to
know about, see below.

ALLIANCE FOR REPRESENTATIVE THEATRE
Inclusive theatre, formerly PEP: Professional Enrichment Program
WEBSITE   <www.culturedisabilitytalent.org>
EMAIL   alchemyworks@aol.com

AXIS DANCE COMPANY   *dance performance and workshop information*
WEBSITE   <www.axisdance.org>
ADDRESS   1428 Alice Street, Suite 200, Oakland, CA 94612
PHONE   510-625-0110

CREATIVE ACCESS
Information about Deaf and hard of hearing artists
WEBSITE   <www.creativeaccess.org>
EMAIL   craccess@aol.com
ADDRESS   100 South Broad Street, Suite 1515, Philadelphia, PA 19110
PHONE   215-569-8311 (Voice/TTY)

CULTURE! DISABILITY! TALENT!
aka Corporation on Disabilities and Telecommunication
SUPERFEST International Media Festival on Disabilities and much more
WEBSITE   <www.culturedisabilitytalent.org>
EMAIL   cdtinfo@aol.com
ADDRESS   CDT, PO Box 1107, Berkeley, CA 94701
PHONE   510-845-5576

DAMON BROOKS ASSOCIATES *Represents talent with disabilities, including Charlene Curtiss, Afi-Tiombe Kambon, Mike Lee, and David Roche*
WEBSITE   <http://www.damonbrooks.com>
EMAIL   info@damonbrooks.com
PHONE   805-604-9017

DEAFMEDIA   *Presenter of Deaf talent*
WEBSITE   <www.deafmedia.org>
ADDRESS   2600 Tenth Street, Berkeley, CA 94710
PHONE   510-841-0165 (TTY), 510-841-0163 (Voice)

THE DISABILITY RIGHTS AND INDEPENDENT LIVING MOVEMENT
COLLECTION *at Bancroft Library, University of California at Berkeley; 300 linear feet of documents, correspondence, photographs*
WEBSITE   <www.bancroft.berkeley.edu/collections/drilm> *oral history texts and illustrative audio and video clips*
NOTE   The Bancroft Library will be remodeling until 2008; the collection is distributed to other locations in the meantime.

EAST BAY MEDIA CENTER *Media services and training*
    WEBSITE   <www.eastbaymediacenter.com>
    EMAIL   maketv@aol.com
    ADDRESS   1939 Addison Street, Berkeley, CA 94704
    PHONE   510-843-3699

EVER WIDENING CIRCLE *Annual showcase of performing artists with disabilities*
    WEBSITE   <www.wid.org> *click on current EWC link*

THE MEDIA ACCESS OFFICE
    Assists people with disabilities in the film, television and theatre industries
    WEBSITE   <http://www.disabilityemployment.org/med_acc.htm
    EMAIL   GCastane@edd.ca.gov (Gloria M. Castañeda)
    ADDRESS   The Media Access Office/EDD, Verdugo Jobs Center, 1255
        South Central Ave., Glendale, CA 91204
    PHONE   818-409-0448 (voice), 711 (CA Relay Service)

MEDIA ACCESS OFFICE – NORTH
    Assists people with disabilities in the film, television and theatre industries
    EMAIL   DGordy@edd.ca.gov (Dr. Douglas Gordy)
    ADDRESS   4071 Port Chicago Hwy, Suite 250, Concord, CA 94520-1157
    PHONE   925-602-7721 (voice), 711 (CA Relay Service)

NATIONAL ARTS AND DISABILITY CENTER (NADC)
    Mass quantities of information on the disability art scene
    WEBSITE   <http://nadc.ucla.edu>
    EMAIL   oraynor@mednet.ucla.edu, bstoffmacher@mednet.ucla.edu
    ADDRESS   NADC, UCLA UCP, 300 UCLA Medical Plaza, Ste. 3330, Los
        Angeles, CA 90095
    PHONE   310-794-1141 (voice), 310-267-2356 (TDD)

NATIONAL CENTER ON DISABILITY AND JOURNALISM (NCDJ)
    Educates about reporting on disability issues
    WEBSITE   <www.ncdj.org>
    ADDRESS   10 Milk Street, Suite 423, Boston, MA 02108
    PHONE   617-728-7772

NATIONAL INSTITUTE OF ART AND DISABILITIES
    Day program for artists with disabilities.
    WEBSITE   <www.niadart.org>
    EMAIL   admin@niadart.org
    ADDRESS   551 23rd Street, Richmond, CA 94804
    PHONE   510-620-0290

SOCIETY FOR DISABILITY STUDIES *Explores issues of disability and chronic illness from scholarly perspective.*
  WEBSITE   <http://www.uic.edu/orgs/sds>
  EMAIL   hammel@uic.edu
  ADDRESS   Dr. Joy Hammel, Deptartment of Disability and Human Development, University of Illinois at Chicago (MC 626), 1640 W. Roosevelt Rd. #236, Chicago IL 60608
  PHONE   312-996-4664

STATE CAREERS IN THE ARTS FORUMS *for people with disabilities began in 2002. These forums support the planning and implementation of activities that (1) assess the education and career needs of artists and arts administrators with disabilities; and (2) develop and implement strategies to overcome barriers and advance careers in the arts for individuals with disabilities. Additional information on the statewide career forums may be found at:*
  WEBSITE   <http://nadc.ucla.edu/StatewideForums.cfm> or NADC (see earlier contact info.)
  <http://www.vsarts.org/x1273.xml> or *See VSA ARTS*

VSA ARTS *Supports inclusion of people with disabilities in the arts; newsletters*
  WEBSITE   <http://www.vsarts.org>
  EMAIL   info@vsarts.org
  ADDRESS   818 Connecticut Ave. NW, Suite 600, Washington, D.C. 20006
  PHONE   202-628-2800 (Voice), 800-933-8721(Toll Free), 202-737-0645 (TDD)

WRY CRIPS DISABLED WOMEN'S THEATER *Info on the availability of their video*
  ADDRESS   c/o Peni Hall, 2951 Derby Street #138, Berkeley, CA 94705
  PHONE   510-548-1645

Books

Many of these publications are books that are available at bookstores or on the internet, and most feature works by artists I have mentioned. If it's out of print, you might find it at your library or through inter-library loans.

BIGGER THAN THE SKY: DISABLED WOMEN ON PARENTING (1999), Edited by Rowen Jade and Michele Wates, *an anthology of writings by women, including Adina Frieden, Corbett O'Toole, Alana Theriault, and Julia Dolphin Trahan*
  WEBSITE   <www.trafalgarsquarebooks.com>
  PHONE   1-800-423-4525

DESIGN FOR ACCESSIBILITY: A CULTURAL ADMINISTRATOR'S GUIDE
  *An NEA publication that was distributed to arts groups throughout the country; can
  be downloaded free or have a hard copy sent to you*
WEBSITE	<http://www.arts.gov/resources/Accessibility/index.html>
PHONE	202-682-5532
NOTE	Lots of other publications are available from AccessAbility (NEA)

GEEK LOVE by Katherine Dunn *(Alfred A. Knopf, Inc., 1983) is available on Amazon
  and in bookstores. (I list this because it is a personal favorite that offers food-for-
  thought in a turn-the-tables way. Not for the faint of heart.)*

KIDS ON WHEELS edited by Jean Dobbs
WEBSITE	http://www.newmobility.com/bookstore.cfm
PHONE	888-850-0344, ext. 209 (Leonard Media Group)

MOVIE STARS AND SENSUOUS SCARS, Essays on the Journey from Disability
  Shame to Disability Pride by Steven E. Brown, Ph.D.
WEBSITE	<www.iuniverse.com>
ADDRESS	2021 Pine Lake Road, Ste. 100, Lincoln, NE 68512
PHONE	402-323-7800 *(Int'l orders: custservice@iuniverse.com)*

  Mark O'Brien's web page with ordering information for his writings:
WEBSITE	<www.pacificnews.org/marko>

"OPENING STAGES" *is a free quarterly newsletter on subjects related to art and
  disability, produced by the John F. Kennedy Center for the Performing Arts; various
  formats*
WEBSITE	<www.kennedy-center.org>
EMAIL	access@kennedy-center.org
ADDRESS	Accessibility Program, Opening Stages, JFK Center for the Performing Arts, 2700 F. Street, NW, Washington, D.C. 20566
PHONE	202-416-8727 (voice), 202-416-8728 (TTY)

REFLECTIONS FROM A DIFFERENT JOURNEY – What Adults with Disabilities
  Wish All Parents Knew, edited by Stan Klein, Ph.D., and John Kemp
WEBSITE	<http://www.disabilitiesbooks.com/reflections>
EMAIL	info@disabilitiesbooks.com
ADDRESS	disABILITIESBOOKS, Inc., 33 Pond Ave. #807, Brookline, MA 02445
PHONE	617-879-0397

SOUND AND MUSIC FOR THE THEATRE by Deena Kaye and James LeBrecht
ADDRESS	Focal Press, 225 Wildwood Avenue, Woburn, MA 01801
AVAILABLE	through Amazon on the internet or many bookstores

STORMS AND ILLUMINATIONS: 18 Years of Access Theatre
by Cynthia Wisehart
ADDRESS   Rod Lathim, 2428 Chapala Street, Santa Barbara, CA 93105
PHONE   805-569-1064

TO LIVE WITH GRACE AND DIGNITY by Lydia Gans
EMAIL   lydiagans@juno.com
PHONE   510-658-4445

WHY I BURNED MY BOOK and Other Essays on Disability
by Paul K. Longmore
WEBSITE   <www.temple.edu/tempress>

Media

Below is just the tip of the iceberg of great media available on disability today.
Many of these distributors have catalogues you can ask for.

ABLE TO LAUGH *Video featuring 6 comedians with disabilities*
WEBSITE   <www.fanlight.com/catalog/films/105_atl.shtml>
ADDRESS   Fanlight Productions, 47 Halifax Street, Boston, MA 02130
PHONE   1-800-937-4113

BREATHING LESSONS *Film featuring Mark O'Brien and some of his work*
AVAILABLE   through Fanlight Productions [SEE ABOVE, "Able to Laugh"]

DISABILITY CULTURE RAP: Disability Identity and Culture *Featuring Cheryl
Marie Wade, who co-produced with Jerry Smith, 2000*
WEBSITE   <www.selfadvocacy.org> (click "online catalogue)
EMAIL   act@selfadvocay.org
ADDRESS   1821 University Ave., Ste. 306-S, St. Paul MN 55104
PHONE   1-800-641-0059

LOOK WHOSE LAUGHING *Features comedians with disabilities*
WEBSITE   <http://www.pdassoc.com>
PHONE   1-800-543-2119
NOTE   Program Development Associates sells works about
               disabilities; one collection is "Open Futures," about workers,
               including artists.

THE POWER OF 504 *An 18-minute documentary video of the 504 demonstrations*
WEBSITE   <www.dredf.org>
EMAIL   dredf@dredf.org
ADDRESS   DREDF, 2212 Sixth Street, Berkeley, CA 94710
PHONE   510-644-2555

SELF-ADVOCACY: Freedom, Equality and Justice for All *Cheryl Marie Wade is featured and was a co-writer with Jerry Smith, 1996*
    AVAILABLE   through ACT [SEE ABOVE, "Disability Culture Rap"]

STORM READING *VHS or DVD, documentary featuring Neil Marcus, 1996*
    ADDRESS   Rod Lathim, 2428 Chapala Street, Santa Barbara, CA 93105
    PHONE   805-569-1064

SUPERFEST INTERNATIONAL MEDIA FESTIVAL ON DISABILITIES *Descriptions and ordering info for winning entries from recent years*
    WEBSITE   <http://www.culturedisabilitytalent.org>
    EMAIL   cdtinfo@aol.com
    ADDRESS   CDT, P.O. Box 1107, Berkeley, CA 94701
    PHONE   510-845-5576

VITAL SIGNS: Crip Culture Talks Back *Cheryl Marie Wade as featured performer*
    AVAILABLE   through Fanlight Productions [SEE ABOVE, "Able to Laugh"]

Leftover,
BUT NOT TO BE LEFT OUT,
Social Security Goodies

SOCIAL SECURITY ADMINISTRATION (SSA) INFORMATION
    WEBSITE   <http://www.ssa.gov/pubs/faxindx1.html> or <www.socialsecurity.gov/work>
    TOLL FREE   1-800-772-1213

SPOTLIGHT ON ARTISTS *SSA has Spotlights on a variety of topics, including one that answers questions about "INCOME FROM THE ARTS"*
    WEBSITE   <www.ssa.gov/notices/supplemental-security-income/spotlights/spot-arts-income.htm>
    NON-WEB   Spotlights are also available from any Social Security office, or you can ask SSA to fax them to you by calling this toll–free number from a touch–tone phone: 1–888–475–7000

THE RED BOOK *is a general reference source about the employment-related provisions of Social Security Disability Insurance and the Supplemental Security Income Programs.*
    WEBSITE   <www.socialsecurity.gov/work/ResourcesToolkit/redbook_page.html>

One more disclaimer for the road: I've worked hard to be as thorough as possible, but a lot goes into writing a book like this. If I have given incorrect information anywhere, I truly apologize. Please send me an email so I can correct it upon reprinting: TalentBridge@aol.com

The author

Pamela Kay Walker is in the process of returning to farm life where she plans to put her shredded writing drafts to good use – lining chicken nests. Although she has written for theater and film, and has had some of her prose, poetry and short fiction published, this is her first offering of a full book. Her word of advice for first-time book writers is, "Don't save the Crumbs for last."